A TESTAMENT
for
OUR TIMES

A TESTAMENT
for
OUR TIMES

C. KENT DUNFORD

Bookcraft
Salt Lake City, Utah

Library of Congress Catalog Card Number: 93-71492
ISBN 0-88494-878-1

First Printing, 1993

Printed in the United States of America

CONTENTS

III. THE BOOK OF MORMON EXPANDS OUR
UNDERSTANDING OF THE GOSPEL

PREFACE

Most Latter-day Saints are familiar with Joseph Smith's high opinion of the Book of Mormon: "I told the brethren that the Book of Mormon was the most correct of any book on earth, and the keystone of our religion, and a man would get nearer to God by abiding by its precepts, than by any other book."[1] A modern Apostle, Bruce R. McConkie, after paying great tribute to the Bible, gave his opinion that "most of the doctrines of the gospel, as set forth in the Book of Mormon, far surpass their comparable recitation in the Bible."[2] I share these opinions; nowhere but in the Book of Mormon can one find the doctrines of the gospel explained in such clarity and depth.

Throughout my career as a teacher in the Church Educational System (CES), I have found myself consistently favoring Book of Mormon explanations of doctrine to those of any of the standard works. Yet, when I began researching the Nephite record in earnest, I was surprised that there were so few thorough studies of Book of Mormon doctrine extant. The book had existed for over a century! Surely that was sufficient time for Latter-day Saints to probe its theological depths. The unpleasant fact is that the early Church had sometimes neglected the book. In an 1832 revelation, the Lord chastised the Saints for having "treated lightly" the things they had received, and placed the Church under condemnation "until they repent and remember the new covenant, even the Book of Mormon" (D&C 84:54, 57). One Latter-day Saint scholar, in examining Church publications for the years 1832 to 1846, discovered that the Bible was "cited nearly twenty times more frequently than the Book of Mormon."[3] In recent years interest in Book of Mormon studies has been flourishing like never before. Numerous scholars have contributed lectures and articles to F.A.R.M.S. (Foundation for Ancient Research and Mormon Studies), Brigham Young University forums, and CES symposiums. President Ezra Taft Benson has specifically called the Church to greater appreciation and study of the Book of Mormon. It remains to be seen if the Church will heed his call and lift the Book of Mormon to its proper status as God's primary revelation to the world of the latter days.

How should we view the Book of Mormon? In addition to the laudatory comments of Joseph Smith and Elder McConkie cited above, as well as the high acclaim given it in President Benson's sermons, canonized modern revelation testifies that (1) the book is true (see D&C 17:6), (2) it contains the word of God (see D&C 19:26), (3) it was translated by divine power (see D&C 20:8), (4) it contains the fulness of the gospel of Jesus Christ (see D&C 20:9; 42:12), (5) it was "given by inspiration, and is confirmed to others by the ministering of angels" (D&C 20:10), (6) it proves to the world that the scriptures are true and that "God does inspire men and call them to his holy work in this age" (D&C 20:11), and (7) those who "receive it in faith . . . shall receive a crown of eternal life" (D&C 20:14).

If the book is so highly prized by the Lord and his prophets, if its precepts will bring us closer to God than any other book, it seems reasonable to suggest that a publication analyzing those precepts would be of significant value. I humbly submit this volume as an attempt to dig deeper into the doctrines of the Book of Mormon, with emphasis on their relevance to those living in the twentieth century. I have spent years unsystematically assembling doctrinal material from the Book of Mormon, at first for myself and my classes, and finally for a possible publication. I knew early in my research that it was impossible to do a definitive study of Book of Mormon doctrine. As long as there are serious students to ponder the divine messages of the Nephite record, so will there continue to be new insights and meanings. My research was greatly stimulated by President Benson's sermons and my own growing excitement for the Book of Mormon. I was struck again and again by the power of the ideas I encountered. Chapter 32 of Alma so wonderfully spoke to my situation when I was struggling for a testimony; chapter 2 of 2 Nephi, which contains statements on the necessity of opposition in all things, was such a sensible explanation of why life is so difficult; chapter 42 of Alma provided me the best explanation of the atonement of Christ when I was earnestly trying to grasp that fundamental doctrine. In graduate school I wrote a paper on the Christian way of living as taught in the Book of Mormon (the basis for chapters 13–17 in this book), a study that provided great excitement and clear guidance. I began to see clearly with President Benson and others that, as Elder Gordon B. Hinckley expressed it, "in its descriptions of the problems of today's society, [the Book of Mormon] is as current as the morning newspaper."[4]

The more I learned about the complexity and profundity of the book, the more my conviction grew that it was not the work of Joseph Smith's imagination, but the work of God. The words the Prophet Joseph used to describe the vision recorded in Doctrine and Covenants 76 accurately express my feelings concerning the Book of Mormon: "The sublimity of the ideas; the purity of the language . . . are so much beyond the narrow-mindedness of men, that every honest man is constrained to exclaim: 'It came from God.'"[5] The day the Book of Mormon came from the Grandin press was the day the book's theology became fixed as the basic doctrinal position of the latter-day Church. No subsequent theological development in the Church could substantially conflict with or deviate from those early concepts without doing damage to the book's claims of divine origin. Surely no twenty-three-year-old youth could accomplish this feat without God's help. This assertion takes on added force when we consider that Joseph produced the book in the brief period of sixty-five to seventy-five working days.[6]

My approach in this study is to let the Book of Mormon speak for itself as much as possible. I believe there is a power in the words and expressions of the ancient American prophets—"the sharpness of the power of the word of God" (2 Ne. 1:26) is the phrase Nephi used. I have intentionally limited citations from other writers, other standard works, and even my own commentary so that what is presented would be as far as possible the unvarnished message of the Book of Mormon itself.

I believe, with President Benson, that the Book of Mormon is not on trial, but the world is on trial. New light has come from heaven! Truth has sprung from the earth! Where much truth is given of God, much is required in turn from his children. How will the world receive the Book of Mormon? How will you receive it?

Part I

THE BOOK OF MORMON SPEAKS TO OUR DAY

Chapter 1

THE MISSION OF THE BOOK OF MORMON TO A WORLD IN RELIGIOUS DECLINE

The Book of Mormon Is a Scripture for Our Time

In 1988 President Ezra Taft Benson spoke these moving words:

> I do not know fully why God has preserved my life to this age, but I do know this: That for the present hour He has revealed to me the absolute need for us to move the Book of Mormon forward now in a marvelous manner. You must help with this burden and with this blessing which He has placed on the whole Church, even all the children of Zion.
>
> . . . God willing, I intend to spend all my remaining days in that glorious effort.[1]

This has been the most urgent message of President Benson's administration as prophet-president of the Church. He has repeatedly reminded us that the Book of Mormon is the "keystone of our religion," the greatest missionary tool we possess, and a record written for our day and problems. He declares that the compiler, Mormon, "saw us in vision and was directed to put into the book those things God felt we would especially need in our time."[2] He has quoted Elder Bruce R. McConkie's statement about there being no greater question facing mankind than the query, "Is the Book of Mormon the mind and will and voice of God to all men?" Unless we elevate the book to its proper place in our personal lives and within the Church, we are still under the Lord's condemnation (see D&C 84:54, 57) for treating lightly this sacred scripture.[3]

Believing these words to be inspired counsel, I submit this volume as an attempt to "move the Book of Mormon forward" as a scriptural witness for our troubled times. This initial chapter will be an overview of the Book of Mormon's mission as seen by its ancient writers.[4]

Mormon and Moroni wrote at a time when their people were being destroyed in the final devastating wars of the Nephite nation; consequently there would have been few Nephite contemporaries to read their writings even if they had been available. During those dark days of Nephite history, Mormon's attention turned increasingly to his book and to its effect on future generations. We can imagine the long hours he spent studying and editing the Nephite records. He had abandoned all hope for his own people (Morm. 5:2), who delighted in the shedding of blood and indulged in great wickedness (Morm. 4:11–12). So he addressed his book to the surviving remnant of his people, "that perhaps some day it may profit them" (W of M 1:1–2; Morm. 3:19; 7:1ff.).

Likewise his son, Moroni, protected the precious plates as he fled from the bloodthirsty Lamanites. Surprised that he had survived so long, Moroni penned his final chapters saying, "I write a few more things, that perhaps they may be of worth unto my brethren, the Lamanites, in some future day" (Moro. 1:4). The Lord had shown him "great and marvelous things concerning . . . that day," so that Moroni spoke as if he knew us personally: "Behold, I speak unto you as if ye were present, and yet ye are not. But behold, Jesus Christ hath shown you unto me, and I know your doing." (Morm. 8:34–35.) The last thing Moroni wrote was the title page. This was an introduction and explanation of the entire record and again stated that it was written to the Lamanite remnant and to the Jews and Gentiles. Moroni then buried the record to await the time when the Lord would bring it forth for a latter-day people.

Surprisingly, it appears that Nephi, who comes at the beginning of Nephite history, saw the last days even more completely than did Mormon and Moroni. He knew and saw that the Book of Mormon would come forth in the latter days as a part of the "marvelous work and a wonder" the Lord was to accomplish (see 1 Ne. 13:34–42; 2 Ne. 3:11–12; 27:6–35). He saw that the book would contain a "revelation from God, from the beginning of the world to the ending thereof" (2 Ne. 27:7, 10), but because of wickedness much of it would be sealed and kept from the eyes of the world (see 2 Ne. 27:8). The Lord would eventually reveal the contents of the sealed part (see 2 Ne. 27:11, 21–22); meanwhile the unsealed portion would bring many to an understanding of God's ways (2 Ne. 27:35) and would be of great worth to all men—"especially unto our seed," Nephi told his brethren, "which is a remnant of the house of Israel" (2 Ne. 28:2).

Further clarification should be made about the Book of Mormon as an abridgment. The first part of the book—1 Nephi through

Omni—is a spiritual record kept by Nephi and others on the small plates of Nephi. On these records Nephi did not attempt to give a full account of Nephite history but was concerned to write "the things of [his] soul" (2 Ne. 4:15), "things which are pleasing unto God and unto those who are not of the world" (1 Ne. 6:5). Nephi left a command to future writers that they should "not occupy these plates with things which are not of worth unto the children of men" (1 Ne. 6:6). Mormon did not abridge these plates but left them intact. The latter part of our Book of Mormon—Mosiah through Moroni—consists mainly of an abridgment of the large plates of Nephi by the prophet Mormon. He reminded his readers that this work was only a small abridgment of the records available to him (see W of M 1:5; Hel. 3:13–14; 3 Ne. 26:6–11). Moroni said the same of the book of Ether (see Ether 15:33). What criteria did Mormon use for selecting his material? There appears to be at least two governing principles: (1) He selected material that he felt would be applicable to the problems of our modern world, and (2) like Nephi he included those things that were "pleasing unto God and unto those who are not of the world" (1 Ne. 6:5).

The Book of Mormon as an Ancient Scripture

All of the above is not to deny that the Book of Mormon records were valuable scripture to the ancient Nephites and Lamanites. Before continuing our discussion of the latter-day worth of the Book of Mormon, let us briefly review its value to the ancient Nephites and Lamanites.

Father Lehi knew the importance of scripture. He sent his sons on a perilous journey of over two hundred miles back to Jerusalem to obtain from Laban the brass plates (essentially the Old Testament up to the Babylonian conquest). Without these records the Nephites would have dwindled and perished in unbelief (see 1 Ne. 4:13). While the brass plates seem to have been the principal scripture used by the Nephites, there are some indications that the Nephite writings were used as well. Nephi suggests that he used his own records along with the brass plates for teaching purposes: "And after I had made these plates [small plates] . . . , I, Nephi, received a commandment . . . that the things which were written should be kept for the instruction of my people . . . and also for other wise purposes, which purposes are known unto the Lord" (1 Ne. 19:3). King Benjamin had his great temple sermon recorded and distributed among the people so that all might be instructed (Mosiah 2:8). Near the end of the book of Alma, we are told that "all those engravings which were in the possession of Helaman were written and sent forth among the children of men throughout all the land, save it were those parts which had been commanded by Alma should not go forth" (Alma 63:12). The records spoken of here presumably included the large and small plates of Nephi.

Nephi once stated that he wrote scripture "for the learning and the profit of my children" (2 Ne. 4:15). When Ammon and his companions proselyted the Lamanites they "expounded unto them all the records and scriptures from the time that Lehi left Jerusalem down to the present time" (Alma 18:38, ca. 90 B.C.). Samuel the Lamanite later testified of the powerful effect the "holy scriptures" had on the conversion of the Lamanites (see Hel. 15:7–8).

Years later Alma the Younger, on the occasion of transferring the sacred records to his son Helaman, spoke of their value for the Nephite and Lamanite people:

> And now, it has hitherto been wisdom in God that these things should be preserved; for behold, they have enlarged the memory of this people, yea, and convinced many of the error of their ways, and brought them to the knowledge of their God unto the salvation of their souls.
>
> . . . Were it not for these things that these records do contain, which are on these plates, Ammon and his brethren could not have convinced so many thousands of the Lamanites of the incorrect tradition of their fathers; yea, these records and their words brought them unto repentance; that is, they brought them to the knowledge of the Lord their God, and to rejoice in Jesus Christ their Redeemer. (Alma 37:8–9.)

Although it is not always clear what scriptures are being referred to in these passages, it seems to me that the large and small plates of Nephi, and maybe other Nephite records we are not aware of, were sometimes used by the ancient Americans. Despite this, all would probably agree that the brass plates were the primary scriptures of the ancient Nephites and Lamanites. Whatever the truth of this issue, these statements do demonstrate the ancient worth of the records that were used in compiling the Book of Mormon, a compilation meant to come forth for the use of those living in the troubled latter days.

Why did these ancient prophets write to us? What did they want us to know? Why did they sacrifice so much that we might be the beneficiaries of their labors? The purpose of this study is to answer those questions and to show that the Book of Mormon prophets knew the problems of our day and proposed divine solutions that we must not ignore.

Does the world need the Book of Mormon? To answer that question we must first understand religious conditions in the contemporary world. Following, therefore, is a survey of the decline of religion in the Western world.

The Secularization of Society

Secularization means the decline of religion's role in society; it is a turning from religious matters to the concerns of this world. It means that religious influence on man's institutions and thinking is decreasing. An important book on the subject, entitled *The Secular City*, says it means "the loosing of the world from religious and quasi-religious understandings of itself, the dispelling of all closed worldviews, the breaking of all supernatural myths and sacred symbols." The author, Harvey Cox, further states, "The age of the secular city, the epoch whose ethos is quickly spreading into every corner of the globe, *is* an age of 'no religion at all.'"[5] Some have characterized history from the Renaissance to the twentieth century as a progressive secularization of society. We will here focus on the principal causes and results of secularization.

Economics

The growth of capitalism, with huge urban centers as its functional base, has transferred man's attention from heaven to economics. Modern man ignores a higher purpose and is preoccupied with calculators, computers, recreation, and the pursuit of personal gain. "From the marketplace to the marital bed, activities are seldom judged in a Christian light," observes author Robin Keeley. "Religion has no business in the laboratory or labour club, the office or the TV studio. The social space is shrinking in which religion is supposed to survive."[6] Most professional people—industrial leaders, politicians, bankers, teachers, musicians—do not see their activities in terms of divine stewardship or service to others, but in terms of personal advancement, profit, efficiency, and control over people and products.

The Transfer of Power and Property to Secular Agencies

The churches have been gradually divested of their political, social, and institutional influence. Government is separated from religion; the church has virtually no political power. Governments in Eastern Europe and the Soviet Union have, until recently, suppressed religion altogether. Many colleges founded by religious organizations have no more connection with their churches. This is not to say that religion is dead; in some areas it shows real vitality. But it still has little control over man's institutions and is essentially limited to the private sphere of life.

The Emergence of Science

Science has been a powerful secularizing force. It is not overgeneralizing to say that the worldview of medieval man was ruled by religion while the worldview of modern man is dominated by science. Science has administered a series of shocks to established, traditional religion that have forced the latter to revise its worldview. These shocks include the work of Copernicus, Kepler, and Galileo, who showed that the earth was not the center of the universe; geological findings suggesting that the earth was extremely old; and the biological theory of Charles Darwin claiming that life evolved from lower forms to their present state. Even more threatening to traditional religion than these particular concepts has been the scientific method of discovering truth. To medieval man the Bible, church creeds, and the theologizing of scholars were the guides to truth. During the seventeenth-century Enlightenment, reason was enthroned, and tradition and revelation were rejected or given secondary importance. Newtonian physics explained the cosmos in terms of natural laws and mechanical principles. Professor W. T. Stace describes this revolutionary change in man's thinking:

> The thought which was born into the world with the new science of the seventeenth century, and which has become a part of the world-picture of the modern mind, is that every small detail of the world's happenings is completely determined by inflexible laws of nature. . . . This basic assumption of science has become, since the seventeenth century, a part of the unconscious mentality of the modern man. And it leaves no room for divine action in the world.[7]

Stace also observes that "science has everywhere substituted natural causes of phenomena for the supernatural causes in which men formerly believed."[8] Man became secular minded; for millions, God is no longer an explanation for the world's phenomena.

Ethical Relativism

With this secular or "naturalistic" view of the world came an accompanying threat to religion. Pre-scientific man believed that the government of the world is in some way a righteous government. God, or some benevolent force, would see that good triumphed over evil. But to the naturalist there is no inherent moral order in the world; the universe as a vast mechanical order is mindless, purposeless, and amoral. According to this view of things, values and moral standards originate with man and vary from age to age and society to society. There are no absolute standards applicable to all men. Morals are a matter of cultural tradition and personal preference. Although it is difficult to say what effect these beliefs have had on actual behavior, it would seem obvious that if morals do not have some objective status, if there is no cosmic accountability for one's actions, then people will be prone to behave in ways that are convenient and expedient. As each person becomes a law unto himself, society's morals will inevitably decay.

The Process of Pluralism

Pluralism is another aspect of the secular society. From the fourth century to the sixteenth, Catholicism held a monopoly in Europe. That monopoly was shattered by the Protestant Reformation. Protestants and Catholics fought wars, persecuted minorities, argued and struggled to maintain their power. A state church was considered a necessity, and for a long time Catholicism held dominance in Italy and France, Anglicanism in England, Presbyterianism in Scotland, Lutheranism in Germany and Scandinavia, Puritanism in New England, and so on. Finally, people became weary of wars and doctrinal contentions. This, plus the sheer pressure of many churches living in geographical proximity, eventually led to the pluralistic state. This is a society in which many different belief systems exist in mutual tolerance. Contributing to this condition, of course, was the intermingling of the world's people brought about by exploration, vast migrations, and improved transportation and communication.

In a pluralistic society it is easy to regard different belief systems as equally true. And it is often unpopular to maintain the exclusive truth of one faith over another. University professor Allan Bloom, who in his book *The Closing of the American Mind* is critical of today's intellectual relativism and supposed openness, provides an apt description of the prevailing mind-set among university students:

> There is one thing a professor can be absolutely certain of: almost every student entering the university believes, or says he believes, that truth is relative. . . . The danger they [the students] have been taught to fear from absolutism is not error but intolerance. . . . Openness—and the relativism that makes it the only plausible stance in the face of various claims to truth and various ways of life and kinds of human beings—is the great insight of our times. The true believer is the real danger. The study of history and of culture teaches that all the world was mad in the past; men always thought they were right, and that led to wars, persecutions, slavery, xenophobia, racism, and chauvinism. The point is not to correct the mistakes and really be right; rather it is not to think you are right at all.[9]

What a powerful secularizing force this way of thinking is! There is no absolute, divine truth; there are only different cultural beliefs.

Biblical Criticism

To early Protestantism the Bible was God's authoritative and (almost) infallible word. Virtually all Christian doctrine depended on its being true. Today, after four centuries of "higher criticism," the holy book does not stand on such solid ground.

Scientific criticism of the Bible is an offshoot of modern historiography, which is an attempt to apply critical standards of secular scholarship to analyze historical texts. It is an effort to use scholarship to discover such things as the original wording of the texts, the authorship, date written, historical setting, and similar things. All that sounds very praiseworthy and legitimate. In reality, however, this approach usually begins with the assumption that the Bible is no different than any other ancient text. Often higher critics of the Bible have been men holding a skeptical scientific worldview that excludes a belief in miracles, prophecy, inspiration, or any form of the supernatural. When one reviews the conclusions of these critics, one finds much that is inimical to the Christian faith. Some of their major findings are:

1. Moses was not the author of the Pentateuch. Much of the religious law contained in these books was written hundreds of years after Moses by different authors with differing purposes.

2. The religion of Israel evolved slowly from animism to polytheism to monotheism.

3. The book of Isaiah was written by several authors at different time periods.

4. The Genesis stories of the Creation, the Garden of Eden, the Fall, the Flood, and the confusion of languages at the Tower of Babel can be relegated to the category of myth.

5. Biblical miracles such as the Flood, the deliverance of the Israelites from Egypt, and the wonders of Moses and Jesus are exaggerations or legends.

6. The Gospels are not accurate historical records written by Jesus' Apostles, but embellished treatises produced by later Christians. They are flawed at best and, at worst, nonhistorical.

Rudolf Bultmann, one of the most noted Bible scholars of the twentieth century, said the following in his study of the teaching of Jesus: "I do indeed think that we can now know almost nothing concerning the life and personality of Jesus, since the early Christian sources show no interest in either, are moreover fragmentary and often legendary."[10] An example of the extremes to which liberal scholars go in their undermining the Gospels is that of the so-called "Jesus Seminar," a panel of contemporary scholars who claim that "more than 80 percent of the words ascribed to Jesus in the Gospels may be apocryphal."[11] In these scholars' published version of the Gospel of Mark they have printed in red the words they believe are authentic sayings of Jesus; words they think he probably spoke are in pink; words they conclude he probably did not say are in gray; and words they think he could not have spoken are colored black. Christians were astonished to find that there is only one red verse in the entire book![12]

Needless to say, such treatment of the Bible has done much to undermine faith in that inspired book and its central character, Jesus Christ.

Liberal Christianity

Because of their disgust with religious superstition, corruption, wars of religion, and endless debates over dogma, men of the Enlightenment sought to create a religion more compatible with the temper of the times. Some developed a "natural" religion based on reason and science and stripped of all superstition. Deism was the popular result. Others desired a restructured Christianity purged of its hard-to-believe elements, preserving only its essence. Thus began Christian liberalism, also called Modernism.

Modernism is the attempt of Christian intellectuals to restate their religion so that it will harmonize with science and modern knowledge. Advocates of this approach have typically accepted scientific findings such as evolution, favored "higher criticism" of the Bible, questioned the full divinity of Jesus, and stressed ethics over dogma. Modernists emphasized only the essentials of the religion and ignored theological speculation. These essentials usually amounted to a belief in God, the brotherhood of man, and the importance of an ethical life.

Three examples will acquaint us more fully with the Modernists' point of view. John Locke (1632–1704), an influential English philosopher of the Enlightenment, tried to present Christianity as the most rational of religions. Most of traditional theology was irrelevant; the only essential doctrine was that Jesus is the Messiah. Friedrich Schleiermacher (1768–1834), an important German theologian, taught that the essence of religion was a "feeling of dependence upon the universe." Creeds and dogma were unnecessary.[13] In early twentieth-century America, Harry Emerson Fosdick (1878–1969), popular liberal writer and preacher, wanted to retain the abiding ideas of Christianity while rejecting the old categories in which these ideas were expressed. An example of his method is revealed in his views concerning the belief that Christ will come a second time to destroy evil and reign in peace. This is too difficult for modern man to believe, taught Fosdick, but we *can* believe that as Christians work to change society and themselves that good will someday triumph. Thus, the old thought form was abandoned and the essence of the idea was retained.[14]

The early twentieth century was the high point of American Christian liberalism. The majority of Protestant seminaries in the North were controlled by liberals, and, according to William R. Hutchison, "by the 1920s, modernists filled enough pulpits and professorships, and controlled so many publications and mission boards, that opponents bitterly characterized modernism as having 'taken over.'"[15]

Liberalism is a diluted (if not deluded) version of Christianity, in danger of losing its distinctiveness. Indeed, we might ask how far it can depart from its roots and still be called Christianity?

Despite the fact that Christianity is still a powerful world religion, real areas of weakness exist within it today. Vast numbers of people have replaced faith with a naturalistic worldview, question the truth of the Bible, and hold that Christianity is no more true than Buddhism, Islam, or Shintoism. Millions keep a superficial contact with their churches while their real lives are immersed in the secular world. In the words of the prophet Alma, they live "without God in the world" and "are in a state contrary to the nature of happiness" (Alma 41:11). A desperate need exists for some new divine evidence to support the Bible, to convince people that Jesus is the Christ and that God has and does speak to prophets. Such is the mission of the Book of Mormon, God's testament for our times.

Religious Apostasy and Moral Decay in the Latter Days

Let us compare the foregoing with the picture of our day as seen by Book of Mormon prophets. These inspired leaders portray the churches of the latter days as being in a state of unbelief and moral degeneracy. It will be a time, says Moroni, "when it shall be said that miracles are done away" (Morm. 8:26), when the Saints will be persecuted (see Morm. 8:27), "when the power of God shall be denied, and churches become defiled" (Morm. 8:28), when people place materialistic values above ethical values—"ye do love money, and your substance, and your fine apparel, and the adorning of your churches, more than ye love the poor and the needy, the sick and the afflicted" (Morm. 8:37). The "holy church of God," he concludes, has therefore become polluted (see Morm. 8:38).

Nephi corroborates this description, saying that the churches will not be built up unto the Lord (see 2 Ne. 28:3). They will "contend one with another," "teach with their learning, and deny the Holy Ghost," "rob the poor," "persecute the meek" (2 Ne. 28:4, 13), and justify themselves in committing evil. "Yea, and there shall be many which shall say: Eat, drink, and be merry, for tomorrow we die; and it shall be well with us" (2 Ne. 28:7; see also Morm. 8:31). These conditions are not restricted to churches. All nations shall be "drunken with iniquity and all manner of abominations" (2 Ne. 27:1; see also 3 Ne. 21:14–19), the devil will "rage in the hearts of the children of men" (2 Ne. 28:20), and the Gentiles will deny the Lord despite his many attempts to redeem them (see 2 Ne. 28:32; 3 Ne. 16:10). The devil and his kingdom ("the great and abominable church") will have so much power over the nations that the numbers of the church of the Lamb of God will be small (see 1 Ne. 14:12; 2 Ne. 28:14). And even among these few, many will be led into error "because they are taught by the precepts of men" (2 Ne. 28:14). Because of these conditions, warns Moroni, "the sword of vengeance hangeth over you" (Morm. 8:41).

Moroni saw other elements that threatened the morality and stability of modern society. He saw the Gadianton type of secret organization existing in our day. After telling us that this order brought about the destructions of the Jaredites and the Nephites (see Ether 8:21), he warns: "Whatsoever nation shall uphold such secret combinations, . . . behold, they shall be destroyed." Then to the future inhabitants of America he speaks with eerie directness:

> Wherefore, O ye Gentiles, it is wisdom in God that these things should be shown unto you, that thereby ye may repent of your sins, and suffer not that these murderous combinations shall get above you. . . .
> Wherefore, the Lord commandeth you, when ye shall see these things come among you that ye shall awake to a sense of your awful situation, because of this secret combination which shall be among you. (Ether 8:22–24.)

Seeing our troubled times, therefore, Book of Mormon prophets and writers produced a book of divine counsel especially designed for our particular problems. Seeing the loss of truth through centuries of apostasy, they told us of God's "marvelous work" of gospel restoration (see chapter 2 herein). They filled their records with marvelous sermons explaining the gospel of Christ (chapters 2, 11–17). Seeing the tragedy of latter-day warfare, they wrote at length about war, its ugliness and its heroes (chapter 3). Knowing the devil's vast power, they warned us of his diabolical plans and methods (chapter 4). Aware of a Christianity that had lost the true concept of God through centuries of endless debate, they provided precious information about a universal, loving Father who gives truth to all nations (chapter 5). Perceiving that false concepts of Christ would proliferate in our time, they produced a record whose major purpose is to be a second witness of the divine Christ (chapters 6, 8, 12). Modern Israel (including Jews and Lamanites) would learn from the book how much God had done for their fathers and how he loved them still and remembered his ancient covenants (chapters 8–9). They wrote of a new promised land called America and discoursed on the important role it would play in God's latter-day work (chapter 10). In a world swayed this way and that by false ideologies, their writings would teach anew that God reveals his will through prophets (chapter 7). And finally, to a world fearful that mortality might be the end of human existence, they would testify of a universal resurrection, of judgment, and of eternal life (chapter 18).

The World Is on Trial

Obviously if the world would accept the Book of Mormon for the purposes for which it was prepared, written, and preserved, it would become an immense blessing to mankind. The world would know its true Savior; it would have its faith in the Bible restored and strengthened; it would become the recipient of additional gospel truths; and it would be vividly aware of its accountability before God for the truth he has revealed in this sacred record. The world is on trial! To reject light from heaven is to take a step toward darkness and damnation. Jesus' words to Nicodemus resonate with truth and relevance: "And this is the condemnation, that light is come into the world, and men loved darkness rather than light" (John 3:19).

The great prophet-writers of the Book of Mormon realized this more keenly than anyone. That is one reason why they sealed their records with forceful testimonies detailing the benefits of their labors and the consequences of rejecting their writings. Nephi stated: "The Lord God promised unto me that these things which I write shall be kept and preserved, and handed down unto my seed, from generation to generation. . . . And the nations who shall possess them shall be judged of them according to the words which are written." (2 Ne. 25:21–22.) Nephi ended his record by telling why he considered it to be of such "great worth" (2 Ne. 33:3).

And the words which I have written in weakness will be made strong unto them [my people]; for it persuadeth them to do good; it maketh known unto them of their fathers; and it speaketh of Jesus, and persuadeth them to believe in him, and to endure to the end, which is life eternal.

And it speaketh harshly against sin, according to the plainness of the truth; wherefore, no man will be angry at the words which I have written save he shall be of the spirit of the devil. . . .

And now, my beloved brethren, and also Jew, and all ye ends of the earth, hearken unto these words and believe in Christ; and if ye believe not in these words believe in Christ. And if ye shall believe in Christ ye will believe in these words, for they are the words of Christ, and he hath given them unto me; and they teach all men that they should do good.

And if they are not the words of Christ, judge ye—for Christ

will show unto you, with power and great glory, that they are his
words, at the last day; and you and I shall stand face to face
before his bar; and ye shall know that I have been commanded of
him to write these things, notwithstanding my weakness. . . .

And you that will not partake of the goodness of God, and respect the words of the Jews, and also my words, and the words
which shall proceed forth out of the mouth of the Lamb of God,
behold, I bid you an everlasting farewell, for these words shall
condemn you at the last day. (2 Ne. 33:4–5, 10–11, 14.)

The Book of Mormon as a Voice of Warning

Moroni promised to meet us at the Judgment, where a reminder
of his warning will be given:

And I exhort you to remember these things; for the time
speedily cometh that ye shall know that I lie not, for ye shall see
me at the bar of God; and the Lord God will say unto you: Did I
not declare my words unto you, which were written by this man,
like as one crying from the dead, yea, even as one speaking out of
the dust?

I declare these things unto the fulfilling of the prophecies.
And behold, they shall proceed forth out of the mouth of the
everlasting God; and his word shall hiss forth from generation to
generation.

And God shall show unto you, that that which I have written
is true. (Moro. 10:27–29.)

Another stern warning by Moroni makes a clear statement of the
book's purpose: "And this [the Book of Mormon] cometh unto you, O
ye Gentiles, that ye may know the decrees of God—that ye may repent, and not continue in your iniquities until the fulness come, that
ye may not bring down the fulness of the wrath of God upon you as
the inhabitants of the land have hitherto done" (Ether 2:11). The
prophet Mormon left this sober exhortation: "Therefore I write unto
you all. And for this cause I write unto you, that ye may know that ye
must all stand before the judgment-seat of Christ, yea, every soul who
belongs to the whole human family." (Morm. 3:20.) Another example
is from the courageous prophet Abinadi, who delivered these words of
the Lord: "And it shall come to pass that except they [the Nephites] repent I will utterly destroy them from off the face of the earth; yet they
shall leave a record [the Book of Mormon] behind them, and I will

preserve them for other nations which shall possess the land; yea, even this will I do that I may discover [reveal] the abominations of this people to other nations" (Mosiah 12:8; see also 28:15).

A final warning voice comes from a latter-day prophet, President Ezra Taft Benson: "Do eternal consequences rest upon our response to this book? Yes, either to our blessing or our condemnation."[16]

Will the World Receive the Book of Mormon?

Will the world receive this record, this other testament of Jesus Christ? The answer to this question is mixed. There is no question that the book is having a major impact on the modern world, yet due to opposition and indifference, that effect will be far from universal. Nephi predicted that many would believe in the record: "For after the book of which I have spoken shall come forth . . . there shall be many which shall believe the words which are written; and they shall carry them forth unto the remnant of our seed" (2 Ne. 30:3). The Lamanite remnant will be greatly influenced by the book (see 2 Ne. 3:23). They will be "restored unto the knowledge of their fathers, and also to the knowledge of Jesus Christ. . . . And then shall they rejoice; for they shall know that it is a blessing unto them from the hand of God." (2 Ne. 30:5–6.) In a great vision showing the future of America, Nephi saw several books of modern scripture, including the Book of Mormon, come forth by God's power to "the convincing of the Gentiles and the remnant of the seed of my brethren, and also the Jews" that the biblical records are true (1 Ne. 13:39).

The wickedness and skepticism existing in the latter days will naturally have a bearing on the reception of the book. Nephi recorded the Lord's prediction that Christian Gentiles would have a tendency to see the Bible as all-sufficient and deny the possibility of any new scripture. "A Bible! A Bible! We have got a Bible, and there cannot be any more Bible," will be their cry. (2 Ne. 29:3.) Moroni, conscious of his weakness in writing, feared that the Gentiles would mock his words (see Ether 12:23, 25). "The things which some men esteem to be of great worth . . . ," Nephi lamented, "others set at naught and trample under their feet" (1 Ne. 19:7). Undoubtedly one reason for this mockery is that Book of Mormon writers did not record those things that were "pleasing unto the world . . . , but the things which are pleasing unto God and unto those who are not of the world" (1 Ne. 6:5). Another reason for its rejection among the wicked is found in the words of Nephi to his wayward brothers: "The guilty taketh the truth to be hard, for it cutteth them to the very center" (1 Ne. 16:2).

The Responsibility of Latter-day Disciples

How is the Book of Mormon to fulfill its great latter-day mission? We members of the restored Church have the burden in our hands; no one else can do it. How is this to be accomplished? Obviously we must first study the book to make it a vital force in our personal lives. Second, we must seek every opportunity to introduce, explain, and promote the book to the world. President Ezra Taft Benson, in one of his many discourses on the Book of Mormon, has given us these guidelines:

"Now God expects us to use the Book of Mormon in several ways. We are to read it ourselves—carefully, prayerfully, and ponder as we read, as to whether this book is the work of God or of an unlearned youth. . . .

"We are to use the Book of Mormon as the basis for our teaching. . . .

"We are to use the Book of Mormon in handling objections to the Church. . . .

". . . We, the members of the Church, and particularly the missionaries, have to be the 'hissers,' or the tellers and testifiers, of the Book of Mormon unto the ends of the earth. . . .

". . . This is *the* instrument which God has given to the missionaries to convince the Jew and Gentile and Lamanite of the truthfulness of our message.

". . . Our families may be corrupted by worldly trends and teachings unless we know how to use the book to expose and combat falsehoods in socialism, rationalism, etc. . . . Our Church classes are not as spirit-filled unless we hold it up as a standard. . . .

"Reading the Book of Mormon is one of the greatest persuaders to get men on missions. We need more missionaries. But we also need better-prepared missionaries coming out of the wards and branches and homes where they know and love the Book of Mormon."[17]

A responsibility weighs upon us to heed a prophet's voice and do all within our power to make the Book of Mormon a force for good in the world.

Chapter 2

THE BOOK OF MORMON
AND THE RESTORATION OF
THE GOSPEL

The conditions of the modern world, described in chapter 1, have left mankind in religious darkness and confusion. Jesus himself spoke of competing ideologies and great deceptions in the last days (see Matt. 24:5, 11). The Apostle Paul characterized modern man as "ever learning, and never able to come to the knowledge of the truth" (2 Tim. 3:7). An angel described to Nephi the latter-day Gentiles as being in an "awful state of blindness" because "plain and most precious" things had been removed from the gospel "by that abominable church" (1 Ne. 13:32).

The countless divisions among Christian churches are not the only manifestation of this confusion; it is a theme that permeates our society's literature, music, and conversation. Psychologist Rollo May spoke of this crisis of meaning in his influential book *Man's Search for Himself:*

> When our society, in its time of upheaval in standards and values, can give us no clear picture of "what we are and what we ought to be," as Matthew Arnold puts it, we are thrown back on the search for ourselves. . . .
>
> . . . People ask . . . , How can anyone attain inner integration in such a disintegrated world? Or they question, How can anyone undertake the long development toward self-realization in a time when practically nothing is certain, either in the present or the future?[1]

The famous vocal group the Beatles used to sing of a "Nowhere Man" who "Doesn't have a point of view, / Knows not where he's going to, / Isn't he a bit like you and me?"

What makes all this a tragedy of major proportions is the fact that people have such a powerful need to find meaning and purpose in their lives. Viktor E. Frankl, world-renowned psychiatrist, bases his therapeutic approach on the premise that the need to "find a meaning in one's life is the primary motivational force in man."[2] Harold Kushner, the Jewish rabbi and best-selling author of *When Bad Things Happen to Good People*, spoke of this need in a follow-up volume:

> What frustrates us and robs our lives of joy is this absence of meaning. Our lives go on day after day. They may be successful or unsuccessful, full of pleasure or full of worry. But do they *mean* anything?
>
> Is there anything more to life than just being alive—eating, sleeping, working, and having children? Are we no different from insects and animals, except that we are cursed with the ability to ask, What does life mean? and as far as we know, other creatures don't have that problem? It is a hard question to answer, but an even harder one to avoid answering. For a few years, perhaps, we can put off answering it while we are distracted with educational, career, and marriage decisions. . . . But sooner or later, we will come face to face with the questions, What am I supposed to do with my life? How shall I live so that my life will mean something more than a brief flash of biological existence soon to disappear forever?[3]

Modern man, with all his vaunted intellectual attainments, is incapable of agreeing on the purpose of his existence. Scientific knowledge is earthbound, limited to an examination and evaluation of physical phenomena. It can offer little help in answering the perplexing problems of human history—the questions of God's existence, the possibility of life after death, the nature of truth, or the correct way to live. Consequently we are faced with a babble of competing opinions and conflicting philosophies. Unable to answer the cosmic questions, we immerse ourselves in the mundane and the worldly. There is no certainty; there are no absolutes. Meaninglessness is the great malady of twentieth-century man.

The Gospel Restoration

The Book of Mormon is part of God's work to dispel the darkness and bring the gospel again to mankind. This is undoubtedly the greatest legacy of the book. An angel told Nephi that God would not "suffer that the Gentiles shall forever remain in that awful state of blindness, which thou beholdest they are in" (1 Ne. 13:32). The Lord said further, "I will be merciful unto the Gentiles in that day, insomuch that I will bring forth unto them, in mine own power, much of my gospel, which shall be plain and precious, saith the Lamb" (1 Ne. 13:34).

Book of Mormon writers frequently wrote of God's plan for his children. "The great plan of happiness" (Alma 42:8), "merciful plan of the great Creator" (2 Ne. 9:6), "plan of redemption" (Jacob 6:8; Alma 17:16; 34:16), "plan of salvation" (Alma 42:5), are samples of Book of Mormon terminology. These expressions suggest that God has a purpose and design that give direction to our mortal existence. This "plan of salvation," wrote Elder Bruce R. McConkie, "for men in this life, is the gospel of Jesus Christ. It comprises all of the laws, ordinances, and performances by conformity to which mortal man is empowered to gain eternal life in the kingdom of God."[4] This plan, this gospel, would be reestablished in the latter days for the benefit of mankind, and this reestablishment would be a "marvelous work and a wonder," as Book of Mormon prophets call the Restoration (see 3 Ne. 21:9; 2 Ne. 25:17; 27:26; 1 Ne. 13:34).

How amazed Joseph Smith must have been as he began to see his work (and himself) as the fulfillment of ancient prophecy! Especially would this be so as he translated Lehi's quotations from the prophecies of Joseph of Egypt, who predicted that a "choice seer" of the latter days (obviously Joseph Smith) would perform a work for the Lord. The work would be of "great worth" to the ancient Joseph's descendants (2 Ne. 3:7). It would be accomplished, said Joseph of old, "by the power of the Lord [and] shall bring my people unto salvation" (2 Ne. 3:15). The seer would "be great like unto Moses," and "out of weakness he shall be made strong" (2 Ne. 3:9, 13). The Lord would bless him, and "they that seek to destroy him shall be confounded" (2 Ne. 3:14). Joseph of Egypt prophesied that this seer would have the same name as his father and of Joseph himself (2 Ne. 3:15). God would bless the seer with "judgment . . . in writing" but would "not make him mighty in speaking." A spokesman would be given him to expound his writings. (2 Ne. 3:17–18.) The seer would have, the Lord told the ancient Joseph, "power to bring forth my word unto the seed of thy loins" and to the "convincing them of my word [the Bible], which shall have already gone forth among them" (2 Ne. 3:11; see also 2 Ne. 3:18–19; 3 Ne. 21:9–11).

This "marvelous work," Nephi prophesied, would be of "great worth unto our seed" (1 Ne. 22:8), to the Gentiles, and to all Israel (1 Ne. 22:9). God will "make bare his arm in the eyes of all the nations, in bringing about his covenants and his gospel unto those who are of the house of Israel. . . . And they shall know that the Lord is their Savior and their Redeemer, the Mighty One of Israel." (1 Ne. 22:11–12.) So great shall this work be that it shall cause the wisdom of the wise to perish, the blind to see, the poor to rejoice; and those who have erred shall "come to understanding" and those who murmured shall "learn doctrine" (see 2 Ne. 27:26, 29, 30, 35).

One aspect of this restoration is the coming forth of a "sealed" book, which contains "a revelation from God, from the beginning of the world to the ending thereof" (2 Ne. 27:7). The sealed portion of the book would not be revealed until the Lord felt the people were ready to receive it (see 2 Ne. 27:21–22). Three witnesses would see the book (see 2 Ne. 27:12; Ether 5:2–4), and a "learned" man would declare his inability to read the words of the book (see 2 Ne. 27:15–18; for the fulfillment of this last prophecy, see JS—H 1:63–64 in the Pearl of Great Price).

This sealed book, the Book of Mormon, will be produced as a support and supplement to the Bible. The Bible needs support because of skepticism concerning its literal truth, and it needs supplementing because a portion of the original record is missing. Originally it "contained the fulness of the gospel of the Lord," but after it went forth unto the Gentiles "many parts which are plain and most precious" were taken away. Because of this, an angel told Nephi, "an exceedingly great many do stumble, yea, insomuch that Satan hath great power over them." (1 Ne. 13:24, 26, 29.) The Book of Mormon will "establish the truth" of the Bible and "make known the plain and precious things which have been taken away" from it. It will also make known to a doubting generation that Jesus Christ "is the Son of the Eternal Father, and the Savior of the world." (1 Ne. 13:40.) The Lord told Joseph of Egypt that the two religious records would "grow together, unto the confounding of false doctrines and laying down of contentions, and establishing peace among the fruit of thy loins, and bringing them to the knowledge of their fathers . . . and also to the knowledge of my covenants, saith the Lord" (2 Ne. 3:12).

It can be seen that one of the great purposes of the Book of Mormon is to corroborate the truth of the Bible and clarify its doctrines. "For behold," wrote Mormon, "this [the Book of Mormon] is written for the intent that ye may believe that [the Bible]; and if ye believe that ye will believe this also; and if ye believe this ye will know concerning your fathers, and also the marvelous works which were wrought by the power of God among them" (Morm. 7:9).

How does the Book of Mormon support the Bible and restore "plain and precious" doctrine? As previously discussed, scientific criticism of the Bible has led many to doubt its miracles, prophecies, historicity, and inspired origin. The Book of Mormon counters these criticisms in every instance. Everywhere the Nephite record supports the validity and historicity of the entire Bible. Everywhere it supports the veracity of the biblical writers in their description of miracles, historical events, and personalities. The Garden of Eden story, for instance, is regarded by the Nephite prophets as literal history, not mythology (see 2 Ne. 2:19–23; Alma 42:2). Adam and Eve were our first parents; "they brought forth children; yea, even the family of all the earth" (2 Ne. 2:19–20). The Fall occurred when Adam and Eve were disobedient and ate of the forbidden fruit. The Book of Mormon supports the miracles of the Bible (see 1 Ne. 17:26–41; 1 Ne. 11:31; 2 Ne. 26:13; Mosiah 3:5); verifies the reality of the Flood story (see Ether 6:7; 13:2) and the Tower of Babel story (see Ether 1; Mosiah 28:17); and supports Moses as the author of the Pentateuch (see 1 Ne. 5:10–11) and Isaiah as the author of the entire book of Isaiah. These are only samples of biblical ideas and facts supported by the Book of Mormon.

We see, therefore, that the Book of Mormon will play a major role in God's marvelous work of restoration. Those accepting it will find their belief in the Bible strengthened, their testimony of Jesus as the Christ fortified, and their knowledge of gospel truth greatly increased.

What is this plan of salvation that has been again restored? Part 3 of this book is an extensive answer to that question, while the remainder of this chapter will focus on the meaning of the term *gospel* as defined by God's inspired spokesmen.

What Is the Gospel?

The word *gospel* comes from the Greek *euangelion* and means "good news," or "glad tidings." What good news? It is the good news that Christ has redeemed us from our fallen condition. Look at this scriptural definition: "And this is the gospel, the glad tidings, . . . that he came into the world, even Jesus, to be crucified for the world, and to bear the sins of the world, and to sanctify the world, and to cleanse it from all unrighteousness; that through him all might be saved" (D&C 76:40–42).

Modern revelation tells us that the Book of Mormon contains a "fulness of the gospel" of Christ (D&C 42:12; 27:5; 20:8–9). This is sometimes confusing when it is discovered that the Book of Mormon does not mention such Latter-day Saint doctrines as our premortal existence, the three degrees of glory, the Word of Wisdom, temple marriage, and endowments. A further understanding of the term *gospel* as used in the Book of Mormon should resolve any misunderstanding. There are three instances in the Book of Mormon when the term is defined; two are brief and one is extensive.

The first definition that we will consider here was spoken by Jesus to his American disciples: "Behold I have given unto you my gospel, and this is the gospel which I have given unto you. . . ." He follows this introduction with a list of the following principles: the Atonement, the Judgment, faith, repentance, baptism of the water and of the Spirit, enduring to the end in following Christ's example, becoming sanctified, and entering into the Lord's rest (3 Ne. 27:13–21; see also v. 27.)

The second passage is from 3 Nephi 11:31–40 and is also from the mouth of the Savior. Jesus calls it "the doctrine which the Father hath given unto me" (v. 32; the "doctrine of Christ" and the "gospel of Christ" are synonymous expressions according to Jacob 7:6). The gospel as defined here consists of the principles of faith, repentance, and baptism of water and of the Holy Ghost. One might ask why there is no specific mention of the Atonement. The answer might be that there are two ways of looking at the gospel: one from the standpoint of Christ's work (the Atonement) and the other from the view of what man must do to make the Atonement effective in his life (faith, repentance, baptism, the gift of the Holy Ghost, having charity, and enduring to the end). Doctrine and Covenants 76, quoted above, views the gospel from the first perspective, and 3 Nephi 11 from the second.

Summarizing what we learn from two brief Book of Mormon passages, then, the gospel of Jesus Christ is the Atonement and the means by which human beings make the Atonement effective in their lives. Human efforts are of no saving efficacy without the Atonement—"it is by grace that we are saved, after all we can do" (2 Ne. 25:23). On the other hand, the sacrifice of Christ is not fully effective unless one lives the principles of the gospel (see Alma 34:16).

Nephi's Discourse on the Strait and Narrow Path

Now, let us consider a third and extensive instance in which the Book of Mormon provides a definition of the gospel. As he neared the end of his record Nephi remarked that he was satisfied with what he had written "save it be a few [final] words which I must speak concerning the doctrine of Christ" (2 Ne. 31:2). He then provides us with one of the finest summaries of the gospel found in scripture.

The example of Christ is the emphasis at the beginning of the sermon. Nephi mentions his baptism, how "he humbleth himself before the Father, and witnesseth unto the Father that he would be obedient unto him in keeping his commandments. . . . It showeth unto the children of men the straitness of the path, and the narrowness of the gate, by which they should enter, he having set the example before them. And he said unto the children of men: Follow thou me." (2 Ne. 31:7, 9–10.)

The emphasis continues: "Wherefore, my beloved brethren, I know that if ye shall follow the Son, with full purpose of heart, acting no hypocrisy and no deception before God, but with real intent, repenting of your sins, witnessing unto the Father that ye are willing to take upon you the name of Christ, by baptism . . . , then cometh the baptism of fire and of the Holy Ghost" (2 Ne. 31:13).

After mentioning the gift of the Holy Ghost, once more the example of Christ is stressed:

> And now, my beloved brethren, I know by this that unless a man shall endure to the end, in following the example of the Son of the living God, he cannot be saved.
>
> Wherefore, do the things which I have told you I have seen that your Lord and your Redeemer should do; for, for this cause have they been shown unto me, that ye might know the gate by which ye should enter. For the gate by which ye should enter is repentance and baptism by water; and then cometh a remission of your sins by fire and by the Holy Ghost. (2 Ne. 31:16–17.)

Nephi uses a common scriptural metaphor, that of the strait and narrow path to salvation. It is only after complying with the first principles and ordinances of the gospel, he says, that one enters through the "gate" onto the "narrow path which leads to eternal life" (2 Ne. 31:18).

Nephi makes clear that there are two important milestones along the path. The first is entrance through the gate, signifying conversion (other scriptural descriptions include being "born again," becoming a "new creature," and we would add becoming a "Christian"). The way to conversion is the application of the first principles and ordinances of the gospel. Each principle and ordinance is designed to bring about a significant change in the human personality:

1. Faith in Christ brings about a change in one's belief system.
2. Repentance brings about a behavioral change.
3. Baptism, signifying new birth, is a change in commitment, or resolve.

4. The gift of the Holy Ghost brings, in the words of the Book of Mormon, "a mighty change of heart." I presume this is essentially an attitudinal and emotional change.

All these combined changes result in a transformed person, a spiritual rebirth, a new creature! It is indeed significant that a person is not on the strait and narrow path just by being a member of the Church or by holding the priesthood or by faith or baptism alone. One must be converted, changed, born again to be on that path to eternal life.

To carry the metaphor further, upon entering through the gate, upon conversion, one has now become a "baby Christian." His objective is to mature as a Christian by daily practice of Christian principles. What are these principles? Nephi gives us a wonderful summary as he discusses the path to the second milestone, which is salvation.

Nephi asks whether, after one has entered onto the path, "all is done" (2 Ne. 31:19). He answers in the negative and then outlines the steps yet to be taken:

> Wherefore, ye must press forward with a steadfastness in Christ, having a perfect brightness of hope, and a love of God and of all men. Wherefore, if ye shall press forward, feasting upon the word of Christ, and endure to the end, behold, thus saith the Father: Ye shall have eternal life.
>
> And now, behold, my beloved brethren, this is the way; and there is none other way nor name given under heaven whereby man can be saved in the kingdom of God. And now, behold, this is the doctrine of Christ. (2 Ne. 31:20–21.)

Nephi is emphatic about this being the *only* way to salvation! Let's take a closer look at this passage. First, Nephi twice stresses the need to "press forward with a steadfastness in Christ." There is no stopping; this is a continuing process with Christ as our beacon. Two of the three great virtues are next mentioned—hope and love. Both the Apostle Paul (see 1 Cor. 13) and Mormon (see Moro. 7) told us that faith, hope, and charity are the supreme Christian virtues. Why? Because faith is "the moving cause of all action,"[5] and faith in Christ motivates a Christian to walk the path ahead; hope is that optimism that sees him through life's difficulties; and love is that virtue which, says Paul, encompasses all others (see Rom. 13:8–10).

What follows in the Book of Mormon seems to be an addendum to Nephi's discourse. He sensed that his brethren still had questions as to what they should do after they had entered onto the path. Referring back to his description of receiving the Holy Ghost and to his charge to feast on the words of Christ, he elaborates:

> Do ye not remember that I said unto you that after ye had received the Holy Ghost ye could speak with the tongue of angels? And now, how could ye speak with the tongue of angels save it were by the Holy Ghost?
>
> Angels speak by the power of the Holy Ghost; wherefore, they speak the words of Christ. Wherefore, I said unto you, feast upon the words of Christ; for behold, the words of Christ will tell you all things what ye should do. . . .
>
> For behold, again I say unto you that if ye will enter in by the way, and receive the Holy Ghost, it will show unto you all things what ye should do.
>
> Behold, this is the doctrine of Christ. (2 Ne. 32:2–3, 5–6.)

Nephi seems to be saying that the "words of Christ," spiritually communicated or written, are the guide that will show Christians all that needs to be done as they walk the path. (The accompanying chart is a graphic depiction of Nephi's gospel summary.)

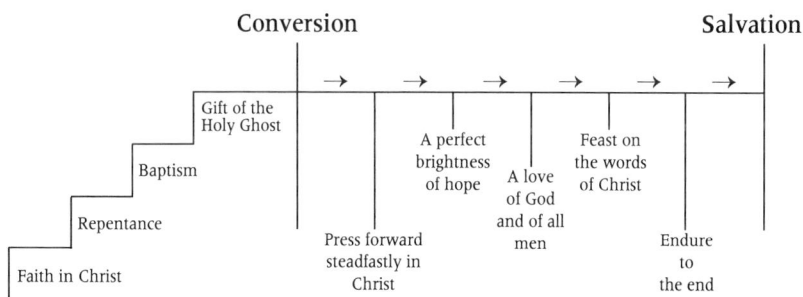

Conclusion

The spiritual darkness that covers the world will be dispelled by the light of the restoration of the gospel of Jesus Christ. This is the "good news," the source of joy and hope for the human race. The Book of Mormon will play a big role in this "marvelous work" of the latter days. It is my conviction that no book teaches the gospel as powerfully as the Book of Mormon.

Chapter 3

COUNSEL FOR
A TIME OF WAR AND
POLITICAL TURMOIL

Is there anything the world hungers for more than peace? Is there anything more antithetical to the message of the Master than war? Then why is there so much war in the Book of Mormon? It is true that Mormon, the principal writer and compiler, was a military man virtually all of his life and therefore interested, if not preoccupied, with such matters. But Mormon was also a prophet who, like Jesus and Nephi before him, saw that the last days would witness "wars and rumors of wars among all the nations and kindreds of the earth" (1 Ne. 14:15). To provide guidance for those in the latter days who must live in an environment of war, Mormon wrote of war's devastation, its evils, and the means by which to prevent it. He showed through teaching and personal example what righteousness means in times of corruption and human conflict.

As history nears its climax, modern revelation tells us, Zion shall be the "only people that shall not be at war one with another" (D&C 45:69). Wars and natural calamities will continue to worsen, we are told in another famous revelation, "until the consumption decreed hath made a full end of all nations" (D&C 87:6). The Christian response to war has always been a major theological problem. We have seen in modern times a whole spectrum of approaches, from Gandhi's and Martin Luther King's nonviolent pacificism to "just war" theories to overt militancy. In a world where humankind has not yet learned to live peacefully, there are few more vital needs than revealed knowledge about war and its prevention. The Book of Mormon supplies us with insightful information on the subjects of war and politics, and since these topics are usually connected, both will be treated in this chapter.

The Purpose of Government

Because people live together they must have some system to promote their corporate welfare, solve problems, and afford protection. Therefore, says a modern political manifesto of the Latter-day Saints, "governments [are] instituted of God for the benefit of man" (D&C 134:1). How should they benefit us? Governments should make laws that will "secure to each individual" the following: (1) "the free exercise of conscience," (2) "the right and control of property," and (3) "the protection of life" (D&C 134:2). Governments "have a right to enact such laws as in their own judgments are best calculated to secure the public interest; at the same time, however, holding sacred the freedom of conscience" (D&C 134:5). And then they must enforce the laws and administer them with "equity and justice" (D&C 134:3). All men are obligated to respect and obey these laws, for "without them peace and harmony would be supplanted by anarchy and terror" (D&C 134:6). Governments must also have limitations. With regard to religion, "men are amenable to [God], and to him only, for the exercise of it, unless their religious opinions prompt them to infringe upon the rights and liberties of others"; but governments do not have a right "to interfere in prescribing rules of worship to bind the consciences of men, nor dictate forms for public or private devotion" (D&C 134:4).

These inspired lines make clear that good government is intended by God to promote the peace and happiness of mankind. The absence of good government brings injustice, chaos, and even war. What can we learn about "good government" from the Book of Mormon?

Nephite Politics

The following chart indicates the various types of governments existing throughout Nephite history. We will consider interesting aspects of each of these in our treatment of Nephite politics.

Patriarchal government (government by head of family)	600 B.C. to ca. 575 B.C. (Approximately 25 years)
Monarchy (government by kings)	ca. 575 B.C. to 91 B.C. (Approximately 484 years)

Republic (government by judges)	91 B.C. to 30 A.D. (121 years)
Tribal government	30 A.D. to 34 A.D. (4 years)
Theocratic government (govern-ment by God-inspired leaders)	34 A.D. to 201 A.D. (167 years)
Unknown	200 A.D. to 385 A.D. (Approximately 185 years)

Father Lehi was the patriarchal leader of his family till the time of his death. His son Nephi, himself developing as a capable leader, never thought of usurping his father's position (see the interesting example in 1 Ne. 16:18–25). Following Lehi's death, the Nephites prevailed upon the reluctant Nephi to be their king (see 2 Ne. 5:18). So effective and benevolent was his administration that they named subsequent kings in his honor (see Jacob 1:10–11). Nothing is known about the kings between Nephi and Mosiah I, but it is probable that few were of the stature of Mosiah's son Benjamin. He is the model king in the Book of Mormon. He sought no wealth from his subjects, taxed them lightly, labored with his own hands to serve them, promoted the gospel, and kept the crime rate to a minimum (see Mosiah 2:12–15).

Mosiah II succeeded Benjamin, and at the end of his administration the government faced a crisis. None of Mosiah's four sons would accept the kingship, because their desire was to be missionaries to the Lamanites. Mosiah feared possible dynastic struggles if someone else was appointed. He therefore advocated the government be changed to the rule of judges. (See Mosiah 29:4–11.) He sent an epistle to his people filled with his political philosophy. If you could always have a righteous king, he wrote, then the best government would be a monarchy (see Mosiah 29:13). But alas, "how much iniquity doth one wicked king cause to be committed," he said, and told them to recall the case of the wicked King Noah (Mosiah 29:17–18). Evil kings often cause their subjects to turn to sin (see Mosiah 29:31). It is virtually impossible to dethrone an evil king, he affirmed, without "much contention, and the shedding of much blood. For behold, he has his friends in iniquity, and he keepeth his guards about him; and he teareth up the laws of those who have reigned in righteousness before him; and he trampleth under his feet the commandments of God." (Mosiah 29:21–22.)

Mosiah urged that there be no more inequality among the people, that this land "be a land of liberty, and every man may enjoy his rights and privileges alike, . . . even as long as any of our posterity remains upon the face of the land" (Mosiah 29:32). Mosiah and Alma the Elder were men of like mind. Years before, when Alma's people had desired him to be their king, he said, "It is not expedient that we should have a king; for thus saith the Lord: Ye shall not esteem one flesh above another, or one man shall not think himself above another; therefore I say unto you it is not expedient that ye should have a king" (Mosiah 23:7). Then he added, like Mosiah, that kings would be desirable if righteous men could always be obtained for the position (see Mosiah 23:8).

To implement these political ideals, Mosiah's advice was accepted and a system of judges replaced the kingship. Judges were to be chosen by the "voice of this people" (Mosiah 29:25), because it was "not common that the voice of the people desireth anything contrary to that which is right . . . ; therefore this shall ye observe and make it your law—to do your business by the voice of the people" (Mosiah 29:26). Then, he warned, "if the time comes that the voice of the people doth choose iniquity, then is the time that the judgments of God will come upon you" (Mosiah 29:27).

Judges were to govern "according to the laws which have been given . . . by our fathers, which are correct, and which were given them by the hand of the Lord" (Mosiah 29:25). Judges may have taken an oath like the one Pahoran took when he was appointed to the judgment-seat in the twenty-fourth year of the reign of the judges. He promised to "judge righteously, and to keep the peace and the freedom of the people, and to grant unto them their sacred privileges to worship the Lord their God, yea, to support and maintain the cause of God all his days, and to bring the wicked to justice according to their crime" (Alma 50:39). The judges would be held accountable; provisions would be made that would make it possible for any who judged unrighteously to be examined and presumably removed from office (see Mosiah 29:28–29).

It is quite evident that the law of Moses was the core of the Nephite legal code (see Alma 30:3 and Mosiah 29:25). Lifted from the Korihor episode, the following passage is quite revealing about the punishments and freedoms that existed among the Nephites: If a man "murdered he was punished unto death; and if he robbed he was also punished; and if he stole he was also punished; and if he committed adultery he was also punished; yea, for all this wickedness they were punished. For there was a law that men should be judged according to their crimes. Nevertheless, there was no law against a man's belief; therefore, a man was punished only for the crimes which he had done; therefore all men were on equal grounds." (Alma 30:10–11.)

If the people wanted to alter the laws they could apparently make their voices heard and submit petitions (see Alma 51:2–3). This happened when the "king-men" wanted to return to a monarchical form of government but were opposed by the "freemen." This matter was settled by some sort of referendum. (Alma 51:5–7.) Under the judges the citizenry was to help carry the burdens of government (see Mosiah 29:34). The government of judges worked well when a chief judge like Alma the Younger ruled and when the populace was righteous. But Alma realized the futility of any political system's solving national problems in times of moral disintegration. Consequently, after eight years he resigned as chief judge in hopes of transforming society by the preaching of the gospel. (See Alma 4:15–20.) His motivation for resigning his political office is closely tied to his motivation for preaching the gospel to the apostate Zoramites about nine years later—"the preaching of the word had a great tendency to lead the people to do that which was just—yea, it had had more powerful effect upon the minds of the people than the sword, or anything else, which had happened unto them" (Alma 31:5; see also Alma 4:19). This is how Jesus Christ brought about the utopian conditions in Nephite-Lamanite society that lasted nearly two centuries.

We know little about the golden age of Nephite society (34–201 A.D.). Presumably a minimum of government regulation was necessary, since "the people were all converted unto the Lord" (4 Ne. 1:2), there was no crime, and there were no class distinctions (see 4 Ne. 1:15–17). One of the great lessons of 4 Nephi is that it is not through government reform, enlightened legislation, or vast bureaucracies that a peaceful and just society is produced; rather it is by the righteousness of each individual.

In summary, we see that Nephite prophets advocated a government that was responsive to the just needs of the people, be it a benevolent monarchy or a democracy. Democratic government was preferred, since there was less probability of tyranny and injustice when government was conducted by the "voice of the people." Political leaders were chosen by the people, and those leaders ruled according to laws based on godly principles and handed down by their fathers. (See Mosiah 29:25–26.)

Causes of Discord

Before we consider war among the Nephites, let us first examine the major causes of discord among these ancient Americans.

Wickedness

The writers of the Book of Mormon are unanimous in teaching that wickedness is the root cause of war and human conflict. In the following passage, Mormon quotes the maxim that the Lord gave to Lehi and then comments on the saying's verification:

> Inasmuch as they shall keep my commandments they shall prosper in the land. But remember, inasmuch as they will not keep my commandments they shall be cut off from the presence of the Lord.
>
> And we see that these promises have been verified to the people of Nephi; for it has been their quarrelings and their contentions, yea, their murderings, and their plunderings, their idolatry, their whoredoms, and their abominations, which were among themselves, which brought upon them their wars and their destructions. (Alma 50:20–21.)

A similar observation was made later at a time of military defeat: "Now this great loss of the Nephites, and the great slaughter which was among them, would not have happened had it not been for their wickedness and their abomination which was among them" (Hel. 4:11). In the light of this truth, is it not obvious that so many of our present plans and policies to bring about a peaceful world miss the point entirely? It is wickedness that brings contention among people; and contention, unless resolved, brings aggression, which can escalate into the mass killing we call war.

Tradition of Resentment and Hatred

To examine a second cause of war among Book of Mormon peoples requires us to look far back into Nephite history. The rebellions of Laman and Lemuel set the political tone of the Book of Mormon story. From the beginning their opposition to Lehi and Nephi seemed to stem from one problem—the right of leadership within the family. The law of primogeniture among the ancient Hebrews designated that the birthright, which included leadership, belonged to the eldest son. The oldest son could disqualify himself through unworthiness, as did Reuben and Esau in the Bible and Laman and Lemuel in the Book of Mormon.

Nephi was divinely designated to be a ruler over his brothers. After Lehi's sons' second unsuccessful attempt to secure the brass plates, an angel appeared and chastised Laman and Lemuel for beating Nephi. He lectured them with these words, "Know ye not that the Lord hath chosen him to be a ruler over you, and this because of your iniquities?" (1 Ne. 3:29.) Laman and Lemuel were not persuaded. Their wrath went to the extent of attempted murder. The broken bow incident and the death of Ishmael brought the little colony to a crisis situation. Laman and Lemuel said to the sons of Ishmael: "Behold, let us slay our father, and also our brother Nephi, who has taken it upon him to be our ruler and our teacher, who are his elder brethren. . . . He has thought to make himself a king and a ruler over us." (1 Ne. 16:37–38.) A similar episode occurred at sea (see 1 Ne. 18:10) and again before their final separation. Here are the words of the elder brothers on the latter occasion: "Our younger brother thinks to rule over us. . . . We will not have him to be our ruler; for it belongs unto us, who are the elder brethren, to rule over this people." (2 Ne. 5:3.) Several hundred years later we find the Lamanites harboring these same views and teaching them to their children:

> And again, they [Laman and Lemuel] were wroth with him [Nephi] when they had arrived in the promised land, because they said that he had taken the ruling of the people out of their hands; and they sought to kill him. . . .
> And thus they have taught their children that they should hate them, and that they should murder them, and that they should rob and plunder them, and do all they could to destroy them; therefore they have an eternal hatred towards the children of Nephi. (Mosiah 10:15, 17; see verses 12–17 for the full context.)

This resentment is one of the persistent causes of conflict between Nephites and Lamanites in the Book of Mormon. Ambitious political dissidents among the Nephites, like Amlici and Amalickiah, would often flee to the Lamanites and, because of their cultural animosity, easily incite them to war against the Nephites.

Secret Combinations

We have yet to consider the single most disastrous cause of war in the Book of Mormon—"secret combinations," which eventually led to the annihilation of both the Nephite and Jaredite nations (see Ether 8:21).

From Book of Mormon descriptions we would probably be accurate to define a secret combination as any secret society whose objective is to gain power and profit, destroy freedom, and hinder the Church of God. Moroni saw secret combinations existing in the latter days and sought to warn us of their evil influence:

> And whatsoever nation shall uphold such secret combinations, to get power and gain, until they shall spread over the nation, behold, they shall be destroyed. . . .
>
> Wherefore, O ye Gentiles, it is wisdom in God that these things should be shown unto you, that thereby ye may repent of your sins, and suffer not that these murderous combinations shall get above you. . . .
>
> Wherefore, the Lord commandeth you, when ye shall see these things come among you that ye shall awake to a sense of your awful situation, because of this secret combination which shall be among you. (Ether 8:22–24.)

We can conclude from Moroni's warning that he felt inspired to describe for us the workings of this movement in order that we would be able to recognize it in our society and hopefully take preventative measures to stop its growth and activity.

How did these secret combinations originate? Let us begin at the beginning. Cain was the first mortal to create a satanic organization when he secretly conspired with the devil to murder his brother Abel (see Moses 5:28–33). Through Cain a subversive crime organization was perpetuated: "For, from the days of Cain, there was a secret combination, and their works were in the dark" (Moses 5:51). The following is said of conditions in the time of Lamech:

> For Lamech having entered into a covenant with Satan, after the manner of Cain, wherein he became master Mahan, master of that great secret which was administered unto Cain by Satan; and Irad, the son of Enoch, having known their secret, began to reveal it unto the sons of Adam;
>
> Wherefore Lamech, being angry, slew him, not like unto Cain, his brother Abel, for the sake of getting gain, but he slew him for the oath's sake.
>
> . . . And thus the works of darkness began to prevail among all the sons of men. (Moses 5:49–50, 55.)

These conditions obviously had a great deal to do with the corruption of all flesh (see Moses 8:29) which in turn brought the Flood upon the inhabitants of the earth.

After the time of the Flood a man named Akish founded the

satanic order among the Jaredites. The oaths he administered to others had been "handed down even from Cain, who was a murderer from the beginning" (Ether 8:15). So powerful did this devilish organization become that, as mentioned above, the Jaredite civilization was destroyed as a result.

Among the Nephites, a professional killer named Kishkumen and the more "talented" Gadianton were founders of the movement. This happened about fifty years before the coming of Christ. They obtained their knowledge of secret oaths and covenants from the devil himself (Hel. 6:26–27), since the Nephite writers had made a conscious effort to keep the "oaths," "covenants," "secret abominations," "signs," and "wonders" of the Jaredite secret orders from their records, lest the people learn of their ways and "fall into darkness also and be destroyed" (Alma 37:27).

The Gadianton society flourished until they obtained "the sole management of the government" about 24 B.C. (Hel. 6:29). They were brought to a temporary end when the prophet Nephi, son of Helaman, asked the Lord to send a famine upon the land, and the people, who became repentant, "swept away the band of Gadianton from amongst them" (Hel. 11:10). The righteous Lamanites of this period were able to eradicate the Gadiantons among them by converting them (see Hel. 6:37). After a few years the organization was revived when Nephite dissenters established their headquarters in the mountains and began to attack Nephite villages (see Hel. 24–26). They became so mighty "that they did defy the whole armies of the Nephites" (Hel. 11:32). The Gadiantons were eventually defeated by the combined efforts of the Nephites and Lamanites, who built a military stronghold in the center of the land and adopted a "scorched earth" policy outside the stronghold. They finally achieved victory after suffering a seven-year siege (see 3 Ne. 2–4). The Gadiantons were dormant during the 167 years of the Nephite "golden age," but reappeared for the last 185 years of Nephite civilization and proved to be the decisive factor in the decline and fall of the Nephite nation.

Turning from this historical survey, let us study the characteristics of these secret combinations, that we might more easily detect their presence in our own society. The following is a summary of their objectives and methods.[1]

Objectives

1. *Gain political power.* "It was his [Kishkumen's] object to murder, and also . . . it was the object of all those who belonged to his band to murder, and to rob, and to gain power" (Hel. 2:8).

2. *Destroy freedom.* "For it cometh to pass that whoso buildeth it up seeketh to overthrow the freedom of all lands, nations, and countries" (Ether 8:25).

3. *Acquire wealth.* "Now the people of Akish were desirous for gain, even as Akish was desirous for power; wherefore, the sons of Akish did offer them money, by which means they drew away the more part of the people after them" (Ether 9:11).

4. *Destroy God's kingdom.* They will shed the blood of the Saints (see Ether 8:22). The devil is the author of the movement (see Hel. 6:26–27).

Methods

1. *Secret oaths, covenants, signs, and group solidarity.* "Behold, Satan did stir up the hearts of the more part of the Nephites, insomuch that they did unite with those bands of robbers, and did enter into their covenants and their oaths, that they would protect and preserve one another in whatsoever difficult circumstances they should be placed, that they should not suffer for their murders, and their plunderings, and their stealings" (Hel. 6:21; see also 6:22–24; 2:3).

2. *Murder and assassination.* "And Cain said: Truly I am Mahan, the master of this great secret, that I may murder and get gain" (Moses 5:31). "And it came to pass that Helaman did send forth to take this band of robbers and secret murderers, they they might be executed according to the law" (Hel. 2:10). There are many examples in the Book of Mormon of Gadiantons killing political leaders in order to obtain power themselves. One example is found in Helaman 8:27–28.

3. *Robbery and plunder.* "And it came to pass that in the nineteenth year Giddianhi [leader of the Gadiantons] found that it was expedient that he should go up to battle against the Nephites, for there was no way that they could subsist save it were to plunder and rob." (3 Ne. 4:5).

4. *Political action.* "And seeing the people in a state of such awful wickedness, and those Gadianton robbers filling the judgment-seats— having unsurped the power and authority of the land; laying aside the commandments of God . . ." (Hel. 7:4).

5. *Bribery and corruption.* The Gadianton robbers who filled the judgment seats were "condemning the righteous because of their righteousness; letting the guilty and the wicked go unpunished because of their money; and moreover to be held in office at the head of government, to rule and do according to their wills, that they might get gain and glory of the world, and, moreover, that they might the

more easily commit adultery, and steal, and kill, and do according to their own wills" (Hel. 7:5).

Hugh Nibley has stated that secret combinations are a symptom of a corrupt people. They cannot thrive without the acceptance or indifference of society. They simply exploit an already sick and evil community.[2]

The characteristics cited here are quite common of evil people throughout history. I will therefore leave it to the reader to identify secret combinations in the contemporary world. I will only say that such attempts at identification usually point to things like organized crime, world communism, terrorist organizations, and drug cartels.

So far in this chapter, three major causes of war have been identified from the Book of Mormon: (1) evil and contentious people, (2) prejudice and hatred passed from generation to generation, and (3) secret criminal organizations that are allowed to thrive by a complacent citizenry. Is there a message and warning for our day in this subject matter? It is evident that Mormon, Moroni, and the God of heaven believed so or it would not have been treated at such length in the sacred Book of Mormon. What about war itself? What can we learn about it from the Book of Mormon?

Warfare in the Book of Mormon

The gospel of Jesus Christ stands for peace and goodwill among men, even to the extent of loving one's enemies (see 3 Ne. 12:43–44) and returning good when evil is done to you (see 3 Ne. 12:39–42). Jesus admonished the Nephites to avoid "disputations" and taught: "He that hath the spirit of contention is not of me, but is of the devil, who is the father of contention, and he stirreth up the hearts of men to contend with anger, one with another" (3 Ne. 11:28–29). He taught an extraordinarily high standard of human relations, one which transcends that normally practiced among humans. As we will see, these principles should also be extended to nation-states. "Renounce war and proclaim peace," was the Lord's commandment to the latter-day Church (D&C 98:16).

Since war is so contrary to everything the gospel teaches, should absolute pacifism be our aim? The answer is no, despite the inspiring example of the pacifistic people of Ammon. They made a solemn covenant with God never to bear arms again. They held killing in such abhorrence that they allowed themselves to be slaughtered rather than become combatants. (See Alma 24:15, 18–22.)

Defensive war *is* justified under certain conditions. What are those conditions? "Now the Nephites were taught to defend themselves against their enemies, even to the shedding of blood if it were necessary; yea, and they were also taught never to give an offense, yea, and never to raise the sword except it were against an enemy, except it were to preserve their lives" (Alma 48:14). As the Nephites prepared for war under General Moroni, the scripture says they did so "reluctantly" (Alma 48:21–22). "They were sorry to take up arms against the Lamanites, because they did not delight in the shedding of blood. . . . Nevertheless, they could not suffer to lay down their lives, that their wives and their children should be massacred by the barbarous cruelty of those who were once their brethren." (Alma 48:23–24.) In connection with an earlier conflict, the record states: "The Nephites were inspired by a better cause, for they were not fighting for monarchy nor power but they were fighting for their homes and their liberties, their wives and their children, and their all, yea, for their rites of worship and their church" (Alma 43:45). In summary, they were following God's instructions, which were: "Inasmuch as ye are not guilty of the first offense, neither the second, ye shall not suffer yourselves to be slain by the hands of your enemies. And again, the Lord has said that: Ye shall defend your families even unto bloodshed. Therefore for this cause were the Nephites contending with the Lamanites." (Alma 43:46–47.)

In modern revelation the Lord reiterated the law that he gave to the ancients (see D&C 98:33). "Behold," he said, "this is the law I gave unto my servant Nephi, and thy fathers, Joseph, and Jacob, and Isaac, and Abraham, and all mine ancient prophets and apostles" (D&C 98:32). This law, as explained in the Doctrine and Covenants, required that "a standard of peace" should be lifted to an enemy. If this offering of peace was rejected up to three times, "then I, the Lord, would give unto them a commandment, and justify them in going out to battle against that nation, tongue, or people." (D&C 98:34–36). In summary, the "Lord's law of warfare" is that a threatened people must try every means to secure peace and only wage war in defense of their lives or when the Lord commands.

The great Nephite generals, like Moroni and Mormon, were usually successful in following these principles. There were times, obviously, when the Nephites were tempted to initiate war, to take the offensive. When they did so the consequences were nearly always disastrous. On one occasion when there was popular support for a preemptive attack, the Nephite general, Gidgiddoni, admonished his people: "The Lord forbid; for if we should go up against them the Lord would deliver us into their hands; therefore we will prepare ourselves in the center of our lands, and we will gather all our armies together, and we will not go against them, but we will wait till they shall come against us; therefore as the Lord liveth, if we do this he will deliver them into our hands" (3 Ne. 3:21). A well-known example of unrighteous, offensive warfare occurred during the final battles of the Nephite nation. After a few victories the Nephites began to delight in the shedding of blood. General Mormon's reaction was to refuse to be their commander (see Morm. 3:11). Later he changed his mind but was "without hope," for his people did not turn from their wickedness (Morm. 5:1–2).

The Nephites were always more successful in battle when they were righteous (see Mosiah 9:18–19; Alma 2:19; 29:23–24; 57:25; 50:21–22). Sometimes the Lord's assistance was dramatic, as in the case of the Nephite forces fighting those of Zerahemnah: "In that selfsame hour that they cried unto the Lord for their freedom, the Lamanites began to flee before them" (Alma 43:50).

The Example of General Moroni

There is no military leader in the Book of Mormon that equals the greatness of General Moroni (Mormon later named his son after this man). A glance at his career will instruct us more fully on the principles of righteous warfare. Only twenty-five years old when he assumed command of the Nephite armies, Moroni worked tirelessly to protect his people from attacks from without and rebellions from within. He was

> a strong and a mighty man; he was a man of a perfect understanding; yea, a man that did not delight in bloodshed; a man whose soul did joy in the liberty and the freedom of his country, and his brethren from bondage and slavery. . . .
> . . . He was a man who was firm in the faith of Christ, and he had sworn with an oath to defend his people, his rights, and his country, and his religion, even to the loss of his blood. (Alma 48:11, 13.)

It was probably Mormon that penned this grand tribute: "If all men had been, and were, and ever would be, like unto Moroni, behold, the very powers of hell would have been shaken forever; yea, the devil would never have power over the hearts of the children of men" (Alma 48:17).

As to his military principles, he did everything possible to avoid armed conflict. Realizing that wickedness was the cause of war, General Moroni did his best to promote righteousness among his people. Another of his principles was the advocacy of a strong defense as a deterrent to war. From the time Nephi used the sword of Laban as a model, the Nephites expended vast effort to produce weapons, protective armor, fortifications, and effective strategy.

Since a strong defense required the support of the people, Moroni exerted himself to keep the Nephites united in defensive efforts. His inspiring leadership, exemplified in the "title of liberty" episode (see Alma 46:11–37), was often sufficient to recruit enough volunteers for the national defense. But later, when a movement of "king-men" refused to support the war effort in the face of a Lamanite invasion, Moroni saw to it that they were "compelled to hoist the title of liberty upon their towers, and in their cities, and to take up arms in defence of their country" (Alma 51:20). Before the "king-men" were brought back into line, four thousand of them had been killed by Moroni's armies (see Alma 51:19; see also Alma 62:9–10 for a similar incident).

Once forced into battle, Moroni could show remarkable restraint and leniency. His benevolent treatment of the Lamanite forces under Zerahemnah is an interesting example. Having surrounded the Lamanite troops and closing in for certain victory, Moroni suddenly commanded a cessation to the fighting. He promised Zerahemnah that his troops could retire in peace if they would surrender their weapons and covenant never to wage war against the Nephites again. Zerahemnah refused the second condition, and the fighting resumed. Before total defeat, the Lamanites were again offered lenient terms by Moroni. This time they accepted. They were allowed to depart in peace with no further punishment or reparations. (See Alma 43–44.)

Moroni's benevolence was also manifested in his humane treatment of prisoners. They were not only treated kindly but also usually allowed to return to their homes at war's end. (See Alma 55:27; 57:15; 44:20; 62:15–17; compare the action of Moroni's son, Moronihah, in Hel. 1:33). It was only occasionally that a war criminal like the Gadianton leader Zemnarihah was executed (see 3 Ne. 4:28; as recorded in Alma 46:35, prisoners were executed when they refused to enter into a covenant to support the cause of freedom). On another occasion Moroni forbade the killing of enemy soldiers who were in a drunken and defenseless position (see Alma 55:19).

Some of Moroni's subordinates were not as moderate as their leader. Teancum, for example, twice assassinated Lamanite commanders in their sleep (see Alma 51:34; 62:36). Nevertheless, he was praised by Mormon as "a man who had fought valiantly for his country, yea, a true friend to liberty" (Alma 62:37).

Although the gospel ideal will always be love, harmony, and peace, the Book of Mormon also teaches that there are many things worth fighting for. Moroni's banner (the "title of liberty") proclaimed some of these—"our God, our religion, and freedom, and our peace, our wives, and our children" (Alma 46:12; see also Alma 43:45). The Nephites felt fully justified in defending the divinely inspired government of the judges, as shown in the cases of Amlici, Amalickiah, and the "king-men." Ammon, a great and righteous missionary, fought and killed in defense of the king's property; of course, he was acting in self-defense.

Is violence justified against an unjust or oppressive government? Like the signers of the Declaration of Independence, Book of Mormon prophets would agree that revolution should not be undertaken for light and transient causes. The popular uprising against the corrupt government of King Noah is one example of a righteous revolution. The American Revolution itself was a divinely supported insurrection. Nephi foresaw in vision that the power of God was with the colonists and the wrath of God was upon the "mother Gentiles" (1 Ne. 13:17–18). Even General Moroni was about to overthrow the government of Pahoran when he mistakenly believed that the chief judge was unsupportive of the war effort. Moroni wrote to Pahoran, the chief judge, "Behold, the Lord saith unto me: If those whom ye have appointed your governors do not repent of their sins and iniquities, ye shall go up to battle against them" (Alma 60:33). Modern scripture says that all men are "bound to sustain and uphold the respective governments in which they reside, *while protected* in their inherent and inalienable rights by the laws of such governments; and that sedition and rebellion are unbecoming every citizen thus protected" (D&C 134:5, emphasis added). It is implied in this passage that men are not bound to sustain their governments *unless* protected in their rights. Of course, "not sustaining" a government and engaging in political rebellion are two different things. Every Christian should do what he can to peacefully transform an unjust government. Violence, to a disciple of Christ, is only an option of last resort.

Conclusion

Although we live in a time when war is often an inescapable necessity, nevertheless we must labor to establish divine principles that govern the interrelationships of individuals and nations. God abhors war and favors a political system that provides peace, security, and equal rights to all people. Since the Constitution of the United States was inspired of God (see D&C 101:80), Latter-day Saints believe that document is closer to gospel principles than any political composition ever penned. Among its inspired features are a "Bill of Rights," which guarantees to each citizen certain basic rights that government cannot deny, and a system of "checks and balances," which prevents the concentration of power in any individual or government department. This latter provision seems especially important since revelation informs us that "it is the nature and disposition of almost all men" to use power unrighteously (D&C 121:39). We begin to see why God has asked his people to befriend and honor this constitution (see D&C 98:6).

After all has been said, the real key to peace is through Jesus Christ. Only by following Christ can the world, and especially this chosen land of America, avert wars and mass destruction (see Morm. 6:17–18; Ether 2:8–9; Alma 37:13). If Christian principles were observed in the world, wars would virtually cease and politics would be transformed. Loving cooperation would replace hostile opposition between individuals and between states. The human race has always longed for a future era of universal peace when men will "beat their swords into plowshares, and their spears into pruninghooks: . . . neither shall they learn war any more" (Isa. 2:4). Regrettably, such ideal conditions may have to wait for the Savior's millennial reign.

Chapter 4

GUIDANCE FOR A DAY
OF DEMONIC POWER

John the Beloved Apostle, after describing the "war in heaven," gives this chilling bit of information: "Woe to the inhabiters of the earth and of the sea! for the devil is come down unto you, having great wrath, because he knoweth that he hath but a short time" (Rev. 12:12). Before the Lord's millennial reign of peace begins, the devil's kingdom will collapse and he will be bound by the righteousness of the people (see 1 Ne. 22:14, 22, 26). Before that day arrives, however, the devil will have his day of power. Nephi said that he would "rage in the hearts of the children of men" (2 Ne. 28:20). His dominion will encircle all nations; evil will engulf the earth. He will fight against the Saints of God, keeping them scattered and their numbers small (see 1 Ne. 14:12–14). Many will stumble because of the precious parts that have been removed from the Bible (1 Ne. 13:24, 29). To the righteous of the latter days, Satan is the anti-Christ. To know about this archenemy, his designs and tactics, needs to be one of our primary lines of defense. The Book of Mormon, with its vital information on the devil, therefore becomes our tactical manual in our struggle with demonic powers.

The Devil's Identity

Who is the devil, and why is he such a threat to our eternal happiness? Latter-day Saint theology teaches that Satan, or Lucifer, was a premortal son of our Heavenly Father, like the rest of mankind. He apparently possessed great ability, persuasive powers, and an enormous ego. In the premortal councils of heaven he proposed to alter the Father's plan, claiming that he would save all mankind (denying them free agency in the process). In return for his efforts, he demanded the glory for himself. (See Moses 4:1–4.) One-third of our Heavenly Father's children supported Satan. A war ensued in which he and his followers were cast down to the earth and denied the experiences of this second estate (see 2 Ne. 9:8). Lehi described Satan as "an angel of God" who had "fallen from heaven; wherefore, he became a devil, having sought that which was evil before God" (2 Ne. 2:17–18).

Satan is now completely, unalterably, and perpetually opposed to everything associated with God. God desires to save his children; the devil seeks to make all mankind miserable like himself (see 2 Ne. 2:18). Christ came into the world to "bear witness unto the truth" (John 18:37); the devil, by contrast, is described as the "father of all lies" (2 Ne. 2:18; see also 2 Ne. 9:9; Ether 8:25). God tries to lead mankind to righteousness; the devil is the "enemy to all righteousness" (Mosiah 4:14), the "author of all sin" (Hel. 6:30). He fights against God and entices men to sin (see Moro. 7:12), influences them to hate each other (see Moro. 9:3; 3 Ne. 11:29), to fight and murder (see 1 Ne. 12:19; Ether 8:25), to stone and kill the prophets of God (see Ether 8:25), to be angry at the words of the prophets (see 2 Ne. 33:5), to seek after harlots (see Alma 29:11), to be puffed up with pride, and to seek for power, riches, authority, and the vain things of the world (see 3 Ne. 6:15). In a word, his objective is to "destroy the souls of men" (Hel. 8:28).

Satan's Methods

Let us look more closely at the devil's "cunning plans which he hath devised to ensnare the hearts of men" (Alma 28:13). One of the most revealing statements on the subject is found in the middle of Nephi's great discourse on evil in the latter days:

> For behold, at that day shall he rage in the hearts of the children of men, and stir them up to anger against that which is good.
>
> And others will he pacify, and lull them away into carnal security, that they will say: All is well in Zion; yea, Zion prospereth, all is well—and thus the devil cheateth their souls, and leadeth them away carefully down to hell.
>
> And behold, others he flattereth away, and telleth them there is no hell; and he saith unto them: I am no devil, for there is none—and thus he whispereth in their ears, until he grasps them with his awful chains, from whence there is no deliverance. (2 Ne. 28:20–22.)

At least two things are very intriguing about this passage. First, the subtlety of Satan's methods. He pacifies and lulls people into "carnal security," thus leading them "carefully down to hell." The devil certainly knows that most good people would recoil at committing a severe crime (like murder), so he might tempt them to criticize and hate, and thus gradually lead them down the path to murder. Christ's second great commandment was that we love one another; the devil, on the other hand, is the "father of contention, and he stirreth up the hearts of men to contend with anger, one with another" (3 Ne. 11:29). Jesus expressly forbade dissension and "disputations" among his disciples (3 Ne. 11:28).

Another striking idea in Nephi's discourse is that Satan, as the father of lies, will attempt to persuade people that there is no devil, no hell (see 2 Ne. 28:22), and no real punishment for sin (see 2 Ne. 28:8). A glance at contemporary religious literature assures us that he has largely succeeded in this endeavor.[1] Disbelief in divine punishment for sin removes one of mankind's greatest restraints to sinning. No wonder Nephi saw latter-day libertines saying, "Eat, drink, and be merry; . . . lie a little, take the advantage of one because of his words, dig a pit for thy neighbor; there is no harm in this; . . . and if it so be that we are guilty, God will beat us with a few stripes, and at last we shall be saved in the kingdom of God" (2 Ne. 28:8).

Another favorite strategy of the devil is to keep people from the truth, for he knows that if someone "follow[s] Christ he cannot be a servant of the devil" (Moro. 7:11). He will use a variety of methods to accomplish this objective. He will teach men not to pray (see 2 Ne. 32:8); bring about secret combinations to keep people in darkness (see Ether 8:16); use his emissaries to ridicule and distort the gospel; try to inhabit the bodies of mankind (see 3 Ne. 7:19; Mosiah 3:6) that he might more effectively control them; and even, on occasion, transform himself into an angel of light (see 2 Ne. 9:9; Hel. 6:26).

Lehi's dream of the tree of life contains interesting information about the pervasive power of the devil. The mists of darkness, the filthy river, and the large and spacious building are satanic elements used to prevent people from partaking of the fruit (see 1 Ne. 8ff.). An angel told Nephi that the "mists of darkness are the temptations of the devil, which blindeth the eyes, and hardeneth the hearts of the children of men, and leadeth them away into broad roads, that they perish and are lost" (1 Ne. 12:17). The filthy river of water represented the "depths of hell" that swallowed up its victims who wandered from the path (1 Ne. 12:16). Those inside the "large and spacious building," representing the "pride of the children of men" (1 Ne. 12:18), mocked and pointed their fingers at those who were partaking of the fruit, causing many of them to be ashamed and fall away from the truth (see 1 Ne. 8:26–28). Judging from the numbers of people that seem to succumb to the devil's methods, it would appear that he is most effective in separating mankind from truth and from partaking fully of the love of God.

There are other examples of the devil turning people away from God's truth. In the account of one of Alma's great missions, the record tells us that the devil "had gotten great hold upon the hearts of the people of the city of Ammonihah; therefore they would not hearken unto the words of Alma" (Alma 8:9).

In 3 Nephi we read that when the new star appeared, along with the night without darkness, to herald the birth of the Savior, "there began to be lyings sent forth among the people, by Satan, to harden their hearts, to the intent that they might not believe in those signs and wonders which they had seen" (3 Ne. 1:22). Not long before this time, in the name of reason and by attributing sinister motives to the true priesthood, the devil obtained great hold upon the hearts of the people (see Hel. 16:16–22). Those whose hearts were thus hardened said this about the true priests of God: "And they will, by the cunning and the mysterious arts of the evil one, work some great mystery which we cannot understand, which will keep us down to be servants to their words, and also servants unto them, for we depend upon them to teach us the word; and thus will they keep us in ignorance if we will yield ourselves unto them, all the days of our lives" (Hel. 16:21). Despite the obvious fulfillment of marvelous prophecies, they argued: "Some things they [the prophets] may have guessed right, among so many; but behold, we know that all these great and marvelous works cannot come to pass" (Hel. 16:16). Why did they argue after this manner? Because they maintained that it was "not reasonable that such a being as a Christ shall come" (Hel. 16:18) and that it was simply a "wicked tradition" passed down to keep them in ignorance (Hel. 16:20).

Anti-Christs

The most prominent of the devil's disciples in the Book of Mormon are the anti-Christs Korihor, Sherem, and Nehor. Let us examine some of their techniques.

Korihor confessed before dying, as did Sherem (see Jacob 7:18), "The devil hath deceived me; for he appeared unto me in the form of an angel" (Alma 30:53). He admitted, "I have taught his words; and I taught them because they were pleasing unto the carnal mind; and I taught them, even until I had much success, insomuch that I verily believed that they were true; and for this cause I withstood the truth, even until I have brought this great curse upon me" (Alma 30:53). It is not surprising that Korihor's words sound very modern; these apostates clearly have their counterparts in the modern world.

Korihor was an agnostic who pronounced false those things that could not be known empirically. He taught that "ye cannot know of things which ye do not see" (Alma 30:15), and further, "No man can know of anything which is to come" (Alma 30:13). He referred to God as "a being who never has been seen or known, who never was nor ever will be" (Alma 30:28), to Christ's future coming as a fiction (see Alma 30), and taught that death was the end of existence (see Alma 30:18). Korihor ridiculed the truth. He called prophecies the "foolish traditions of your fathers" (Alma 30:14) and the result of a "frenzied mind" (Alma 30:16). Priests, he said, have traditionally used ritual and ordinances to usurp power over people and keep them in ignorance (see Alma 30:23).

In arguing with Alma, Korihor stated, "I do not deny the existence of a God, but I do not believe that there is a God; and I say also, that ye do not know that there is a God; and except ye show me a sign, I will not believe" (Alma 30:48). He got his sign; he was struck speechless by the power of God according to Alma's word. As a consequence he was forced to admit in writing, "I know that nothing save it were the power of God could bring this upon me; yea, and I always knew that there was a God. But behold, the devil hath deceived me; for he appeared unto me in the form of an angel." (Alma 30:52–53.)

Sherem's career was a similar case. He is described as a learned man with a "perfect knowledge of the language of the people; wherefore, he could use much flattery, and much power of speech, according to the power of the devil" (Jacob 7:4). He was a believer in the law of Moses but maintained that the prophet Jacob had twisted it into the worship of some unknown deity named Christ who would come in the future. Like Korihor, he held that no man could know the future. (See Jacob 7:7.) Again, like Korihor, he demanded a sign before he would believe (see Jacob 7:13). God's power struck him to the ground, and before he died he "confessed the Christ," and said that he had been "deceived by the power of the devil" (Jacob 7:17–18). He died a frightened man, saying that he feared that he had "committed the unpardonable sin" (Jacob 7:19).

The devil abandons his disciples when they cease to be useful to him. After telling how Korihor was brutally trodden to death by a Zoramite mob, the Book of Mormon record states, "And thus we see that the devil will not support his children at the last day, but doth speedily drag them down to hell" (Alma 30:60).

Nehor's heretical teachings were less extreme, it seems, than Korihor's, yet he, like the devil (see 2 Ne. 28:22), taught that people "need not fear nor tremble," because "in the end, all men should have eternal life" (Alma 1:4). In addition, however, Nehor was guilty of murder, having killed the righteous Gideon when he "withstood [Nehor] with the words of God" (Alma 1:9).

Many deductions could be drawn from these examples; I will mention a few that are striking to me. It is frightening how thoroughly Satan took over the minds and actions of these men. They spoke his words and were captive to his will. An interesting characteristic of their teachings is its similarity to modern scientific and humanistic arguments against religion. Agnosticism, with its typical reluctance to accept any argument that is not empirically verifiable, is a common feature of such arguments then as well as now. Finally, the effort to discredit God's servants and their ideas through ridicule was a favorite ploy of these Book of Mormon anti-Christs and is an all-too-common technique of the adversary in today's world. I cannot resist one final observation. Korihor, Sherem, and Nehor apparently were educated, capable people, but their learning made them no less vulnerable to Satan's power. Jacob's famous warning that learning can be dangerous comes to mind: "O that cunning plan of the evil one! O the vainness, and the frailties, and the foolishness of men! When they are learned they think they are wise, and they hearken not unto the counsel of God, for they set it aside, supposing they know of themselves, wherefore, their wisdom is foolishness and it profiteth them not. And they shall perish. But to be learned is good if they hearken unto the counsels of God." (2 Ne. 9:28–29.)

In a related but ultimately happier account in the Book of Mormon, we are told of a man named Zeezrom who, though under Satan's influence for a time, was converted by the powerful preaching of Alma and Amulek. Zeezrom was one of the wicked lawyers of Ammonihah who stirred up trouble among the people in order to have more business. He was "expert in the devices of the devil" (Alma 11:21) and used argument, lying, and bribery to turn the people against the missionaries. Alma told Zeezrom that this effort was a plan of the "adversary, and he hath exercised his power in thee" (Alma 12:5). Then, speaking to all who were gathered there, Alma said, "This was a snare of the adversary, which he has laid to catch this people, that he might bring you into subjection unto him, that he might encircle you about with his chains, that he might chain you down to everlasting destruction, according to the power of his captivity" (Alma 12:6). Fortunately Zeezrom came to realize that he had been used by Satan to blind the minds of the people (see Alma 14:6). After his conversion he turned his talents to working for the kingdom of God (see Alma 31:6).

Evil Institutions
("The Great and Abominable Church")

The devil works not only through individuals but also through institutions. Secret criminal organizations like the Gadianton robbers trace their origin to him (see Hel. 6:26–27). Much of the devil's power operates through the "great and abominable church" (1 Ne. 14:9). There are other names for this demonic movement, such as the "mother of abominations" (1 Ne. 14:10, 16), the "whore of all the earth" (1 Ne. 14:10), and the "kingdom of the devil" (2 Ne. 28:19).

What is this "great and abominable church"? Some have tried to identify it with a specific organization, but it seems more likely that Nephi designates it as a force manifesting itself in many different organizations. Here is one of Nephi's clear declarations on the subject: "All churches which are built up to get gain, and all those who are built up to get power over the flesh, and those who are built up to become popular in the eyes of the world, and those who seek the lusts of the flesh and the things of the world, and to do all manner of iniquity; yea, in fine, all those who belong to the kingdom of the devil are they who need fear, and tremble, and quake" (1 Ne. 22:23). This statement clearly categorizes all evil "churches" under the phrase "kingdom of the devil." This is obviously the intent of the angel's words to Nephi in the following famous utterance: "Behold there are save two churches only; the one is the church of the Lamb of God, and the other is the church of the devil" (1 Ne. 14:10; see also Alma 5:39). Probably the simplest definition was provided by the prophet Jacob, who quoted the Lord's words as follows: "Wherefore, he that fighteth against Zion, both Jew and Gentile, both bond and free, both male and female, shall perish; for they are they who are the whore of all the earth" (2 Ne. 10:16). The two principal Book of Mormon chapters on this subject (1 Nephi 13 and 14) speak of fighting God as the dominant quality of the devil's kingdom.

In 1 Nephi 13 a potential problem for interpreters arises when the angel, speaking to Nephi, singles out a specific church that is "most abominable above all other churches" (1 Ne. 13:5, 26). Gold, silver, silks, scarlets, precious clothing, and harlots are associated with this church, and so is brutality as this entity persecutes the Saints of God.

Before the Bible goes forth to the Gentile nations, this demonic institution will delete many of its great truths. (See 1 Ne. 13:5ff. and 26ff.) This is done to "pervert the right ways of the Lord" and to "blind the eyes and harden the hearts of the children of men" (1 Ne. 13:27). The Bible that results, while true and precious, is nevertheless rather incomplete, and as a consequence "an exceedingly great many do stumble, yea, insomuch that Satan hath great power over them" (1 Ne. 13:29). This situation will be remedied, in part, when the Book of Mormon comes forth to confirm the truth of the Bible and help "make known the plain and precious things which have been taken away from" it (1 Ne. 13:40).

Since Nephi saw these events occurring during a particular period of history—the period of apostasy from the primitive Church of Jesus Christ—some have been prone to identify the church "most abominable above all other churches" as the Roman Catholic church. Many Church leaders are opposed to this interpretation, however, and surely there are other reasonable possibilities. The apostate Gnostics, the Roman Empire, or Hellenistic Christianity in general have all been suggested by other interpreters.[2] As for the Roman Catholic church, it could be argued that it was the result of the Apostasy, not its cause. In the book of Revelation, the same term is used for the devil's kingdom as is used in 1 Nephi 14, that term being the "whore," and the "whore" is associated with the city of Rome (see Rev. 17:1, 18), Rome being a central demonic power persecuting the Saints at the time. Some see Rome further identified with the "whore" when in the book of Revelation an angel interprets the seven heads of the beast as the seven "mountains" (or hills) of the city and seven "kings" (or emperors) who had ruled the empire (see Rev. 17:9–10).

Based on our earlier definition of the great and abominable church, we might conclude that the devil may have worked to fight the Saints through all of the above-mentioned organizations at one time or another.

The great and abominable church of the last days, described in 1 Nephi 14, is again characterized as multitudes and nations that "fight against the Lamb of God" (1 Ne. 14:13). It has "dominion over all the earth" (1 Ne. 14:11), and so great is its influence that the Saints of God, though scattered throughout the world, will be small in numbers (see 1 Ne. 14:12). As the end of the world draws close, all the nations which belong "to the mother of abominations" (1 Ne. 14:16) will fight among each other (see 1 Ne. 22:13), and Nephi assures us that "every nation which shall war against thee, O house of Israel, shall be turned one against another, and they shall fall into the pit which they digged to ensnare the people of the Lord. And all that fight against Zion shall be destroyed, and that great whore, who hath perverted the right ways of the Lord, yea, that great and abominable church, shall tumble to the dust and great shall be the fall of it." (1 Ne. 22:14.) "The time cometh speedily," Nephi concludes, quoting another prophet, probably Zenos, "that Satan shall have no more power over the hearts of the children of men" (1 Ne. 22:15); the Lord will come in glory; evil will be destroyed; and the devil will have no power, "because of the righteousness of [the Lord's] people" (1 Ne. 22:26).

Nephi refrained from writing more about the end of the world, since it would be written in John's book of Revelation (see 1 Ne. 14:20–27). Still, both sources give abundant testimony of the ultimate destruction of the devil's kingdom (see 1 Ne. 22:14 and Rev. 18).

How Can We Fortify Ourselves Against the Devil?

While awaiting (and contributing to) the eventual demise of the devil's kingdom, how can we effectively protect ourselves from his temptations? Here are a few suggestions:

1. The devil will eventually have no power, "because of the righteousness of [the Lord's] people" (1 Ne. 22:26). Hence, personal righteousness will keep the devil at bay. Joseph Smith said, "The devil has no power over us only as we permit him. The moment we revolt at anything which comes from God, the devil takes power."[3]

2. We can become informed about his tactics and objectives, and this chapter has been written with that in mind. The best general rule for detecting the works of the devil was given by Mormon: "But whatsoever thing persuadeth men to do evil, and believe not in Christ, and deny him, and serve not God, then ye may know with a perfect knowledge it is of the devil; for after this manner doth the devil work, for he persuadeth no man to do good, no, not one; neither do his angels; neither do they who subject themselves unto him" (Moro. 7:17).

3. We must build our lives on the foundation of Christ. Quoted earlier was Mormon's great statement that if someone "follow[s] Christ he cannot be a servant of the devil" (Moro. 7:11). Because of this truth, one of the most important pieces of advice in scripture are these words of Helaman to his sons:

> And now, my sons, remember, remember that it is upon the rock of our Redeemer, who is Christ, the Son of God, that ye

must build your foundation; that when the devil shall send forth his mighty winds, yea, his shafts in the whirlwind, yea, when all his hail and his mighty storm shall beat upon you, it shall have no power over you to drag you down to the gulf of misery and endless wo, because of the rock upon which ye are built, which is a sure foundation, a foundation whereon if men build they cannot fall (Hel. 5:12).

4. Since there are both good and evil spirits at work, it is incumbent upon each of us to learn to detect the difference. Moroni 7:16–17 surely applies to good and evil spirits. Modern revelation and Joseph Smith's counsel on the subject are also wonderful guides as we strive to sort out the influences that come to us.[4]

Part II

THE BOOK OF MORMON TEACHES OF GOD AND HIS DEALINGS WITH THE NATIONS

Chapter 5

THE GOD OF NATIONS

We live in a time when millions find it difficult to believe in God. There are many atheists, agnostics, and even leftovers from the "God-is-dead" movement of the sixties. We are so immersed in the scientific method that anything that cannot be known empirically seems unreal. Modern man is, in the words of Joe David Brown, "more at home with visible facts than unseen abstractions."[1]

It takes only a quick glance at history to elicit sympathy for this dilemma. Through the ages people have worshiped countless deities, including forces of nature, fertility gods, gods of war, mother gods, and animal gods. Some scholars see in human history an evolutionary development from animism, totemism, polytheism, to monotheism. A common interpretation of Jehovah of the Old Testament is that he began as an angry tribal god of the Hebrews (one god among many) and developed into the ethical monotheistic God of the later prophets. Then Christianity added a mystifying element by claiming that God came to earth in the person of Jesus of Nazareth. Centuries of debate among Christians finally resolved the relationship of the Father, the Son, and the Holy Ghost by declaring that they were "one God in three divine persons" and a pure spirit that filled all of space. Theologians then and since have shown such a dislike for the notion of an anthropomorphic (humanlike) God that their descriptions have become increasingly abstract, such as theologian Paul Tillich's definition of God as the "ultimate ground of being."

What has happened to the traditional Christian concept of God is humorously described in the well-known story of two explorers coming upon a garden in the middle of the jungle. One explorer believes the condition of the garden is clear evidence that a gardener is tending the plot. The other explorer disagrees and says there is no gardener.

So they pitch their tents and wait and no gardener appears. The believer is undaunted and argues that perhaps the gardener is invisible. So they put an electric fence around the garden and patrol it with bloodhounds. But there are no shrieks suggesting an intruder has entered the enclosure and the bloodhounds do not bark. Still the believer maintains his conviction: "There is a gardener, invisible, intangible, insensible to electric shocks, a gardener who has no scent and makes no sound. . . . At last the skeptic despairs, 'But what remains of your original assertion? Just how does what you call an invisible, intangible, eternally elusive gardener differ from an imaginary gardener or even from no gardener at all?'"[2] As in this story about an "elusive gardener," God as conceptualized by traditional Christianity has been abstracted nearly out of existence.

If the world will listen, the Book of Mormon can teach much about the true nature of God. It should be said at the outset that Book of Mormon prophets do not discuss the question of God's existence; they always assume it. They do, however, have much to tell us about his attributes.

The "Oneness" of God

Latter-day Saints teach that the Godhead consists of three divine personages: the Father; the Son, Jesus Christ; and the Holy Ghost. The Father and the Son have tangible bodies, and the Holy Ghost is a body of spirit (see D&C 130:22). These divine beings are spoken of in the scriptures as being manlike, personal, benevolent, all-powerful, and all-knowing.

The Book of Mormon tells us little about the Father directly. Most references to God in the book refer to Jesus Christ, who is the Creator, the God of ancient Israel, the divine administrator of the Godhead to the peoples of the earth. Among the many Book of Mormon names for Christ appear the exalted titles "Almighty God" (Jacob 2:10), "Creator of all things" (Mosiah 3:8), and the "Eternal Father" (Alma 11:38, 39). When Samuel the Lamanite spoke of Jesus coming to earth, he referred to him as "the Son of God, the Father of heaven and of earth, the Creator of all things from the beginning" (Hel. 14:12). The title page of the Book of Mormon calls Christ the "Eternal God, manifesting himself unto all nations."

Notwithstanding this, there is abundant evidence that the Nephites understood that Christ was the Son of God the Father and that the Father and the Son had separate identities. The common language of the Nephite prophets makes this clear. Nephi's early revelations taught him that the virgin Mary would be the mother of the Son of God, after the manner of the flesh" (1 Ne. 11:18). He was told that her baby would be "the Lamb of God, yea, even the Son of the Eternal Father" (1 Ne. 11:21). Later Nephi predicted that "the Only Begotten of the Father" would come to earth and be crucified. He foresaw that the Jews will someday "be persuaded to believe in Christ, the Son of God," and will "look not forward any more for another Messiah" to come. The Messiah's name, said Nephi, "shall be Jesus Christ, the Son of God." (2 Ne. 25:12, 13, 16, 19.)

Numerous Book of Mormon examples could be produced in which God and Christ are commonly spoken of as separate beings (for instance, see Jacob 4:4–5; Alma 5:48; 11:44; 12:33–34), but for present purposes one more example will suffice. In one of his final discourses, speaking of Jesus' baptism, Nephi wrote that Jesus "humbleth himself before the Father, and witnesseth unto the Father that he would be obedient unto him in keeping his commandments" (2 Ne. 31:7). Continuing, Nephi distinguished between the Father and the Son in verses 10 through 13 and in verse 18. The latter verse reads, in part: "Ye have done according to the commandments of the Father and the Son; and ye have received the Holy Ghost, which witnesses of the Father and the Son."

Nephi closed the above discourse with a comment on the oneness of the Godhead, saying, "And now, behold, this is the doctrine of Christ, and the only and true doctrine of the Father, and of the Son, and of the Holy Ghost, which is one God, without end. Amen." (2 Ne. 31:21.) As is the case with the Bible, there are Book of Mormon passages that speak of the Godhead as one; but several passages from the Book of Mormon, the Bible, and the Doctrine and Covenants clearly show that *oneness* is often a synonym for *unity*. For instance, the scriptures speak of the oneness of a husband and wife (see Mark 10:8) and of the need for Church members to be one (see D&C 38:27). Jesus spoke of that oneness to those on the American continent in these words: "Behold, I am Jesus Christ the Son of God. I created the heavens and the earth, and all things that in them are. I was with the Father from the beginning. I am in the Father, and the Father in me; and in me hath the Father glorified his name." (3 Ne. 9:15.) Later he said, "And thus will the Father bear record of me, and the Holy Ghost will bear record unto him of the Father and me; for the Father, and I, and the Holy Ghost are one" (3 Ne. 11:36). On another occasion, having gone "a little way off" (3 Ne. 19:27) to pray while his Nephite disciples also prayed, Jesus spoke of oneness (in connection with the disciples as well as all who believed on the disciples' words) in language reminiscent of that which he used in prayer while with his Jerusalem Apostles: "Father, I pray not for the world, but for those whom thou hast given me out of the world, because of their faith, that they may be purified in me, that I may be in them as thou, Father, art in me, that we may be one, that I may be glorified in them" (3 Ne. 19:29; compare John 17:20–22). It would be ludicrous to assume that Jesus was praying that the disciples would somehow merge their physical beings with his own. So, likewise, is it folly to interpret Jesus and the Father's oneness as some kind of mysterious sameness of being. The oneness of the Godhead is that the three divine beings think, act, and work together as one!

Jesus as the Father

Another controversial matter that is sometimes used to find fault with the Book of Mormon is a number of references speaking of Jesus as the Father. When Zeezrom, the scheming attorney of Ammonihah, inquired, "Is the Son of God the very Eternal Father?" Amulek replied, "Yea, he is the very Eternal Father of heaven and of earth, and all things which in them are." (Alma 11:38–39.) Jesus said to the brother of Jared, "I am the Father, I am the light, and the life, and the truth of the world" (Ether 4:12). Abinadi even spoke of Jesus as "the Father and Son" (Mosiah 15:3).

In 1916 the First Presidency of the Church issued an official statement explaining this issue.[3] The statement shows that Jesus can be called the Father in three different ways:

1. He is the Father because of his role as the Creator. Under the father's direction he created the worlds (see Moses 1:31–33; 7:30); consequently the Book of Mormon refers to Jesus as "the Father of heaven and earth, the Creator of all things from the beginning" (Mosiah 3:8).

2. He is the Father of all those who are spiritually born of God. A good example of this is found in the words of King Benjamin to his converted subjects: "Because of the covenant which ye have made ye shall be called the children of Christ, his sons, and his daughters; for behold, this day he hath spiritually begotten you; for ye say that your hearts are changed through faith on his name; therefore, ye are born of him and have become his sons and his daughters" (Mosiah 5:7).

3. Finally, the Savior is the Father by "divine investiture of authority," which means that he is fully authorized by the Father to speak and act for him.

The Attributes of God

There are times in the Book of Mormon when it is difficult to determine which member of the Godhead is being discussed. King Benjamin, for example, urged his people, "Believe in God; believe that he is, and that he created all things, both in heaven and in earth; believe that he has all wisdom, and all power, both in heaven and in earth" (Mosiah 4:9). Was he speaking of the Father or the Son? Since they act as one, and since Jesus taught that to know him is to know the Father (see John 14:9), it is probably not so important that we know who is being spoken of in every instance. Much of the material that follows, therefore, will speak of God in general and make no attempt to identify which member of the Godhead is being referred to in each instance.

Book of Mormon prophets uniformly teach the existence of a God who is all-powerful (see Jacob 2:5). In a masterful discourse on God's powers, Mormon says:

> Yea, behold at his voice do the hills and the mountains tremble and quake. . . .
> Yea, by the power of his voice doth the whole earth shake. . . .
> Yea, and if he say unto the earth—Move—it is moved.
> Yea, if he say unto the earth—Thou shalt go back, that it lengthen out the day for many hours—it is done. . . .
> And behold, also, if he say unto the waters of the great deep—Be thou dried up—it is done.
> Behold, if he say unto this mountain—Be thou raised up, and come over and fall upon that city, that it be buried up—behold it is done. (Hel. 12:9, 11, 13–14, 16–17.)

God has created all things (see 2 Ne. 2:14); controls natural elements (see Hel. 11:12ff.); and knows all things (see Moro. 7:22; Alma 26:35, 37; 2 Ne. 2:24; 9:20; Mosiah 4:9), including future events (see Alma 13:3, 7) and even the thoughts and intents of our hearts (see Alma 12:3; 18:32; 12:14).

God is the embodiment of perfect morality. The prophet Mormon told us that "all things which are good cometh of God. . . . Wherefore, every thing which inviteth and enticeth to do good, and to love God, and to serve him, is inspired of God." (Moro. 7:12–13.) The Lord is "a God of truth" and cannot lie (Ether 3:12). "He cannot walk in crooked paths; neither doth he vary from that which he hath said; neither hath he a shadow of turning from the right to the left, or from that which is right to that which is wrong; therefore, his course is one eternal round" (Alma 7:20). God's word is completely trust-worthy: "He never doth vary from that which he hath said" (Mosiah 2:22); and "it is impossible for him to deny his word" (Alma 11:34). He is not partial or changeable (see Moro. 8:18).

The Universality of God's Love

"God is mindful of every people, whatsoever land they may be in; yea, he numbereth his people, and his bowels of mercy are over all the earth" (Alma 26:37). These were the words of Ammon to his fellow missionaries. This wonderful truth is taught throughout the Book of Mormon. One of the most powerful sermons on this theme is by Nephi:

> He [the Lord God] doeth not anything save it be for the benefit of the world; for he loveth the world, even that he layeth down his own life that he may draw all men unto him. Wherefore, he commandeth none that they shall not partake of his salvation. . . .
>
> Behold, hath the Lord commanded any that they should not partake of his goodness? Behold I say unto you, Nay; but all men are privileged the one like unto the other, and none are forbidden. . . .
>
> . . . He inviteth them all to come unto him and partake of his goodness; and he denieth none that come unto him, black and white, bond and free, male and female; and he remembereth the heathen; and all are alike unto God, both Jew and Gentile. (2 Ne. 26:24, 28, 33.)

God's goodness and love are manifested in his untiring efforts to bring happiness and salvation to his children. Nephi told us that "the Lord hath created the earth that it should be inhabited; and he hath created his children that they should possess it" (1 Ne. 17:36). Our mortal life is a time for growth and testing, a "probationary state," a "time to prepare for that endless state . . . which is after the resurrection" (Alma 12:24). God gives us a plan to live by—Alma calls it "the great plan of happiness" (Alma 42:8)—and will finally judge us according to how well we follow the plan. In the context of describing our fate "if we have hardened our hearts against the word" (Alma 12:13), Alma makes it clear that God's judgment will be fair:

We must come forth and stand before him in his glory, and in his power, and in his might, majesty, and dominion, and acknowledge to our everlasting shame that all his judgments are just; that he is just in all his works, and that he is merciful unto the children of men, and that he has all power to save every man that believeth on his name and bringeth forth fruit meet for repentance (Alma 12:15).

In his divine wisdom, God gives to nations and individuals the amount of truth they are prepared to receive. Nephi taught that "the Lord esteemeth all flesh in one" (1 Ne. 17:35) and that he "manifesteth himself unto all those who believe in him, by the power of the Holy Ghost; yea, unto every nation, kindred, tongue, and people, working mighty miracles, signs, and wonders, among the children of men according to their faith" (2 Ne. 26:13). Alma the Younger declared that "the Lord doth grant unto all nations, of their own nation and tongue, to teach his word, yea, in wisdom, all that he seeth fit that they should have" (Alma 29:8). On another occasion he revealed that the level of truth people received was determined by their worthiness:

It is given unto many to know the mysteries of God; nevertheless they are laid under a strict command that they shall not impart only according to the portion of his word which he doth grant unto the children of men, according to the heed and diligence which they give unto him.

And therefore, he that will harden his heart, the same receiveth the lesser portion of the word; and he that will not harden his heart, to him is given the greater portion of the word, until it is given unto him to know the mysteries of God until he know them in full.

And they that will harden their hearts, to them is given the lesser portion of the word until they know nothing concerning his mysteries; and then they are taken captive by the devil. (Alma 12:9–11.)

Under this principle of revelation, virtually all nations obtain some measure of God's truth. Some Church leaders have applied this truth to say that God has granted to people such as Confucius, Buddha, Mohammed, the Protestant Reformers, and even some secular teachers a measure of his truth.[4] The Lord gave expression to this principle while chastising the latter-day Gentiles for refusing the Book of Mormon:

And I do this that I may prove unto many that I am the same yesterday, today, and forever; and that I speak forth my words according to mine own pleasure. And because that I have spoken one word ye need not suppose that I cannot speak another; for my work is not yet finished; neither shall it be until the end of man, neither from that time henceforth and forever. . . .

For I command all men, both in the east and in the west, and in the north, and in the south, and in the islands of the sea, that they shall write the words which I speak unto them. . . .

For behold, I shall speak unto the Jews and they shall write it; and I shall also speak unto the Nephites and they shall write it; and I shall also speak unto the other tribes of the house of Israel, which I have led away, and they shall write it; and I shall also speak unto all nations of the earth and they shall write it. (2 Ne. 29:9, 11–12.)

Where are these divine writings produced by "all nations of the earth"? Could this be referring to the sacred writings of the various world religions?

All of religious history, then, is the story of God's attempts to save his people, and it clearly reveals God to be a being of supreme love and mercy. One of the difficult questions of theology is the extent to which God intervenes in the affairs of humankind to bring about his purposes. Is he "transcendent"—that is, above and removed from the world—or is he "imminent," meaning actively involved in world affairs? The Book of Mormon teaches that God is an active participant in historical events. Nephi taught his brothers that God "raiseth up a righteous nation, and destroyeth the nations of the wicked. And he leadeth away the righteous into precious lands, and the wicked he destroyeth, and curseth the land unto them for their sakes." (1 Ne. 17:37–38).

The allegory of Zenos, in chapter 5 of the book of Jacob, is a remarkable account of God's dealings with humanity throughout history. It is a story of workers laboring to bring an olive vineyard into fruitful productivity. It is scriptural history in microcosm.

Jacob quoted this allegory because he saw prophetically that the Jews would reject Christ, "the only sure foundation" upon which they could build (see Jacob 4:16–18). The allegory portrayed God's untiring efforts to save them (and all mankind). Indeed, to me, the most moving part of the allegory is when the grieving Lord asks:

But what could I have done more in my vineyard? Have I slackened mine hand, that I have not nourished it? Nay, I have nourished it, and I have digged about it, and I have pruned it, and I have dunged it; and I have stretched forth mine hand almost all the day long, and the end draweth nigh. And it grieveth me that I should hew down all the trees of my vineyard, and cast them into the fire that they should be burned. (Jacob 5:47.)

In his commentary that followed, Jacob assured Israel that the Lord would not forget them and would "set his hand again the second time to recover" them (Jacob 6:2). Therefore, he implored his people: "After ye have been nourished by the good word of God all the day long, will ye bring forth evil fruit, that ye must be hewn down and cast into the fire? Behold, will ye reject these words?" (Jacob 6:7–8.) Clearly, Jacob was trying to turn Israel to righteousness by applying the insights of Zenos's allegory.[5]

A God of Justice

We have been examining God's love and mercy, but every student of the Book of Mormon knows that he is also a God of justice. He will not let his mercy rob justice of its rightful claims; otherwise, say the scriptures, he "would cease to be God" (Alma 42:13). He will not limit man's agency in order to prevent evil and sin. He sometimes destroys the wicked and, on occasion, even allows the righteous to perish. Not knowing the mind of God, we are forced to admit that the Lord's ways are not always the same as our ways. "For as the heavens are higher than the earth, so are my ways higher than your ways," said the Lord to the prophet Isaiah (Isa. 55:9).

Many people are inclined to blame calamities on God. But when Samuel the Lamanite predicted that celestial signs, tempests, and destructions would occur in America, he also declared that an angel had assured him that those who were destroyed in the turmoil would bring that destruction upon themselves:

And the angel said unto me that many shall see greater things than these, . . . to the intent that there should be no cause for unbelief among the children of men—

And this to the intent that whosoever will believe might be saved, and that whosoever will not believe, a righteous judgment might come upon them; and also if they are condemned they bring upon themselves their own condemnation.

And now remember, remember, my brethren, that whosoever perisheth, perisheth unto himself; and whosoever doeth iniquity, doeth it unto himself; for behold, ye are free; ye are permitted to act for yourselves; for behold, God hath given unto you a knowledge and he hath made you free. (Hel. 14:28–30.)

Samuel said further, "The people of Nephi hath [the Lord] loved, and . . . in the days of their iniquities hath he chastened them because he loveth them" (Hel. 15:3). When chastening occurs, no doubt even many God-fearing mortals might not interpret their experience as a manifestation of God's love—but again, God's ways are not always our ways.

There is an amazing Book of Mormon story concerning the missionaries Alma and Amulek. The wicked people of Ammonihah were slaughtering the two missionaries' converts, casting them into the fire and making Alma and Amulek witness the carnage.

> And when Amulek saw the pains of the women and children who were consuming in the fire, he also was pained; and he said unto Alma: How can we witness this awful scene? Therefore let us stretch forth our hands, and exercise the power of God which is in us, and save them from the flames.
>
> But Alma said unto him: The Spirit constraineth me that I must not stretch forth mine hand; for behold the Lord receiveth them up unto himself, in glory; and he doth suffer that they may do this thing, or that the people may do this thing unto them, according to the hardness of their hearts, that the judgments which he shall exercise upon them in his wrath may be just; and the blood of the innocent shall stand as a witness against them, yea, and cry mightily against them at the last day. (Alma 14:10–11.)

Amulek's reaction was a very human one; Alma's reply is beyond our full comprehension, but he assured his bewildered companion that the hardened people of Ammonihah were permitted to commit these atrocities that the judgments of God might be just.

We learn in the Book of Mormon that God destroys those who become "ripened in iniquity" (Ether 2:9), that he "slayeth the wicked to bring forth his righteous purposes" (1 Ne. 4:13), that he led Joshua to drive the wicked Canaanites from the promised land of Palestine (see 1 Ne. 17:32–35), and that he caused that the wicked Nephites should be destroyed:

> Behold, it came to pass that three hundred and twenty years had passed away, and the more wicked part of the Nephites were destroyed.

> For the Lord would not suffer, after he had led them out of
> the land of Jerusalem and kept and preserved them from falling
> into the hands of their enemies, yea, he would not suffer that the
> words should not be verified, which he spake unto our fathers,
> saying that: Inasmuch as ye will not keep my commandments ye
> shall not prosper in the land.
>
> Wherefore, the Lord did visit them in great judgment; never-
> theless, he did spare the righteous that they should not perish,
> but did deliver them out of the hands of their enemies. (Omni
> 1:5–7.)

The Lord poured out great destructions upon the face of America
prior to his ministry to the Nephites (see 3 Ne. 8, 9). At other times
he had smitten some "with famine and sore afflictions, to stir them
up in remembrance of their duty" (Mosiah 1:17; see also Hel.
11:4–7). He allowed the Lamanites to enslave Alma's people, for "the
Lord seeth fit to chasten his people; yea, he trieth their patience and
their faith" (Mosiah 23:21). Yet he made their burdens light (see
Mosiah 24:15) and finally freed them through his divine intervention
(see Mosiah 24:19–25). Let us not overlook the fact that God at times,
according to his wisdom, intervenes to save the innocent.

Let us affirm our conviction that God is loving and just; but let us
also recognize that in our finite wisdom we cannot always tell how
these virtues are manifest in world affairs. From the knowledge we
have of God, we can surely say, with Paul, "We know that all things
work together for good to them that love God" (Rom. 8:28).

Chapter 6

JESUS CHRIST, THE HEART OF THE BOOK OF MORMON

Nothing could be of greater value to the modern world than an authentic second witness for Jesus Christ. Skepticism concerning his divinity is pervasive in the Western world, and he is not well known in the Eastern Hemisphere, where Christianity is still a minority religion.

A few years ago conservative Christians staged a national protest over a movie called *The Last Temptation of Christ.* In it Christ was depicted as a human weakling, confused as to his mission and identity. A student acquaintance inquired how it was possible to present Christ so contrary to the portrait found in the biblical Gospels. The truth is that many people today question the accuracy of that biblical portrait and therefore feel at liberty to construct some other identity for the Savior. There actually exists a bewildering number of opinions about who and what Jesus was—a messianic pretender, an eschatological prophet, a magician, a Galilean charismatic, to name a few.

In connection with the furor generated by *The Last Temptation of Christ,* an article appeared in *Time* magazine entitled, "Who Was Jesus?" It asserted that "the search for the historical Jesus . . . rests on one fundamental issue: How reliable are the Gospels?"[1] The article went on to say: "In the view of numerous academicians, the anonymous authors of the four Gospels (later conventionally labeled *Matthew, Mark, Luke* and *John*) were working from second- and third-hand materials, passed along by word of mouth for some decades before being written down. Consequently, the Gospels cannot be taken as gospel; that is, they cannot in every instance be considered as describing actual events."[2] As discussed in chapter 1, this is not an unusual interpretation of the Gospels.

In light of this skepticism, how urgently does the world need the Book of Mormon's testimony of Christ?

The Centrality of Christ

The primary objective of Book of Mormon prophets was to testify of the divinity of Christ, to "make known to all kindreds, tongues, and people, that the Lamb of God is the Son of the Eternal Father, and the Savior of the world; and that all men must come unto him, or they cannot be saved" (1 Ne. 13:40). The Book of Mormon mentions over twenty people by name who saw Jesus; he was the heart of the Book of Mormon people's religion; his future ministry and atonement were the focus of their hopes and dreams. Centuries before the Savior's appearance, men like Nephi knew of him and labored "diligently to write, to persuade our children, and also our brethren, to believe in Christ" (2 Ne. 25:23). Said Nephi, "We talk of Christ, we rejoice in Christ, we preach of Christ, we prophesy of Christ, and we write according to our prophecies, that our children may know to what source they may look for a remission of their sins" (2 Ne. 25:26). Nephi was concerned not only about his contemporaries but also about future generations. "The fulness of mine intent," he said concerning his writings, "is that I may persuade men to come unto the God of Abraham, and the God of Isaac, and the God of Jacob, and be saved" (1 Ne. 6:4). In a similar expression, he wrote, "I, Nephi, have written these things unto my people, that perhaps I might persuade them that they would remember the Lord their Redeemer" (1 Ne. 19:18). Two other major writers of the Book of Mormon had similar hopes. Mormon must have spent hundreds of hours abridging the records of his people so that a future generation might come to know that "Jesus is the Christ, the Son of the living God" (Morm. 5:14). Moroni carried on his father's work, abridging the Jaredite record, writing a chapter of his own, and finally appending a title page to the completed volume. This last item declared that the book's purpose, in part, was to convince "Jew and Gentile that Jesus is the Christ, the Eternal God, manifesting himself unto all nations."

What about the other prophets? Jacob, brother of Nephi, said that "none of the prophets have written, nor prophesied, save they have spoken concerning this Christ" (Jacob 7:11). Abinadi also argued that all past prophets have spoken of Christ: "Did not Moses prophesy unto them [the children of Israel] concerning the coming of the Messiah, and that God should redeem his people? Yea, and even all the prophets who have prophesied ever since the world began—have they not spoken more or less concerning these things?" (Mosiah 13:33.)

Here are some further examples demonstrating Book of Mormon prophets' central interest in Christ: Nephi loved the writings of Isaiah because that prophet would "more fully persuade" his brethren "to believe in the Lord their Redeemer" (1 Ne. 19:23). Apparently one of Abinadi's favorite scriptures was the suffering-servant prophecy of Isaiah 53 (see Mosiah 14), which poetically described Jesus' suffering for the sins of the world. Zenock, Neum, and Zenos—prophets not mentioned in the Old Testament but whose writings appeared on the more complete plates of brass—knew of Jesus' crucifixion and burial, as pointed out by Nephi (see 1 Ne. 19:10). The reason why Mormon was so impressed with the small plates of Nephi and part of the reason why he attached them to his own abridgment is that they contained many prophecies of Christ (see W of M 1:4).

Recent statistical studies have proved just how thoroughly the Book of Mormon is a Christ-centered book. Monte S. Nyman of Brigham Young University has shown that of 239 chapters in the Book of Mormon, only 6 make no mention of the Savior![3] Susan Easton Black of Brigham Young University discovered that the Book of Mormon's 6,607 verses contain 3,925 references to Christ.[4] She has found 101 different names or titles for Jesus Christ in the Book of Mormon, concluding that there is "some form of his name on an average of every 1.7 verses" in the book.[5]

There are many other ways in which Jesus Christ is presented as central to Book of Mormon religion. The following are illustrative: The Book of Mormon teaches that (1) only through the atonement of Jesus Christ can the world be saved (see Alma 21:9; 2 Ne. 10:24; 9:23); (2) Christ is the object of our faith (see Moro. 7:26); (3) in baptism the recipient makes a covenant to serve Christ and keep his commandments (see Mosiah 18:10, 13; 21:35; Alma 7:15–16); (4) in taking the sacrament, disciples constantly renew covenants to take upon themselves the name of Christ, to always remember him, and to keep Christ's commandments (see Moro. 4:3; 3 Ne. 18:7–11); (5) Christ is the father of the spiritually reborn (see Mosiah 5:7); (6) Jesus taught that the Church should be named after himself (see 3 Ne. 27:1–8); and (7) Christ declared himself the model for Christian behavior—"What manner of men ought ye to be?" he asked the Nephite disciples. "Verily I say unto you, even as I am." (3 Ne. 27:27.)

In 1982 the Church gave the Book of Mormon a subtitle, "Another Testament of Jesus Christ." Nothing could more accurately describe the contents of the book.

What the Book of Mormon Teaches About Christ

The Book of Mormon teaches us of Christ's divine identity. All of Jesus' titles found in the Book of Mormon tell us something of his person and mission. Among the titles are "Almighty God" (Jacob 2:10), God's "Beloved Son" (2 Ne. 31:11), "Creator of all things" (Mosiah 3:8), "Eternal Father" (Alma 11:38), "God of Abraham, and Isaac, and Jacob" (Mosiah 7:19), "Holy Messiah" (2 Ne. 2:6), "Mediator" (2 Ne. 2:28), "Only Begotten of the Father" (Alma 5:48), "Prince of Peace" (2 Ne. 19:6), "Savior" (1 Ne. 10:4), "Son of the most high God" (1 Ne. 11:6), "God of miracles" (2 Ne. 27:23), "good shepherd" (Alma 5:38), and "truth of the world" (Ether 4:12).

Possibly the best description is the one Jesus applied to himself when his voice was heard by the survivors of the destructions occurring on the American continent:

> Behold, I am Jesus Christ the Son of God. I created the heavens and the earth, and all things that in them are. I was with the Father from the beginning. I am in the Father, and the Father in me; and in me hath the Father glorified his name. . . .
>
> . . . By me redemption cometh, and in me is the law of Moses fulfilled.
>
> I am the light and the life of the world. I am Alpha and Omega, the beginning and the end. . . .
>
> Behold, I have come unto the world to bring redemption unto the world, to save the world from sin. (3 Ne. 9:15, 17, 18, 21.)

The Book of Mormon teaches about Jesus' earthly ministry. Nephi, desirous of learning the interpretation of his father's dream, was given a vision of Christ's ministry (was the tree a symbol of Christ?) (see 1 Ne. 11:7, 21). Nephi had learned from Lehi that Christ would come to earth in six hundred years from the time Lehi left Jerusalem (see 1 Ne. 10:4). In his vision Nephi saw Jesus' "beautiful" mother (see 1 Ne. 11:13–18); he also saw John the Baptist preparing the way, and he saw the Savior's baptism, his rejection by the people, the Twelve Apostles, his miracles, and his crucifixion (see 1 Ne. 11:27–29, 31–33). Nephi saw that Christ's death would be marked by destructions and that the Savior would make a personal visit to America (see 1 Ne. 12:1–10; see also 2 Ne. 26:1–9).

King Benjamin (see Mosiah 3:3ff.), Alma the Younger (see Alma 7:7ff.), and Samuel the Lamanite (see Hel. 14:2ff.) also foresaw the Savior's coming. An angel gave to King Benjamin a remarkable summary of Jesus' life, part of which reads:

> For behold, the time cometh, and is not far distant, that with power, the Lord Omnipotent who reigneth, who was, and is from all eternity to all eternity, shall come down from heaven among

the children of men, and shall dwell in a tabernacle of clay, and shall go forth amongst men, working mighty miracles. . . .

And lo, he shall suffer temptations, and pain of body, hunger, thirst, and fatigue, even more than man can suffer, except it be unto death. . . .

And he shall be called Jesus Christ, the Son of God, the Father of heaven and earth, the Creator of all things from the beginning; and his mother shall be called Mary.

And lo, he cometh unto his own, that salvation might come unto the children of men even through faith on his name; and even after all this they shall consider him a man, and say that he hath a devil, and shall scourge him, and shall crucify him. (Mosiah 3:5, 7–9.)

Samuel the Lamanite, who lived near the time of Christ, predicted that the signs of Christ's birth would be a day and a night and a day without darkness (see Hel. 14:3–4), a "new star," and "many signs and wonders in heaven" (Hel. 14:5–6). At the time of the Crucifixion, the sun would be darkened and the moon and the stars would refuse to give their light for three days. Frightening destructions would occur, such as thunderings, lightnings, great tempests, and the shaking of the earth. (See Hel. 14:20ff.) These spectacular wonders would be given for the "intent that there should be no cause for unbelief among the children of men" (Hel. 14:28).

Jesus' American Ministry

Jesus' ministry to America was a short one. He spent only three full days there, with brief appearances thereafter. We are not told how many, but we do know that he filled what hours he had with teaching, blessing, healing, organizing the Church, and introducing ordinances.

Jesus' teachings were extensive. Mormon wrote that Jesus "did expound all things unto them, both great and small" (3 Ne. 26:1). In fact, "he did expound all things, even from the beginning until the time that he should come in his glory" (3 Ne. 26:3). Unfortunately, we have only a small digest of what Jesus taught the Nephites. Originally "the more part of the things which [Jesus] taught the people" was recorded on the large plates of Nephi (3 Ne. 26:7). Yet Mormon was instructed to write only a small portion on his plates because the Lord wanted to "try the faith" of future readers (see 3 Ne. 26:11).

"And if it shall so be that they shall believe these things," wrote Mormon, "then shall the greater things be made manifest unto them" (3 Ne. 26:9).

It is irresistible to draw contrasts and parallels between Jesus' Palestinian and American ministries. One of the greatest dissimilarities is seen in the spiritual receptivity of the people. In Palestine, much of the Savior's time was spent trying to convince his listeners that he was the Savior. In America, the wicked were destroyed, and those who remained, awed by the dramatic events that preceded his coming, were completely receptive to the gospel. This explains the amazing outpouring of spiritual power to the Nephites, the ability of Jesus to perform healing miracles (among the Jews he was unable to perform such great miracles "because of their unbelief" [3 Ne. 19:35]), Jesus' description of events to the end of the world, and the Christian utopia (the society of Zion) that resulted from the righteousness of the people (see 4 Ne.).

Destructions Preceding the Ministry

In the beginning of the thirty-fourth year A.D., there arose the greatest storm anyone had ever seen. There were thunderings, lightnings, and earthquakes. Cities were destroyed, buildings toppled, highways broken up, and the "whole face of the land was changed" (3 Ne. 8:12; all further references in this chapter are from 3 Nephi unless otherwise designated). These three hours of terror were followed by three days of "thick darkness" in which not even a fire could be ignited (8:20–21).

Suddenly through the darkness a voice was heard. The people heard these words: "Wo, wo, wo unto this people; wo unto the inhabitants of the whole earth except they shall repent; for the devil laugheth, and his angels rejoice, because of the slain of the fair sons and daughters of my people; and it is because of their iniquity and abominations that they are fallen!" (9:2.) The voice enumerated the destructions that had occurred, called the survivors to repentance, and then identified himself: "Behold, I am Jesus Christ the Son of God. I created the heavens and the earth. . . . I am the light and the life of the world. . . . Behold, I have come unto the world to bring redemption unto the world, to save the world from sin." (9:15, 18, 21.)

In their astonishment, the people ceased their lamentations, and "there was silence in all the land for the space of many hours" (10:2). Obviously such events stirred every soul to the depths of his being.

After the Lord's voice was heard again and after the three days had passed, the darkness dispersed and rejoicing was heard throughout the land.

Not long after this,[6] while a large group of people were assembled at the temple in Bountiful, a voice was heard: "Behold my Beloved Son, in whom I am well pleased, in whom I have glorified my name—hear ye him" (11:7). As the people looked heavenward they beheld a glorious being descend and identify himself as Jesus Christ. He allowed them individually to touch his wounds to prove that he had "been slain for the sins of the world" (11:14). Thus assured with a certain witness that a God was among them, the multitude cried, "Hosanna! Blessed be the name of the Most High God!" The record continues, "And they did fall down at the feet of Jesus, and did worship him." (11:17.) Such was the majestic beginning of Christ's American ministry.

The Events of Jesus' American Ministry

The first thing Jesus did after inviting the multitude to see and touch his wounds was to call twelve disciples to assist with the work of the kingdom. Nephi, an experienced prophet, and eleven others were selected from the multitude, taught the ordinance of baptism, and given power to minister in Christ's name. Mormon made this comment about their authority: "Whoso receiveth not the words of Jesus and the words of those whom he hath sent receiveth not him; and therefore he will not receive them at the last day" (28:34). Later the Church was organized and named after Christ. When questioned about the proper name of the Church, Jesus declared, "And how be it my church save it be called in my name? For if a church be called in Moses' name then it be Moses' church." (27:8). So successful were Jesus and his ministers that everyone became converted and the Church expanded into an ideal, or Zion, society that existed for over one hundred and fifty years.

Jesus Taught the Gospel

The gospel of salvation was the core of Jesus' message. "Behold I have given unto you my gospel," he testified during an appearance to his Nephite disciples, "and this is the gospel which I have given unto you—that I came into the world to do the will of my Father, because my Father sent me. And my Father sent me that I might be lifted up upon the cross; and after that I had been lifted up upon the cross, that I might draw all men unto me." (27:13–14.) His definition of the gospel also included the first principles and ordinances as well as enduring to the end—"that ye may be sanctified by the reception of the Holy Ghost, that ye may stand spotless before me at the last day" (see 27:13–20).

Two highlights of Jesus' gospel teaching were the Sermon on the Mount (or Sermon at the Temple, as some call the American version) and his quintessential rule for Christian living—"The works which ye have seen me do that shall ye also do. . . . Therefore, what manner of men ought ye to be? Verily I say unto you, even as I am." (27:21, 27.) Because several principles from the Sermon on the Mount (or Sermon at the Temple) are discussed elsewhere in this book (see chapters 15–17), the present discussion will only point out some interesting differences between the sermon as found in the Bible (see Matt. 5–7) and the Book of Mormon version (see 3 Ne. 12–14).[7] (1) To the first beatitude—"blessed are the poor in spirit"—is added the words "who come unto me" (3 Ne. 12:3). (2) To the fourth beatitude— "blessed are all they who do hunger and thirst after righteousness"— is added, "for they shall be filled with the Holy Ghost" (3 Ne. 12:6). (3) There are places where obvious references to features of Jerusalem society of the first century A.D. are omitted from the Book of Mormon sermon. For example, in the Book of Mormon there is no mention of scribes and Pharisees (comp. Matt. 5:20 and 3 Ne. 12:20); the word *senine* is used instead of *farthing* (comp. Matt. 5:26 and 3 Ne. 12:26); the word *Jerusalem* (found in Matt. 5:35) is omitted (see 3 Ne. 12:35); and references to publicans (found in Matt. 5:46–47) are omitted (see 3 Ne. 12:45–48). (4) In the Bible version the Lord commands that we should not be angry with our brother "without a cause" (Matt. 5:22). Third Nephi (along with the best New Testament manuscripts[8]) omits this phrase (see 3 Ne. 12:22). (5) Instead of the counsel to pluck out an eye or cut off a hand if one is tempted to licentious behavior (see Matt. 5:29–30), in the Book of Mormon sermon the Savior says: "Behold, I give unto you a commandment, that ye suffer none of these things to enter into your heart; for it is better that ye should deny yourselves of these things, wherein ye will take up your cross, than that ye should be cast into hell" (3 Ne. 12:29–30). (6) In Palestine, before his resurrection, Jesus said, "Be ye therefore perfect, even as your Father which is in heaven is perfect" (Matt. 5:48); in America, however, after his resurrection, the Savior said, "Therefore I would that ye should be perfect even as I, or your Father who is in heaven is perfect" (3 Ne. 12:48). (7) The phrases "thy kingdom come" and "give us this day our daily bread" (Matt. 6:10–11) are omitted from the Lord's Prayer in the Book of Mormon (see 3 Ne. 13:9–13). (8) The counsel to "take no thought for your life, what ye shall eat, or what ye shall drink" in the Book of Mormon is directed to the twelve disciples, not the multitude (3 Ne. 13:25). These items constitute the main differences between the two sermons. The question arises, Why are the two sermons so much alike, most of the wording being exactly the same? Some have hypothesized that Joseph Smith used Matthew's wording, altering it only when he saw differences on the plates of Mormon.

Additional Teachings of Jesus

Following Jesus' sermon at the temple in Bountiful, some were puzzled about the "fulfilling" of the law of Moses, that "old things had passed away, and that all things had become new" (15:2). The law of Moses had been their religious standard for centuries; was it to be swept away? "Behold, I am he that gave the law," said Jesus, "and I am he who covenanted with my people Israel; therefore, the law in me is fulfilled, for I have come to fulfil the law; therefore it hath an end" (15:5).

Jesus taught his Nephite disciples much about the history of the world and their role in that history. They were a remnant of the tribe of Joseph, and God had given them the promised land. They were the "other sheep" that he had spoken of to his Jewish followers, but the Jews had thought he was speaking of the Gentiles. (See 15:15–22.) Jesus further explained that he had still "other sheep, which are not of this land, neither of the land of Jerusalem," that he must visit (16:1, 3).

Jesus spoke of the scattering and gathering of Israel (see 20:29–33), of the rise of a powerful Gentile nation who would be both a curse and a blessing to the Lamanite remnant on this continent. That nation was warned to repent lest the "remnant of Jacob" prove to be a destructive force among them (see 3 Ne. 16; also 20:16 and 21:12). Finally, the New Jerusalem would be built on this land and the ten tribes would return from the north before the Savior's second coming (see 20:22; 21:23–24).

Many of these concepts Jesus taught from the writings of Isaiah. "Search these things diligently," he said; "for great are the words of Isaiah" (23:1). Searching the Nephite scriptures, Jesus discovered some deficiencies. Samuel the Lamanite's prophecy of many others being resurrected along with Jesus was omitted. This he commanded to be added to the record; and he also dictated to them Malachi's words about Jesus' second coming, so that these too could be added. (See 23:6–14; 24:1.) He instructed that a careful chronicle of his ministry also be attended to (see 27:23). The Savior's interest in the scriptural record must have left a lasting impression concerning the value of scripture and scripture study.

The Ministry as a Spiritual Feast

Toward the end of the first day, Jesus perceived that the people did not fully understand what he had taught them, so he told them to return to their homes and "ponder upon the things which I have said, and ask of the Father, in my name, that ye may understand, and prepare your minds for the morrow, and I come unto you again" (17:2–3). Jesus, the Master Teacher, was well aware of the learning readiness of his audience.

At that moment Jesus intended to visit the lost tribes of Israel, but when he saw tears in the eyes of the people, he yielded to their unspoken entreaties that he stay longer. He invited their sick to come to him and all were healed. What a contrast to his home in Nazareth where "he did not many mighty works . . . because of their unbelief"! (Matt. 13:58.)

Next, Jesus called for their little children. Everyone knelt and heard Jesus pour out his soul in mighty prayer. So powerful was the Spirit that all were "overcome" with joy (17:18). Jesus himself wept. He blessed the children; angels ministered to them, and they were encircled with celestial fire (see 17:21–24).

The sacrament was introduced while Jesus explained that the people's participation was "a testimony unto the Father that ye do always remember me. And if ye do always remember me ye shall have my Spirit to be with you." (18:7.) The unworthy were not to partake lest they eat and drink damnation to their souls (see 18:28–29), but neither were they to be cast out of the synagogues, "for unto such shall ye continue to minister; for ye know not but what they will return and repent, and come unto me with full purpose of heart, and I shall heal them; and ye shall be the means of bringing salvation unto them" (18:32).

There is an obvious emphasis on prayer and the sacrament during Jesus' ministry. The sacrament keeps us in the narrow way by repeatedly binding disciples to a covenant relationship with Christ. Worthy participation in the sacrament brings the Savior's promise that we will always have his Spirit to be with us (see 18:7). Prayer and the sacrament, properly applied, can keep Christ's followers spiritually alive during the days of their mortal sojourn.

The Savior's day's work completed, a cloud settled on the multitude and Jesus ascended through it toward heaven. What a memorable experience! All who made covenant to "always remember him" would never forget the events and feelings of that day.

Many were active during the night, alerting others to the blessing of being with the Savior. A greatly enlarged assembly gathered near the temple by early morning. The twelve disciples divided them into groups, and taught and baptized them; whereupon "the Holy Ghost did fall upon them" (19:13). Jesus appeared and began his second day by calling upon the multitude and the disciples to pray. Jesus departed a little distance and had his own communication with the Father. Three times he returned to them as they continued praying; he commented that he had never seen such great faith among the Jews (see 19:35). He finally told them to stop praying verbally but "that they should not cease to pray in their hearts" (20:1). Wine and bread for the sacrament were miraculously produced, and it was again administered. This was followed by a period of teaching, listening to Jesus expound on the future of the kingdom of God, largely from the writings of Isaiah and Malachi.

After the three days, Jesus appeared often, teaching, breaking bread, healing their sick, and encouraging his disciples in their ministry. The people became so righteous that they had all their goods and possessions "common among them, every man dealing justly, one with another" (26:19).

Before the Savior's final departure he expressed satisfaction over that generation because "none of them are lost" (27:20); yet by the fourth generation, he warned, there would be a return to evil (see 27:32). His last act was to promise his faithful assistants, the Nephite Twelve, the desires of their hearts. Nine wished to come speedily into Christ's kingdom following their deaths. Seeing the other three hesitating, Jesus discerned their longing to continue their ministry until he should come again. The Savior granted their desire with the added promises of immunity from physical pain and of instant resurrection when he returned. These three performed a miraculous ministry (see 3 Ne. 28) and were probably removed from the earth as the Nephites ripened in iniquity (see Morm. 8:10–11).

Thus did Jesus' American ministry come to a close. Rarely had a people so thoroughly embraced the gospel of Christ. For the next century and a half the people lived in perfect happiness, prosperity, and peace (see 4 Ne.).

Praise and Testimony of Christ

We have reviewed the Christ-message of the Book of Mormon. Here is a long succession of prophets telling us that the Lord Omnipotent—the Creator, Redeemer, Teacher, and Exemplar—came to earth to save us in God's eternal kingdom. Still, there is much more than can be told in a single chapter. Chapters 7–11 of this study will explain how the Savior has worked with the Father throughout history to bring salvation to mankind. Chapter 12 will examine how American prophets explained his crowning work, the Atonement. Chapters 13–17 will explore the new way of life that he taught. An angel testified to Nephi that "the words of the Lamb shall be made known in the records of thy seed" (1 Ne. 13:41). The final chapter will consider the penalty or blessings that await all people in the life to come, all of which is ultimately determined by each person's response to Christ.

Could any personage be of greater importance than Christ? Could anything be more valuable than his message or the book that contains his message? Overpowered by the greatness of Christ, Book of Mormon prophets often gave utterance to beautiful words of praise. Nephi expressed his gratitude by writing, "Rejoice, O my heart, and cry unto the Lord, and say: O Lord, I will praise thee forever; yea, my soul will rejoice in thee, my God, and the rock of my salvation" (2 Ne. 4:30). As Nephi's brother Jacob described the magnitude of the Atonement, he exclaimed: "O how great the goodness of our God, who prepareth a way for our escape from the grasp of this awful monster; yea, that monster, death and hell, which I call the death of the body, and also the death of the spirit" (2 Ne. 9:10).

The divine Creator-God, Jesus Christ, laid aside his greatness and glory and came to earth to experience mortal conditions that he might become our Advocate and Savior. Alma said that the Savior would "go forth, suffering pains and afflictions and temptations of every kind" as he took upon himself "the pains and the sicknesses of his people." Alma continued: "And he will take upon him death, that he may loose the bands of death which bind his people; and he will take upon him their infirmities, that his bowels may be filled with mercy, according to the flesh, that he may know according to the flesh how to succor his people according to their infirmities." (Alma 7:11–12.) No wonder the angel introduced Nephi's vision of Christ's ministry with these words: "Look and behold the condescension of God!" (1 Ne. 11:26.)

The Book of Mormon is a precious testament of Christ because it contains the teachings and testimonies of numerous prophets about

Christ's life and work. As a fitting conclusion to this chapter we will scrutinize their testimonies a little closer.

John W. Welch of Brigham Young University has found that Book of Mormon prophets such as Nephi, Jacob, Abinadi, Benjamin, Alma, and Moroni all express what he calls a "foundational testimony of Christ" in their writings. In addition to this basic testimony, each of these prophets' witnesses has some distinctive, individual elements. The "foundational testimony," Welch claims, has seven identifiable features: Jesus (1) is the Son of God, (2) would live as a mortal on the earth, (3) would heal the sick, cast out devils, and suffer, (4) would redeem his people by his suffering and death, (5) would die by crucifixion and then be resurrected, (6) would thus bring about the resurrection of all mankind, and (7) would judge all people by their works.[9]

Three of the most impressive testimonies concerning Christ are those recorded by Nephi, Mormon, and Moroni at the conclusion of their respective writings. It is significant that they chose to end their accounts on this most important of all topics.

Nephi's Final Words

In chapter 2 we highlighted Nephi's wonderful summary of the gospel. In that summary there is a strong emphasis on the dominant role of Christ. Nephi's principal metaphor is a "strait and narrow path" that Christians must walk to return to the presence of God. The "Lamb of God, which should take away the sins of the world" (2 Ne. 31:4), followed that path and

> notwithstanding he being holy, he showeth unto the children of men that, according to the flesh he humbleth himself before the Father, and witnesseth unto the Father that he would be obedient unto him in keeping his commandments. . . .
>
> And again, it showeth unto the children of men the straitness of the path, and the narrowness of the gate, by which they should enter, he having set the example before them. . . .
>
> Wherefore, my beloved brethren, I know that if ye shall follow the Son, with full purpose of heart, acting no hypocrisy and no deception before God, but with real intent, repenting of your sins, witnessing unto the Father that ye are willing to take upon you the name of Christ, by baptism . . . behold, then shall ye receive the Holy Ghost. (2 Ne. 31:7, 9, 13.)

Nephi then reiterated the need to follow Christ's example: "And now, my beloved brethren, I know by this that unless a man shall endure to the end, in following the example of the Son of the living God, he cannot be saved" (2 Ne. 31:16).

After one enters through the gate onto the strait and narrow path (see 2 Ne. 31:18), there is still much to do. "Ye have not come thus far," Nephi continues, "save it were by the word of Christ with unshaken faith in him, relying wholly upon the merits of him who is mighty to save" (2 Ne. 31:19). Now one must apply the principles of Christian living, which include the need to "press forward with a steadfastness in Christ" and "feasting upon the word of Christ" (2 Ne. 31:20).

Finally, Nephi implores, "My beloved brethren, and also Jew, and all ye ends of the earth, hearken unto these words and believe in Christ; and if ye believe not in these words believe in Christ. And if ye shall believe in Christ ye will believe in these words, for they are the words of Christ, and he hath given them unto me; and they teach all men that they should do good. And if they are not the words of Christ, judge ye—for Christ will show unto you, with power and great glory, that they are his words, at the last day." (2 Ne. 33:10–11.)

Mormon's Final Words

After lamenting over the barbarity of his people, their atrocities, and their certain destruction, Mormon exhorts his son Moroni in a letter to remain faithful despite the hardness of the Nephites' hearts. Further on in the letter come these words of comfort: "My son, be faithful in Christ; and may not the things which I have written grieve thee, to weigh thee down unto death; but may Christ lift thee up, and may his sufferings and death, and the showing his body unto our fathers, and his mercy and long-suffering, and the hope of his glory and of eternal life, rest in your mind forever" (Moro. 9:25).

Moroni's Final Words

Apparently Moroni intended these words to be his final testimony:

And now I, Moroni, bid farewell unto the Gentiles, yea, and also unto my brethren whom I love, until we shall meet before the judgment-seat of Christ, where all men shall know that my garments are not spotted with your blood.

And then shall ye know that I have seen Jesus, and that he hath talked with me face to face. . . .

And now, I would commend you to seek this Jesus of whom the prophets and apostles have written, that the grace of God the Father, and also the Lord Jesus Christ, and the Holy Ghost, which beareth record of them, may be and abide in you forever. Amen. (Ether 12:38–39, 41.)

However, Moroni lived on to write another segment to the plates— his own book of Moroni. He closes this record with a stirring exhortation: "Yea, come unto Christ, and be perfected in him, and deny yourselves of all ungodliness . . . , that by his grace ye may be perfect in Christ. . . . And again, if ye by the grace of God are perfect in Christ, and deny not his power, then are ye sanctified in Christ by the grace of God, through the shedding of the blood of Christ. . . . And now I bid unto all, farewell." (Moro. 10:32–34.)

These great prophet-writers knew the Lord Jesus Christ as the heart of the gospel, and they have left us powerful testimonies of his work and glory. They would advise, with Helaman, that the only sure foundation on which to build our lives is the foundation of Christ. If this be our foundation, said Helaman, "when the devil shall send forth his mighty winds, yea, his shafts in the whirlwind, yea, when all his hail and his mighty storm shall beat upon you, it shall have no power over you to drag you down to the gulf of misery and endless wo, because of the rock upon which ye are built, which is a sure foundation, a foundation whereon if men build they cannot fall." (Hel. 5:12.)

Of all the things God has done to bless his children, the most important is the sending of his Son as the Savior—"God so loved the world, that he gave his only begotten Son" (John 3:16). Knowing this, may we, like the great Nephi, "talk of Christ, . . . rejoice in Christ, . . . preach of Christ, . . . prophesy of Christ" (2 Ne. 25:26), and look to Him as our exemplar, our mentor, and our Savior.

Chapter 7

HOW GOD WORKS THROUGH ANGELS, PROPHETS, AND THE PRIESTHOOD

The Principle of Revelation

How can mortal man learn about the infinite God unless God chooses to reveal himself? Without revelation mankind would be left in darkness. The Prophet Jacob said, "It is impossible that man should find out all his [God's] ways. And no man knoweth of his ways save it be revealed unto him; wherefore, brethren, despise not the revelations of God." (Jacob 4:8.) The Book of Mormon is a record of God's revelations to ancient American prophets. It proves "that God does inspire men and call them to his holy work in this age and generation, as well as in generations of old" (D&C 20:11).

In the religious apostasy prevailing in the latter days, Nephi saw a skepticism concerning revelation and heavenly manifestations: "They shall teach with their learning, and deny the Holy Ghost" (2 Nephi 28:4). Other Book of Mormon prophets warned us about this dangerous attitude. Helping his son Corianton to understand the need for revelation about Christ's mission *before* the Savior's mortal advent, Alma queried, "Is it not as easy at this time for the Lord to send his angel to declare these glad tidings unto us as unto our children, or as after the time of his coming?" (Alma 39:19.) Moroni was especially emphatic that revelation and spiritual gifts would never cease as long as someone had faith in Christ. "I would exhort you," he pleaded, "that ye deny not the power of God. . . . that ye deny not the gifts of God, for they are many. . . . All these gifts of which I have spoken, which are spiritual, never will be done away, even as long as the world shall stand, only according to the unbelief of the children of men." (Moroni 10:7, 8, 19; see also 7:36.)

Modern Christian churches are virtually unanimous in believing that there were no prophets and revelation after the Bible was completed. A typical creedal statement by Protestants is the following: "The whole counsel of God, concerning all things necessary for his own glory, man's salvation, faith, and life, is either expressly set down in Scripture [the Bible], or by good and necessary consequence may be deduced from Scripture: unto which nothing at any time is to be added, whether by new revelations of the Spirit, or traditions of men."[1]

A popular Catholic book on doctrine states that the doctrine of papal infallibility does not include revelation.

> The infallibility of the Popes does not signify that they are in-spired. The Apostles were endowed with the gift of inspiration, and we accept their writings as the revealed Word of God. No Catholic, on the contrary, claims that the Pope is inspired or en-dowed with Divine revelation properly so called . . .
>
> The Pope, therefore, be it known, is not the maker of Divine law; he is only its expounder. He is not the author of revelation, but only its interpreter. All revelation came from God alone through His inspired ministers, and it was complete in the begin-ning of the Church.[2]

This stance of modern Christianity is the polar opposite of the Book of Mormon position. American prophets taught that God re-veals to each nation the amount of truth it is prepared to receive (see Alma 12:9–11; 2 Ne. 29:6ff.). He "manifesteth himself unto all those who believe in him, by the power of the Holy Ghost; yea, unto every nation, kindred, tongue, and people" (2 Ne. 26:13). If anyone denies revelation and other gifts of the Spirit, that person, according to Mo-roni, "knoweth not the gospel of Christ," nor does he understand the scriptures (Morm. 9:7–8). "Wo be unto him," warned Nephi, "that shall say: We have received the word of God, and need no more of the word of God, for we have enough!" (2 Ne. 28:29.)

How does God reveal himself to man! There are several ways spo-ken of in the Book of Mormon. The following list is a summary:

1. *Personal appearances of heavenly beings:* The premortal Jesus ap-peared to the brother of Jared (see Ether 3:13). The "Spirit of the Lord" conversed with Nephi (see 1 Ne. 11:11). Angels appeared to King Benjamin (see Mosiah 3:2), to Laman and Lemuel (see 1 Ne. 3:27–30), to Alma (see Alma 8:14–15), to Alma and the sons of Mosiah (see Mosiah 27:11), and to others.

2. *An audible voice:* When Nephi and Lehi, sons of Helaman, were imprisoned in the land of Nephi, "a still voice of perfect mildness" spoke to their enemies and it "did pierce even to the very soul" (see Hel. 5:29–33). The Father spoke in a similar manner before Jesus' ap-pearance to the Nephites (see 3 Ne. 11:3).

3. *A voice inside one's mind:* Enos said that the "voice of the Lord came into [his] mind" and conveyed a message (Enos 1:10).

4. *Visions:* Lehi's dream is a prime example (see 1 Ne. 1:8–15). Amulek saw a vision of an angel (see Alma 8:20). The brother of Jared had a vision of the earth's history (see Ether 3:25).

5. *Promptings of the Spirit or of the Holy Ghost:* The most common type of revelation is when the Spirit of God (usually the Holy Ghost is meant by this term) gives a person ideas, impressions, feelings, or even words and sentences. In discussing the contents of the brass plates with his brothers, Nephi explained that "they were manifest unto the prophet by the voice of the Spirit; for by the Spirit are all things made known unto the prophets, which shall come upon the children of men according to the flesh" (1 Ne. 22:2). Nephi implied that normally the Spirit works through our feelings rather than by visual or audible revelations. The Lord had spoken to his brothers in a "still small voice," said Nephi, "but ye were past feeling, that ye could not feel his words" (1 Ne. 17:45). Preaching to the people of Zarahemla, Alma testified that what he taught was made known to him "by the Holy Spirit of God. Behold, I have fasted and prayed many days that I might know these things of myself. And now I do know of myself that they are true; for the Lord God hath made them manifest unto me by his Holy Spirit; and this is the spirit of revelation which is in me." (Alma 5:46.) Lehi taught according to the workings of the Spirit (see 2 Ne. 1:16). Nephi prophesied according to the Spirit in him (see 2 Ne. 25:4; 28:1). Jacob likewise prophesied by the Spirit's promptings (see Jacob 4:15). When an inspired person speaks, the Holy Ghost carries the word into the hearts of others (see 2 Ne. 33:1). Moroni says the Holy Ghost can convince one of the truthfulness of the Book of Mormon and other gospel principles (see Moro. 10:4–5). Nephi was led by the Spirit to obtain the brass plates (see 1 Ne. 4:6, 18).

6. *Dreams:* "The Lord warned Omer in a dream that he should depart out of the land" (Ether 9:3).

7. *Special instruments:* Not only did the Liahona lead Lehi's family in the proper direction, but divine messages appeared on it from time to time (see 1 Ne. 16:28–29). Mosiah used the Urim and Thummim ("holy interpreters") to translate the plates of Ether (see Mosiah 28:13, 17).

Recipients of Revelation

The scriptures teach that every individual is entitled to guidance from the Lord. All people born into the world receive the "Spirit of

Christ" to assist them in distinguishing between good and evil (Moro. 7:16). As people progress in righteousness they qualify for greater and greater revelatory influences.

Although everyone can receive guidance, or revelation, from God to some degree, only the righteous are given it in abundant measure. Nephi desired to know and see the divine things seen by his father, Lehi, and he knew that these things could be seen and known "by the power of the Holy Ghost, which is the gift of God unto all those who diligently seek him. . . . For he that diligently seeketh shall find; and the mysteries of God shall be unfolded unto them, by the power of the Holy Ghost, as well in these times as in times of old." (1 Ne. 10:17, 19.) Overcome with joy at the conclusion of his mission, the prophet Ammon asked: "What natural man is there that knoweth these things?" Answering his own question, he declared that the ex-alted feelings and understanding they experienced came to only "the penitent. Yea, he that repenteth and exerciseth faith, and bringeth forth good works, and prayeth continually without ceasing—unto such it is given to know the mysteries of God; yea, unto such it shall be given to reveal things which never have been revealed." (Alma 26:21–22.)

It was Jesus who said, "Seek, and ye shall find; knock, and it shall be opened unto you" (3 Ne. 14:7), but seeking and knocking appar-ently means righteous living and diligent searching. Numerous Book of Mormon examples prove that God withholds his revelations when people are unworthy. Mormon was restrained from recording more of Jesus' teachings (see 3 Ne. 26:8–11) and directed to seal one-third of the plates because of the unreadiness of future readers. Nephi's ut-terance was stopped by the Spirit, all because of the "unbelief, and the wickedness, and the ignorance, and the stiffneckedness of men; for they will not search knowledge, nor understand great knowledge, when it is given unto them in plainness, even as plain as word can be" (2 Ne. 32:7).

The Ministering of Angels

God uses mortals as well as non-mortals to assist him in his work. His non-mortal helpers (excepting Jesus Christ and the Holy Ghost) are called angels, and there are at least four types: (1) premortal spir-its, who are yet to experience life on earth (2) spirit beings who have completed their mortal life but have not yet been resurrected: (3) those who have received their resurrected bodies, and finally (4) translated, or "transfigured," personages.[3]

What is the ministry of angels? Mormon said that "the office of their ministry is to call men unto repentance, and to fulfil and to do the work of the covenants of the Father, . . . to prepare the way among the children of men, by declaring the word of Christ unto the chosen vessels of the Lord, that they may bear testimony of him" (Moro. 7:31). Earlier in his discourse, Mormon mentioned one more responsibility of angels: "For behold, God knowing all things, being from everlasting to everlasting, behold, he sent angels to minister unto the children of men, to make manifest concerning the coming of Christ" (Moro. 7:22). This is the way, continued Mormon, that "the Lord God prepareth the way that the residue of men may have faith in Christ" (Moro. 7:32).

Angels are therefore intermediaries between God and man. They manifest "themselves unto them of strong faith and a firm mind in every form of godliness" (Moro. 7:30). This includes any righteous individual. Alma reminded us that God "imparteth his word by angels unto men, yea, not only men but women also. Now this is not all; little children do have words given unto them many times, which confounded the wise and the learned." (Alma 32:23.)

The Book of Mormon contains numerous examples of angelic ministrations. In the generous sampling that follows we can see that angels are fulfilling the responsibilities of their ministry by calling people to repentance, declaring the words of Christ unto the prophets, and helping to fulfill the Lord's covenants.

1. Angels ministered to all these "chosen vessels" of the Book of Mormon: Nephi (see 2 Ne. 4:24); Jacob (see Jacob 7:5); King Benjamin (see Mosiah 3:2); Alma (see Alma 9:21); Alma and Amulek (see Alma 8:14–21); Nephi and Lehi, sons of Helaman (see Hel. 5:48); the Nephite Twelve (see 3 Ne. 19:13–15); and the Nephite children (see 3 Ne. 17:21–24).

2. Angels called Book of Mormon people to repentance: Laman and Lemuel were rebuked by an angel (see 1 Ne. 3:29). Alma and the sons of Mosiah were chastised by an angel and threatened with destruction unless they repented (see Mosiah 27:11–17; Alma 38:7). Amulek preached that God cries repentance to people "by the voice of his angels" (Alma 10:20–21). Alma spoke these words to the people of Ammonihah: "And now for this cause, that ye may not be destroyed, the Lord has sent his angel to visit many of his people, declaring unto them that they must go forth and cry mightily unto this people, saying: Repent ye, for the kingdom of heaven is nigh at hand" (Alma 9:25). Helaman taught that God sent angels to declare conditions of repentance (see Hel. 5:11).

3. Other Book of Mormon examples of angels assisting the

prophets to do the Lord's work are as follows: Alma was visited by an angel and told to return to Ammonihah to preach the gospel (see Alma 8:14–18). Amulek had a vision of an angel who told him of the coming of a holy man (see Alma 8:20). Amulek told Zeezrom that he received his testimony from an angel (see Alma 11:31). Samuel the Lamanite said that an angel had taught him what to teach the Nephites (see Hel. 13:7).

More should be said about the final category of angels mentioned above, namely translated beings. The few mortals who have been translated apparently experience a kind of suspended mortality. John the Beloved Apostle (see 3 Ne. 28:6), the three Nephite disciples (see 3 Ne. 28:4–9), and possibly Alma the Younger (see Alma 45:18–19), Nephi the son of Helaman (3 Ne. 1:3), and the prophet Ether (Ether 15:34) are examples of translated beings. The prophet Mormon gave this description of the condition of the three Nephite disciples:

> Therefore, that they might not taste of death there was a change wrought upon their bodies, that they might not suffer pain nor sorrow save it were for the sins of the world.
>
> Now this change was not equal to that which shall take place at the last day; but there was a change wrought upon them, insomuch that Satan could have no power over them, that he could not tempt them; and they were sanctified in the flesh, that they were holy, and that the powers of the earth could not hold them.
>
> And in this state they were to remain until the judgment day of Christ; and at that day they were to receive a greater change, and to be received into the kingdom of the Father to go no more out, but to dwell with God eternally in the heavens. (3 Ne. 28:38–40.)

Jesus indicated that the above-mentioned "greater change" would be a quick transformation from mortality to immortality (see 3 Ne. 28:8).

The following interesting bit of information about the status of translated beings was contributed by the Prophet Joseph Smith: "Many have supposed that the doctrine of translation was a doctrine whereby men were taken immediately into the presence of God, and into an eternal fullness, but this is a mistaken idea. Their place of habitation is that of the terrestrial order, and a place prepared for such characters He held in reserve to be ministering angels unto many planets, and who as yet have not entered into so great a fullness as those who are resurrected from the dead."[4]

The three Nephite disciples ministered to their own people until the Nephites became too wicked (see Morm. 8:10–11). Subsequently, they were to perform a "great and marvelous work" (3 Ne. 28:32) among the Gentiles as well as minister to the Jews and "unto all nations, kindreds, tongues and people" (3 Ne. 28:28–29). Mormon noted that they would be unknown as they labored among the Gentiles and Jews (see 3 Ne. 28:27–28).

It can be seen from the foregoing that angels have an important role to play in the work of the Lord.

The Role of the Prophets

The Book of Mormon is a prophet's record as well as a record of prophets, dating from Lehi, who escaped Jerusalem in 600 B.C., to Moroni, who buried the records in about A.D. 421. A prophet has been defined as a spokesman for God; following are three examples that illustrate this role: Jacob, a prophet and the brother of Nephi, once wrote these words: "For behold, as I inquired of the Lord, thus came the word unto me, saying: Jacob, get thou up into the temple on the morrow, and declare the word which I shall give thee unto this people" (Jacob 2:11). After being cast out of Zarahemla, Samuel the Lamanite was told by the "voice of the Lord . . . that he should return again, and prophesy unto the people whatsoever things should come into his heart" (Hel. 13:3). This is said of the Jaredite prophet named Ether: "And Ether was a prophet of the Lord; wherefore Ether came forth in the days of Coriantumr, and began to prophesy unto the people, for he could not be restrained because of the Spirit of the Lord which was in him" (Ether 12:2; see also 13:20).

The role of angels, as already noted, is to declare "the word of Christ unto the chosen vessels of the Lord, that they may bear testimony of him" (Moro. 7:31). A prophet is one who receives revelation from God and delivers it to others in either spoken or written form. Jacob told us why he kept the records: "For this intent have we written these things, that they may know that we knew of Christ, and we had a hope of his glory many hundred years before his coming; and not only we ourselves had a hope of his glory, but also all the holy prophets which were before us. . . . Wherefore, we search the prophets, and we have many revelations and the spirit of prophecy." (Jacob 4:4, 6.) Mormon testified that he made his record "according to the knowledge and the understanding which God has given me" (W of M 1:9). The primary role of prophets is to teach us of Christ, the Redeemer. An angel declared to Benjamin, the Nephite prophet-king, that "the Lord God hath sent his holy prophets among all the children of men, to declare these things [Christ's ministry] to every kindred, nation, and tongue, that thereby whosoever should believe that Christ should come, the same might receive remission of their sins, and rejoice with exceedingly great joy" (Mosiah 3:13).

Some prophets are also seers. King Limhi observed that "a seer is greater than a prophet" (Mosiah 8:15). The king had sent forty-three scouts northward to Zarahemla in hopes of obtaining help to rescue his people from Lamanite bondage. By accident these men bypassed Zarahemla and discovered the remains of the Jaredite civilization. They returned with a Jaredite record—the twenty-four gold plates of Ether. Ammon, who had led an expedition from Zarahemla and had thus found Limhi's people, confessed that he had no ability to decipher the records but was confident that the prophet and seer King Mosiah could do the job. Ammon explained that King Mosiah possessed some miraculous "interpreters" into which he could "look, and translate all records that are of ancient date" (Mosiah 8:13). This ability made him a "seer." A "seer is a revelator and a prophet also," explained Ammon; "and a gift which is greater can no man have, except he should possess the power of God. . . . But a seer can know of things which are past, and also of things which are to come, and by them shall all things be revealed, or, rather, shall secret things be made manifest, and hidden things shall come to light, and things which are not known shall be made known by them, and also things shall be made known by them which otherwise could not be known." (Mosiah 8:16–17.)

As a seer's powers are superior to those of a prophet's, so are some prophets given greater divine gifts than others. Ammon the son of Mosiah was able to read the thoughts of King Lamoni (see Alma 18:18); the brother of Jared was literally empowered to move a mountain (see Ether 12:30); and Nephi the son of Helaman, because of his faithful and unwearying service, was told by the Lord: "All things shall be done unto thee according to thy word." One reason why the Lord could trust him with so much power was that the Lord knew that Nephi would "not ask that which is contrary to [God's] will." (Hel. 10:5.)

Prophets and seers, therefore, have a special ability to understand the things of God. If people want to learn of divine things, they must look to the prophets. This is why the scriptures repeatedly counsel us to trust in the prophets and be wary of uninspired teachers. Alma the Elder told us to "trust no one to be your teacher nor your minister, except he be a man of God, walking in his ways and keeping his commandments" (Mosiah 23:14). Speaking to us who live in the latter days, Nephi warned, "Cursed is he that putteth his trust in man, . . . or shall hearken unto the precepts of men, save their precepts shall be given by the power of the Holy Ghost" (2 Ne. 28:31). He told us that God would provide us with new scripture, warned us about false teachers, and declared: "Wo be unto him that shall say: We have received the word of God, and we need no more of the word of God, for we have enough!" (2 Ne. 28:29.) To reject the word of God is to reject God himself. The same principle applies to anyone who rejects God's spokesmen, the prophets, as Mormon indicated: "And wo be unto him that will not hearken unto the words of Jesus, and also to them whom he hath chosen and sent among them; for whoso receiveth not the words of Jesus and the words of those whom he hath sent receiveth not him; and therefore he will not receive them at the last day" (3 Ne. 28:34; in the New Testament, see Matt. 10:14–15 and Luke 10:16).

Priesthood and Church Organization

To organize and facilitate his work, God established a church among the Nephites. The Church is an instrument through which God's mortal servants can teach, administer saving ordinances, and nurture souls in the gospel. Those who operate the Church do so by the power and authority of the holy priesthood. The Book of Mormon does not provide us with a detailed account of the Church and its functions; nevertheless its pages contain valuable information on this subject.

There is no direct mention of the Church's existence among the Jaredites or during the first 450 years of Nephite history. Despite this, it is difficult to believe that Lehi, Nephi, Jacob, and others did not know something about the concept of the Church. Nephi and his father saw in vision the ministry of the Savior (see 1 Ne. 10:7–10; 11:13–34); Nephi wrote of the "great and abominable church" (see 1 Ne. 13), of corrupt churches in the latter days (see 2 Ne. 28:3), and— surprisingly to students of the Old Testament—of a church among the Jews of 600 B.C. (see 1 Ne. 4:26).

We do read of the existence of the priesthood at this early period. Nephi tells of consecrating his brothers Jacob and Joseph to be "priests and teachers over the land of my people" (2 Ne. 5:26). Jacob later remarks that he was "ordained" after God's "holy order" by the hand of his brother (2 Ne. 6:2). Since the Nephites were not descendants of Aaron and there were no Levites among them, President Joseph Fielding Smith concluded that they held the Melchizedek Priesthood.[5] It should be mentioned, however, that the Book of Mormon speaks neither of Aaronic or Melchizedek priesthoods but uses the term "the high priesthood of the holy order of God" or some variation of this term.

In describing the activities of Alma the Elder and his people, the Book of Mormon calls Alma the "founder of their church" (Mosiah 23:16; see also 29:47). Alma, a former priest of the wicked King Noah, was converted by the preaching of Abinadi and fled with his flock of fellow believers to the Waters of Mormon. Here he baptized about 204 souls, who were called the "church of God, or the church of Christ" (Mosiah 18:17). Alma gave some structure to the Church by ordaining "one priest to every fifty of their number" for the purpose of teaching the gospel (Mosiah 18:18). Although we are not told how Alma received his authority (likely from Abinadi), all priests and teachers among his people received their priesthood from him (see Mosiah 23:17). After Alma and his people were united with the main body of Nephites, King Mosiah, the prophet and seer, granted Alma the privilege of establishing churches throughout the Zarahemla area:

> And it came to pass that king Mosiah granted unto Alma that he might establish churches throughout all the land of Zarahemla; and gave him power to ordain priests and teachers over every church. . . .
>
> Therefore they did assemble themselves together in different bodies, being called churches; every church having their priests and their teachers, and every priest preaching the word according as it was delivered to him by the mouth of Alma.
>
> And thus, notwithstanding there being many churches they were all one church, yea, even the church of God; for there was nothing preached in all the churches except it were repentance and faith in God. (Mosiah 25:19, 21–22.)

Priests were taken from the ranks of the common people. They were "not to depend upon the people for their support" but were to labor for their own livelihood (see Mosiah 18:24, 26).

When Alma grew old he conferred his office of high priest upon his brilliant son, Alma the Younger, who also was "appointed to be the first chief judge." His father gave him "charge concerning all the affairs of the church." (Mosiah 29:42; see also Alma 5:3.) After functioning for a time in the offices of both high priest and chief judge, Alma the Younger resigned his judgeship, "but he retained the office of high priest unto himself" and "confined himself wholly to the high priesthood of the holy order of God" (Alma 4:18, 20). During his mission to the people of Ammonihah, Alma preached what is probably the best sermon on priesthood in the Book of Mormon (see Alma

13). He referred to the priesthood as the "high priesthood of the holy order of God" (Alma 13:6), or the "holy order, which was after the order of his Son" (Alma 13:1). Those receiving this priesthood were "called and prepared from the foundation of the world according to the foreknowledge of God, on account of their exceeding faith and good works" (Alma 13:3). Their calling is to preach the gospel (see Alma 13:1), and their callings typify Christ's calling in such a way that the people might thereby look forward to the coming of the Son of God for a remission of their sins (see Alma 13:16). Those who received the priesthood were called with a "holy calling" and were "ordained with a holy ordinance" (Alma 13:8). Alma taught that the priesthood was eternal—"from eternity to all eternity" (Alma 13:7)—and that it was the same priesthood held by the great Melchizedek (see Alma 13:14).

When the resurrected Christ appeared in America he proceeded to establish his church by ordaining twelve disciples (Apostles) and giving them authority to baptize and bestow the Holy Ghost (see 3 Ne. 18:37). These leaders apparently took the place of the high priests as head of the Church. Other Apostles were "ordained in their stead" when they died (4 Ne. 1:14). One other valuable piece of information given by Jesus was that the true Church must be named after him (see 3 Ne. 27:7–8). Although we assume that the Church was established in its completeness, the Book of Mormon neither mentions all the offices familiar to us today nor gives any details of their various functions. It seems that the prophet Moroni noticed this lack of information and intentionally supplied some of the missing details in his closing chapters. He described the method by which the Holy Ghost was conferred, the manner of ordaining priests and teachers, the way to administer the sacrament, the way in which Church meetings were conducted, and the manner of receiving new members. (See Moro. 2–6.)

From time to time in Book of Mormon history false prophets and priests rose up in opposition to the true priesthood. Nehor was one of the first prominent anti-Christs. He preached that "every priest and teacher ought to become popular; and they ought not to labor with their hands, but that they ought to be supported by the people. And he also testified unto the people that all mankind should be saved at the last day, and that they need not fear nor tremble." (Alma 1:3–4.) This man began an apostate movement among the Nephites that was called "the order of the Nehors." Many subsequent apostates are mentioned as belonging to this order, such as Amlici (see Alma 2:1) and the Amalekites and Amulonite apostates (see Alma 21:4; 24:28). At Nehor's trial, Alma, the chief judge, accused him of introducing "priestcraft" among the Nephites, and if "priestcraft [were] to be enforced among this people it would prove their entire destruction" (Alma 1:12). Nephi explained that "priestcrafts are that men preach and set themselves up for a light unto the world, that they may get gain and praise of the world; but they seek not the welfare of Zion" (2 Ne. 26:29). Priestcrafts were instrumental in bringing about the cruci-fixion of the Savior (see 2 Ne. 10:5); and both Jesus and Moroni warned that priestcrafts would be found among the people in the lat-ter days (see 3 Ne. 16:10; 21:19; 30:2; Morm. 8:32–33, 36–39). A modern revelation to the Prophet Joseph Smith warned us that the priesthood should only be used in righteousness, and that if we use it to "gratify our pride, our vain ambition," or to exercise "unrighteous dominion" over other men's souls, then such priestcrafts would lead to a forfeiture of priesthood power (see D&C 121:36–40).

The Reception of Prophets

A prophet's calling, though glorious, is usually difficult. They are often called to tell people of their sins and the consequences of sinful living—obviously not popular topics. Lehi told an evil Jerusalem that destruction awaited if the people persisted in wickedness. He was mocked, his life was threatened, and even his older sons accused him of being carried away by the "foolish imaginations of his heart" (see 1 Ne. 1:19, 20; 2:11). Abinadi had a similar mission to the Nephites and was burned to death for his testimony (see Mosiah 17:18–20). Nephi spoke of his "afflictions in the wilderness" (2 Ne. 4:20); Aaron, Omner, and Himni suffered a cruel imprisonment (see Alma 20:28–29); Alma the Younger was reviled, spat on, and cast out of the city of Ammonihah (see Alma 8:13); and much of Moroni's life was spent in hiding to escape his bloodthirsty enemies (see Moro. 1:1–4).

Not only do God's servants encounter difficulty, but their success is often very limited. Very few missions produce results like those achieved during the mission of Mosiah's sons to the Lamanites or those brought about by the ministry of Jesus to America. This will es-pecially be the case in the latter days when, in the midst of wicked-ness, only a "few" faithful Saints will exist (see 2 Ne. 28:14; 1 Ne. 13:12). There is an element of sadness in such teachings as the Sav-ior's parable of the sower (see Matt. 13) or Levi's vision of the tree of life (see 1 Ne. 8), for they indicate that of all those offered the gospel, only a few make an affirmative response.

Lehi's magnificent vision illustrates the various responses people make to the gospel, and a closer look at that vision seems appropriate here.

First, let us review the essential elements of the dream. Lehi was led through a "dark and dreary" wasteland by a man in a white robe. After earnest prayer, he beheld a "large and spacious field" and a "tree, whose fruit was desirable to make one happy" (1 Ne. 8:7–10). Reaching the tree, Lehi partook of the fruit and it filled his "soul with exceedingly great joy; wherefore, [he] began to be desirous that [his] family should partake of it also" (1 Ne. 8:12). His wife, Sariah, and his sons Sam and Nephi came forward and ate of the fruit, while Laman and Lemuel refused to come. Lehi then described other symbols in the dream: He saw a "strait and narrow path" leading to the tree, and a kind of handrail, or "rod of iron," along the path. The path came from a "large and spacious field, as if it had been a world," and passed by a fountain. (1 Ne. 8:20.) Along the path ran a river—which Nephi would later see was a river of "filthy water" (1 Ne. 12:16)—and across the river, standing in the air, was a "great and spacious building" (1 Ne. 8:26) full of nicely dressed people mocking those who were walking along the path. Masses of people walked through the field attempting to find the path and reach the tree. Mists of darkness covered much of the field and the beginnings of the path, and many were lost in the mist as a result. A few caught hold of the iron rod and made it to the tree, but among those some became ashamed, wandering off to forbidden paths, and were lost. Throngs of people headed directly toward the great and spacious building, others drowned in the river, and many more lost their way by wandering on strange roads.

We are indebted to Nephi and his report of his own vision for the interpretation of Lehi's dream (see 1 Ne. 11:21–36; 12:16–18; 15:21–36). The following chart is an outline of the symbols found in the dream and their meanings (all scripture references in this chart are from 1 Nephi):

Symbol	Interpretation
Large and spacious field (8:9, 20)	The world (8:20)
The mist of darkness (8:23)	Temptations of the devil (12:17)
River of water (8:13), or "fountain of filthy water" (12:16)	Hell and the depths thereof (12:16; 15:26–36)
Great and spacious building (8:26)	Pride and wisdom of the world (11:34–36; 12:18)
The rod of iron (8:19)	The word of God (15:24)
The tree of life and its fruit (8:10–12; 11:25; 15:21–22)	The love of God (11:21–22)

The tree and its fruit are the most important symbols of the dream. They represent "the love of God, which sheddeth itself abroad in the hearts of the children of men" (1 Ne. 11:22), with the fruit symbolizing particularly "the greatest of all the gifts of God" (1 Ne. 15:36). When Nephi asked to see the same things his father had, the angel spoke of the tree and its fruit and showed them to Nephi. Then, when Nephi asked to know the meaning of the tree, he was shown a vision of the Christ child, and he realized that the tree represented the "love of God." Since the tree symbolizes the love of God, it seems likely that the angel was showing Christ as the greatest example of God's love. Subsequently, Nephi was shown a great vision of Christ's ministry. (See 1 Ne. 11.)

The essential meaning of the dream, therefore, is to convey the idea that if an individual can pass through the devil's temptations (the mist), resist the sinful allurements of the world (great and spacious building), cling to the word of God (the rod of iron) steadfastly, he can partake of the love of God as manifested through the mission of his Son Jesus Christ. In addition to finding Christ, the end result of this journey is the insight and happiness one feels when realizing God's love—with the ultimate and greater result, or fruit, being eternal life.

Now let us summarize the various responses made by the people in Lehi's vision:

1. 1 Nephi 8:17–18. Laman and Lemuel represent the many who refuse to come to the tree. They are possibly content to stay in the field or go directly to the great building.
2. 1 Nephi 8:21–23. There are "numberless concourses of people" who begin on the path but are led off the path by the devil's power (mists of darkness).
3. 1 Nephi 8:24–28. Some make it to the tree and eat of the fruit, but because of ridicule, persecution, public opinion (mockery of those in the great building), they become ashamed and are lost.
4. 1 Nephi 8:30. Multitudes of people press forward, constantly guided by the word of God ("continually holding fast to the rod of iron"), and rejoice in their redemption (eat of the fruit).
5. 1 Nephi 8:31–33. "Other multitudes" are attracted by the ways of the world (go straight to the building); many are completely dominated by the devil (drowned in the filthy water); others choose behavior patterns incompatible with Christian living ("wandering in strange roads"); and a great many join those who persecute the righteous (join the scoffers in the spacious building).

Why do so few, relatively speaking, accept and live the gospel? No wonder prophets like Nephi and Mormon sometimes were pained over the wickedness of mankind. Said Nephi, "I am left to mourn because of the unbelief, and the wickedness, and ignorance, and the stiffneckedness of men; for they will not search knowledge, nor understand great knowledge, when it is given unto them in plainness, even as plain as word can be" (2 Ne. 32:7). Lamenting the condition of the Nephites not long before Christ's coming to America, Mormon exclaimed: "O how foolish, and how vain, and how evil, and devilish, and how quick to do iniquity, and how slow to do good, are the children of men; yea, how quick to hearken unto the words of the evil one, and to set their hearts upon the vain things of the world!" (Hel. 12:4.) Alma, one of God's greatest missionaries, cried out that his ability to convert people was so limited: "O that I were an angel, and could have the wish of mine heart, that I might go forth and speak with the trump of God, with a voice to shake the earth, and cry repentance unto every people!" (Alma 29:1.) Then, upon reflection, he realized that he did "sin in [his] wish" and that he ought to be content with what the Lord had allotted him (Alma 29:3), because God allows only that amount of truth to people that they are prepared for (see Alma 29:8). Therefore, he concluded, "why should I desire more than to perform the work to which I have been called?" (Alma 29:6.)

We have seen that God's saving works are accomplished through angels, prophets, priesthood, and Church organization. All these are directed by divine revelation. "Great and marvelous are the works of the Lord. How unsearchable are the depths of the mysteries of him; and it is impossible that man should find out all his ways. And no man knoweth of his ways save it be revealed unto him; wherefore, brethren, despise not the revelations of God." Those powerful words were spoken by the prophet Jacob, who further on gives this admonition: "Wherefore, brethren, seek not to counsel the Lord, but to take counsel from his hand. For behold, ye yourselves know that he counseleth in wisdom, and in justice, and in great mercy, over all his works." (Jacob 4:8, 10.)

Chapter 8

JESUS CHRIST, THE GOD OF ANCIENT ISRAEL

Moderns often have difficulty figuring out the relationship of the Old Testament to the New, the law of Moses to the gospel of Christ, and the God of Israel to the Jesus of the Gospels. The truth taught by the Book of Mormon differs strikingly from traditional ideas—the Nephite record teaches that Jesus is the "God of Israel," the "God of the whole earth" (3 Ne. 11:14). It was Christ who gave the law to Moses and who led the children of Israel out of Egyptian bondage (see 1 Ne. 19:10). God's covenant people are not exclusively the ancient Israelites but also include the New Testament Saints, the Nephites, and anyone who chooses to accept the gospel of Christ. This chapter will explore these ideas in greater detail.

From the Beginning

Jesus declared to the Nephites that he had "created the heavens and the earth, and all things that in them are" (3 Ne. 9:15; see also Mosiah 3:8; 4:2; Hel. 14:12). It was Christ who guided the patriarchs of ancient Israel and led the Jaredites to the New World. At least two thousand years before his earthly ministry, Jesus Christ appeared to the brother of Jared, a man with such great faith that "he could not be kept from beholding within the veil; and he saw the finger of Jesus" (Ether 3:19). Jesus identified himself to this man in these words: "Behold, I am he who was prepared from the foundation of the world to redeem my people. Behold, I am Jesus Christ. I am the Father and the Son. In me shall all mankind have life, and that eternally, even they who shall believe on my name. . . . Behold, this body, which ye now behold, is the body of my spirit; and man have I created after the body of my spirit; and even as I appear unto thee to be in the spirit will I appear unto my people in the flesh." (Ether 3:14, 16.)

Nephi learned early in his ministry that "the God of our fathers, who were led out of Egypt, out of bondage, and also were preserved in the wilderness by him, yea, the God of Abraham, and of Isaac, and the God of Jacob" was none other than he who would come to earth as the Messiah, the Savior of the world. The prophets Zenock and Neum foresaw his crucifixion, and Zenos declared that he would be "buried in a sepulchre." (See 1 Ne. 19:8–10.) Thus it was that the Savior, even Jesus Christ, announced to the Nephites, "I am he that gave the law, and I am he who covenanted with my people Israel; therefore, the law in me is fulfilled, for I have come to fulfil the law; therefore it hath an end" (3 Ne. 15:5).

The Abrahamic Covenant

Despite the Savior's love for all nations, he has, for reasons not fully understood, chosen the family of one great man to do his work on earth. That family is Abraham's. From his day to the present the children of God have belonged literally or spiritually to Abraham's family. We can be assured that this does not contradict what has been said concerning God's universal love. The idea of a "chosen people" is not the elevating of one race to a status of superiority, but the selection of a people for special service and responsibility.

The Lord's covenant to Abraham consisted of the following provisions:

1. "I will make of thee a great nation, and I will bless thee above measure."

2. "Thy seed . . . shall bear this ministry and Priesthood unto all nations; . . . for as many as receive this Gospel shall be called after thy name, and shall be accounted thy seed."

3. "I give unto thee a promise that this right shall continue in thee, and in thy seed after thee (that is to say, the literal seed, or the seed of the body) shall all the families of the earth be blessed, even with the blessings of the Gospel, which are the blessings of salvation even of life eternal." (Abr. 2:9–11; see also Gen. 17:1–14; Ex. 19:3–6.)

4. Among the promises were choice lands for an eternal inheritance (see Gen. 17; 22:15–18; Gal. 3).

This covenant was renewed with Abraham's son Isaac (see Gen. 24:60; 26:1–4, 42) and with his grandson Jacob, or Israel (see Gen. 28; 35:9–13; 48:3–4). The Old Testament is a history of this covenant people, and the Book of Mormon is an account of one branch of this family. During the Savior's American ministry he applied the covenant identity to the Nephites: "Ye are of the house of Israel; and ye are of the covenant which the Father made with your fathers, saying unto Abraham: And in thy seed shall all the kindreds of the earth be blessed. The Father having raised me up unto you first, and sent me to bless you in turning away every one of you from his iniquities; and this because ye are the children of the covenant." (3 Ne. 20:25–26.) This covenant was to continue throughout history (see 1 Ne. 15:18; 22:9).

It is important to note that this covenant was to continue with the righteous, regardless of family lineage. The Apostle Paul made this clear in New Testament times (see Gal. 3:19–29; Rom. 9–11), as did the Nephite prophets: "I say unto you that as many of the Gentiles as will repent are the covenant people of the Lord; and as many of the Jews as will not repent shall be cast off; for the Lord covenanteth with none save it be with them that repent and believe in his Son, who is the Holy One of Israel" (2 Ne. 30:2). So, God's real covenant people are those who truly embrace the gospel of Jesus Christ. The original words of the covenant were, in part: "As many as receive this Gospel shall be called after thy name, and shall be accounted thy seed" (Abr. 2:10).

The Law of Moses

By the time of Moses, a different element entered into God's dealings with his covenant people. This was an amended version of the gospel called the law of Moses. The Book of Mormon, we have seen, teaches us that God gives to people the amount of truth that they are prepared to receive. We know from the book of Exodus that Moses had a particularly stubborn and spiritually immature group of people to lead. Although the Lord desired to make of Israel a "kingdom of priests, and an holy nation" (Ex. 19:6), and to provide them with the Melchizedek Priesthood and the fulness of the gospel that they might see the face of God, they proved unworthy of the blessing. When Moses decended from Mount Sinai and saw the revelry, the idol worship, he destroyed the tablets and later returned with a modified law. (See D&C 84:23–26 and JST, Ex. 34:1–3.) The Lord took away the higher priesthood and part of the gospel, and added a system of rules and ceremonies called "the law of carnal commandments" (D&C 84:26).

There were apparently two major parts to the law of Moses: (1)

moral laws that are a permanent part of the gospel (although much of this was a terrestrial standard), and (2) the carnal commandments "added because of transgressions" (Gal. 3:19), consisting of dietary rules, sanitation laws, cleanliness laws, and an elaborate system of special sacrifices and ceremonies.

This law was so precious to the family of Lehi that they went to great lengths to retrieve the brass plates. As they studied the pages of this record they found it to be of "great worth unto us, insomuch that we could preserve the commandments of the Lord unto our children" (1 Ne. 5:21). The Nephites offered animal sacrifices (see 1 Ne. 2:7; 5:9; Mosiah 2:3), built temples (see 2 Ne. 5:16; Mosiah 2:2; 7:17; 3 Ne. 11:1), and observed the law even though it was often "dead" to them because they possessed the fulness of the gospel. About forty years after their departure from Jerusalem, Nephi wrote that "notwithstanding we believe in Christ, we keep the law of Moses, and look forward with steadfastness unto Christ, until the law shall be fulfilled. For, for this end was the law given; wherefore the law hath become dead unto us, and we are made alive in Christ because of our faith; yet we keep the law because of the commandments." (2 Ne. 25:24–25.) When the sons of Mosiah converted thousands of Lamanites to the gospel of Christ, those Lamanites were, nevertheless, taught to

> keep the law of Moses; for it was expedient that they should keep the law of Moses as yet, for it was not all fulfilled. But notwithstanding the law of Moses, they did look forward to the coming of Christ, considering that the law of Moses was a type of his coming, and believing that they must keep those outward performances until the time that he should be revealed unto them.
>
> Now they did not suppose that salvation came by the law of Moses; but the law of Moses did serve to strengthen their faith in Christ. (Alma 25:15–16.)

Although we are given very little information as to how the law of Moses and the gospel existed simultaneously during Nephite history, the above scriptural passages give the essential relationship: the Nephites observed the "outward performances" of the law, not because it would bring them salvation, but because it pointed to the Savior, Jesus Christ. Therefore, the law was "dead" to them while their understanding and expectation of Christ was the vital element in their religion.

The greatest insight into the nature of the law of Moses is provided by the Book of Mormon prophet Abinadi. While the evil priests of King Noah held him in custody, Abinadi taught them the meaning of the law. He chastised them for not living the Ten Commandments. His boldness offended them and they sought to kill him, but he announced that God's power was upon him and his life could not be taken until he had delivered his message. He testified that "salvation doth not come by the law alone; and were it not for the atonement, . . . they must unavoidably perish, notwithstanding the law of Moses." He then gave this interesting explanation of the law:

> And now I say unto you that it was expedient that there should be a law given to the children of Israel, yea, even a very strict law; for they were a stiffnecked people, quick to do iniquity, and slow to remember the Lord their God;
> Therefore there was a law given them, yea, a law of performances and of ordinances, a law which they were to observe strictly from day to day, to keep them in remembrance of God and their duty towards him.
> But behold, I say unto you, that all these things were types of things to come. (Mosiah 13:28–31.)

This suggests that the less religiously advanced a people are, the stricter the rules and the greater the regimentation needed to govern them. The daily sacrifices, the "kosher" food rules, the myriad observances kept the Israelites constantly aware of their relationship with God. Therefore, their minds were continually focused on religious matters, and as a consequence they were less likely to become involved in sin.

The Law Pointed to Christ

Abinadi ended his powerful sermon with an emphasis on Christ: "Therefore, if ye teach the law of Moses, also teach that it is a shadow of those things which are to come—teach them that redemption cometh through Christ the Lord, who is the very Eternal Father. Amen." (Mosiah 16:14–15.)

Virtually all the Book of Mormon prophets taught that the law of Moses was a preparation for Christ. Several hundred years before the appearance of Christ, the prophet Nephi exclaimed: "Behold, my soul delighteth in proving unto my people the truth of the coming of Christ; for, for this end hath the law of Moses been given; and all things which have been given of God from the beginning of the world, unto man, are the typifying of him" (2 Ne. 11:4). Amulek said that this was the "whole meaning of the law, every whit pointing to that great and last sacrifice; and that great and last sacrifice will be the Son of God, yea, infinite and eternal" (Alma 34:14). Jarom wrote: "Wherefore, the prophets, and the priests, and the teachers, did labor diligently, exhorting with all long-suffering the people to diligence; teaching the law of Moses, and the intent for which it was given; persuading them to look forward unto the Messiah, and believe in him to come as though he already was. And after this manner did they teach them." (Jarom 1:11.)

The Nephites saw symbols of Christ in many of their religious experiences. The miraculous director called the Liahona, which led Lehi's family in the wilderness, was interpreted by the prophet Alma as a symbol of the words of Christ. Counseling his son Helaman, he said: "Is there not a type in this thing? For just as surely as this director did bring our fathers, by following its course, to the promised land, shall the words of Christ, if we follow their course, carry us beyond this vale of sorrow into a far better land of promise." (Alma 37:45.) Moses' "brazen serpent" was another such symbol. As the Israelites needed only to look at the serpent to be healed, similarly all must look to Christ to be saved (see Alma 33:19ff.; Hel. 8:14–15). Nephi went so far as to declare that "all things" that God has given to man are "the typifying" of the Savior (2 Ne. 11:4).

Despite this intent of the law of Moses—its religious sacrifices and ceremonies being symbols of Christ and his mission—many Israelites did not and still do not see Christ as a part of the law. The angel lamented this fact in his words to King Benjamin: "Yet the Lord God saw that his people were a stiffnecked people, and he appointed unto them a law, even the law of Moses. And many signs, and wonders, and types, and shadows showed he unto them, concerning his coming; and also holy prophets spake unto them concerning his coming; and yet they hardened their hearts, and understood not that the law of Moses availeth nothing except it were through the atonement of his blood." (Mosiah 3:14–15.)

The prophet Jacob gives us an intriguing explanation as to why the Jews did not recognize Jesus as the prophesied Messiah. They were "a stiffnecked people; and they despised the words of plainness, and killed the prophets, and sought for things that they could not understand. Wherefore, because of their blindness, which blindness came by looking beyond the mark, they must needs fall; for God hath taken away his plainness from them, and delivered unto them many things which they cannot understand, because they desired it. And because they desired it God hath done it, that they may stumble." (Jacob 4:14.) What could this mean? I will hazard a guess. For two hundred years before and after Christ, the Jews, in their zeal to "build a hedge around the law," expanded the Mosaic code into thousands of minute rules and practices. This oral law (later to become the heart of the Talmud) was denounced by Jesus as emphasizing the "letter" of the law and missing the "spirit." Could it be that all this commentary obscured the "plainness" of the law (that it pointed to Christ) and by so doing caused the Jews to "look beyond the mark" (Christ)? Thus was rejected, said Jacob, "the only sure foundation, upon which the Jews can build" (Jacob 4:16).

Jesus Fulfills the Law

There was a time, shortly after the birth of Christ, that some Nephites felt that it was no longer necessary to obey the law of Moses, but they were soon convinced of their error when they realized that it had not been completely fulfilled (see 3 Ne. 1:24–25). This was still to be accomplished by Christ during his earthly mission. Subsequently, to the Nephites the voice of the Savior announced: "And ye shall offer up unto me no more the shedding of blood; yea, your sacrifices and your burnt offerings shall be done away, for I will accept none of your sacrifices and your burnt offerings. And ye shall offer for a sacrifice unto me a broken heart and a contrite spirit." (3 Ne. 9:19–20.) Later, during his visit to the Nephites, Jesus perceived that some did not understand his saying that "old things had passed away, and that all things had become new" (3 Ne. 15:2), and they were still wondering what he would do about the law of Moses. He then taught the following: "Marvel not that I said unto you that old things had passed away, and that all things had become new. Behold, I say unto you that the law is fulfilled that was given unto Moses. Behold, I am he that gave the law, and I am he who covenanted with my people Israel; therefore, the law in me is fulfilled, for I have come to fulfil the law; therefore it hath an end." (3 Ne. 15:3–5.)

We may not know everything Jesus had in mind when he said that he fulfilled the law. Certainly the New Testament Church had difficulties deciding what aspects of the law should be abandoned and what parts perpetuated. But we can say that it was essentially the "law of carnal commandments" that came to an end—no more blood sacrifices, no circumcision, no cleanliness and food laws and the ceremonies associated with them. These reminders were unnecessary under the new covenant of the gospel.

Jeremiah, a contemporary of Lehi, gave the Lord's word regarding a new covenant that He would someday make: "Behold, the days come, saith the Lord, that I will make a new covenant with the house of Israel, . . . not according to the covenant that I made with their fathers in the day that I took them by the hand to bring them out of the land of Egypt; which my covenant they brake . . . : but this shall be the covenant that I will make with the house of Israel; After those days, saith the Lord, I will put my law in their inward parts, and write it in their hearts; and will be their God, and they shall be my people" (Jer. 31:31–33). This may mean that under the new covenant (gospel of Christ), the compulsion of the law of Moses will be replaced by the willing consent of the heart that has been transformed by the Holy Ghost.

Conclusion

The law of Moses was a divine legal code and was a great advancement for the times. It was observed by millions on two continents for hundreds of years. But alas, its major purpose—to act as a "schoolmaster" to bring people to Christ (Gal. 3:24)—was not universally realized. The Book of Mormon, we have seen, sheds considerable light on our interpretation of the law of Moses, along with the successes and failures of the Israelites in relation to that law.

Chapter 9

THE HOUSE OF ISRAEL: TRAGEDY AND DESTINY

What is the destiny of God's ancient covenant people? Will the lost tribes return? What of the blood of Israel scattered among the nations? Will the Jews continue gathering to their ancestral homeland? Will their gathering aggravate political tensions and lead the region down the road to Armageddon? Will the Lamanites "blossom as the rose"? (D&C 49:24.)

The title page of the Book of Mormon declares that a major purpose of the record is to show to latter-day Israel "what great things the Lord hath done for their fathers; and that they may know the covenants of the Lord, that they are not cast off forever." God's work in the latter days includes the renewal of his covenants with Israel and gathering the various branches of this historic family. It appears that there will be four distinct phases of their gathering: (1) the assembling of the dispersed of Israel into the Church by the labors of the missionaries, (2) the return of the Jews to Palestine, (3) the conversion of the Lamanites, and (4) the coming of the lost ten tribes from the north.

Before considering latter-day Israel, we will provide an overview of ancient Israel, with emphasis on their dispersion throughout the world.

The Scattering of Israel

God made his covenant with Abraham, Isaac, and Jacob and revealed his law to the Israelites under Moses. The Old Testament is a record of how they departed from that covenant and turned to wickedness. Nephi spoke of apostasy in pre-exilic Israel:

And he [the Lord] loveth those who will have him to be their God. Behold, he loved our fathers, and he covenanted with them, yea, even Abraham, Isaac, and Jacob; and he remembered the covenants which he had made; wherefore, he did bring them out of the land of Egypt. . . .

And they did harden their hearts from time to time, and they did revile against Moses, and also against God; nevertheless, ye know that they were led forth by his matchless power into the land of promise.

And now, after all these things, the time has come that they have become wicked, yea, nearly unto ripeness; and I know not but they are at this day about to be destroyed; for I know that the day must surely come that they must be destroyed, save a few only, who shall be led away into captivity.

Wherefore, the Lord commanded my father that he should depart into the wilderness; and the Jews also sought to take away his life. (1 Ne. 17:40, 42–44.)

It wasn't long after this prediction that Nephi learned that the destruction of the Jews had indeed taken place. Father Lehi, shortly after their landing in America, informed his family that he had "seen a vision" in which he knew that Jerusalem was destroyed; and had they remained in Jerusalem they also would have perished (2 Ne. 1:4). The survivors were transported to Babylon; this "Babylonian Captivity" (580 B.C.) was the second great conquest of the Israelite people. The first one occurred over one hundred years earlier (722 B.C.) when the armies of Assyria conquered the northern kingdom of Israel and took the ten tribes into Mesopotamia.

Nephi now realized that his family's arrival in America was a part of the Lord's design to scatter the family of Israel throughout the world. He and others in his little band were naturally curious about the ultimate destiny of the Israelite people (see 1 Ne. 22:1–3; 15:2ff.) That is one reason why they turned to the prophecies of Isaiah and Zenos on the brass plates, because they discovered that these prophets spoke about, in the words of the Savior, "all things concerning my people which are of the house of Israel" (3 Ne. 23:2). When Nephi was asked by his brothers the meaning of his readings from the brass plates, he replied: "It appears that the house of Israel, sooner or later, will be scattered upon all the face of the earth, and also among all nations" (1 Ne. 22:3). Even now, he continued, "the more part of all the tribes have been led away; and they are scattered to and fro upon the isles of the sea; and whither they are none of us knoweth"

(1 Ne. 22:4). Nephi was fully aware that their little group of wanderers was spoken of in these prophecies (see 1 Ne. 22:6). No doubt he took great comfort in Isaiah's repeated assurances of God's love and future concern for the people of the house of Israel. They had been chastened, but not forsaken. "Hearken, O ye house of Israel," wrote Isaiah, "all ye that are broken off and are driven out because of the wickedness of the pastors of my people; yea, all ye that are broken off, that are scattered abroad, who are of my people, O house of Israel" (1 Ne. 21:1);[1] for the Lord will yet "have mercy upon his afflicted. . . . For can a woman forget her sucking child? . . . Yet will I not forget thee, O house of Israel." (1 Ne. 21:13, 15.)

Father Lehi must have studied the writings of Zenos on the brass plates, for one of Lehi's teachings, possibly based on Zenos's allegory, was that the "house of Israel . . . should be compared like unto an olive-tree, whose branches should be broken off and should be scattered upon all the face of the earth" (1 Ne. 10:12). Lehi also knew that someday Israel would be grafted back into the natural olive tree (see 1 Ne. 10:14). It was after Lehi's death that his son Jacob recorded Zenos's allegory in full, along with some related comments of Jacob's own (see Jacob 5–6).

The Scattering of the Jews

In Israel's initial scattering, the ten tribes were lost to history and the tribe of Judah spent seventy years of servitude in Babylon. At the end of the period covered by the Old Testament the Jews were freed from Babylon and allowed to return to their homeland. Several hundred years later the Jews again turned their backs to God's redemptive outreach—they rejected the Savior. Nephi foresaw this: "When the day cometh that the Only Begotten of the Father, yea, even the Father of heaven and of earth, shall manifest himself unto them [the Jews] in the flesh, behold, they will reject him, because of their iniquities, and the hardness of their hearts, and the stiffness of their necks. Behold, they will crucify him." (2 Ne. 25:12–13.) Jacob said that Christ would "come among the Jews, among those who are the more wicked part of the world," and that there was "none other nation on earth that would crucify their God" (2 Ne. 10:3). "Because of their iniquities," Jacob explained, "destructions, famines, pestilences, and bloodshed shall come upon them; and they who shall not be destroyed shall be scattered among all nations" (2 Ne. 10:6). Elsewhere in the Book of Mormon we read that the Jews would be persecuted by the nations, "become a hiss and a byword, and be hated among all nations" (1 Ne. 19:13–14). Jesus prophesied, we read in the Bible, that "Jerusalem shall be trodden down of the Gentiles, until the times of the Gentiles be fulfilled" (Luke 21:24). Since the Romans destroyed the city of Jerusalem in A.D. 70, the city has known a succession of rulers: Romans, Moslems, Ottoman Turks, Great Britain, Palestinian Arabs, and now the Jews.

The Jews have been one of the world's most tragic people, suffering persecution and hatred while keeping alive the hope of someday returning to Palestine. With their scattering, God always held out a promise of future blessing and gathering if they would only repent and turn to Christ (see 2 Ne. 10:7). That long-awaited gathering is taking place in our time.

When Will Israel Be Gathered?

Nephi capsulized the doctrine of the gathering in these words: "And after the house of Israel should be scattered they should be gathered together again; or, in fine, after the Gentiles had received the fulness of the Gospel, the natural branches of the olive-tree, or the remnants of the house of Israel, should be grafted in, or come to the knowledge of the true Messiah, their Lord and their Redeemer" (1 Ne. 10:14).

Notice that the gathering of Israel will occur *after* the Gentiles have received the fulness of the gospel. This time sequence is important because the Gentile nations will play a major role in bringing about the gathering. They will send missionaries to search out scattered Israel and, to both Jews and Lamanites, will be like "nursing fathers and mothers" because of the assistance they give to them.

Another clue to the time period of the gathering was given by Jesus during his American ministry. "I give unto you a sign," he stated, "that ye may know the time when these things shall be about to take place—that I shall gather in, from their long dispersion, my people, O house of Israel, and shall establish again among them my Zion." He went on to indicate that "when these things," meaning the Book of Mormon and the Restoration, shall come forth, and when "thy seed shall begin to know these things—it shall be a sign unto them, that they may know that the work of the Father hath already commenced unto the fulfilling of the covenant which he hath made unto the people who are of the house of Israel." (3 Ne. 21:1, 2, 3, 7.) So, the gathering is to happen concurrently with the latter-day restoration of the gospel. Jesus further emphasized the point in the same chapter: "And then shall the work of the Father commence at that day, even when this gospel shall be preached among the remnant of this people. Verily I say unto you, at that day shall the work of the Father commence among all the dispersed of my people, yea, even the tribes which have been lost, which the Father hath led away out of Jerusalem. Yea, the work shall commence among all the dispersed of my people." (3 Ne. 21:26–27.)

It was no less a prophet than Moses who appeared to Joseph Smith in the Kirtland Temple and bestowed upon him the keys (or divine authorization) for the gathering of Israel (see D&C 110:11).

A prerequisite for the gathering is that the people of Israel turn to Christ (see 2 Ne. 6:11; 30:7–8; 3 Ne. 5:24–26; 20:29–31; 21:27–29; Morm. 5:14). Nephi wrote: "When that day cometh, saith the prophet [Zenos], that they no more turn aside their hearts against the Holy One of Israel, then will he remember the covenants which he made to their fathers. Yea, then will he remember the isles of the sea; yea, and all the people who are of the house of Israel, will I gather in, saith the Lord." (1 Ne. 19:15–16.) Israel was scattered for rejecting the Holy One of Israel; they will be gathered and again become the covenant people when they accept the Savior.

The Return of Scattered Israel

The restoration of the gospel to the Gentiles, discussed above, will commence the great latter-day work of Israel's restoration. A major feature of this work will be the sending of missionaries to the nations to gather Israel through the preaching of the gospel. In the book of Jeremiah we read: "Turn, O backsliding children, saith the Lord; . . . and I will take you one of a city, and two of a family, and I will bring you to Zion" (Jer. 3:14). As stated previously, true Israel is not so much a matter of lineage as it is of righteousness; consequently any who accept the gospel are those who constitute modern Israel. The Lord has referred to modern Church members as being "the children of Israel, and of the seed of Abraham" (D&C 103:17). All faithful Latter-day Saints, therefore, should "rise up and bless [Abraham], as their father" (Abr. 2:10).

The Return of the Jews

Must the Jews convert to Christ before they return to their ancestral lands? At this writing, great numbers of Jews have returned to Palestine. The recent collapse of communism has led thousands of

Jews to migrate from the former Soviet Union to Palestine. It seems incredible that any large number of them would convert to Christianity. I believe it is doubtful that the Jews will accept Jesus through the teachings of traditional Christianity, even with the aid of the New Testament. There have been too many centuries of bitterness for the Jews to embrace a religion whose adherents historically have so often been their persecutors. Yet many will be influenced by a "new witness" for Christ. One reason for the Book of Mormon's existence is to be a witness for Christ to the Jews. Mormon, the compiler of the book, prophesied that his record would "go unto the unbelieving of the Jews; and for this intent shall they go—that they may be persuaded that Jesus is the Christ, the Son of the living God; that the Father may bring about, through his most Beloved, his great and eternal purpose, in restoring the Jews, or all the house of Israel, to the land of their inheritance" (Morm. 5:14).

Nephi had much to say on this theme. After the resurrection of Christ, he wrote, Jerusalem would be destroyed and the Jews would be scattered among all nations.

> And after they have been scattered, and the Lord God hath scourged them by other nations for the space of many generations, yea, even down from generation to generation until they shall be persuaded to believe in Christ, the Son of God, and the atonement, which is infinite for all mankind—and when that day shall come that they shall believe in Christ, and worship the Father in his name, with pure hearts and clean hands, and look not forward any more for another Messiah, then, at that time, the day will come that it must needs be expedient that they should believe these things.
>
> And the Lord will set his hand again the second time to restore his people from their lost and fallen state. Wherefore, he will proceed to do a marvelous work and a wonder among the children of men.
>
> Wherefore, he shall bring forth his words unto them, which words shall judge them at the last day, for they shall be given them for the purpose of convincing them of the true Messiah, who was rejected by them; and unto the convincing of them that they need not look forward any more for a Messiah to come, for there should not any come, save it should be a false Messiah. (2 Ne. 25:16–18.)

How the Book of Mormon will accomplish this goal is not completely clear. The prophet Jacob predicted that the time would come when the Jews would "be restored to the true church and fold of God," but left the time indefinite (2 Ne. 9:2). A statement from Jesus seems to indicate that their acceptance of him was required before their gathering. He stated, "And they [the Israelites] shall believe in me, that I am Jesus Christ, the Son of God." A little further on he declared, "Then will the Father gather them together again, and give unto them Jerusalem for the land of their inheritance." (3 Ne. 20:31, 33.) Nephi provides some clarification on this point: "And it shall come to pass that the Jews which are scattered also shall begin to believe in Christ; and they shall begin to gather in upon the face of the land; and as many as shall believe in Christ shall also become a delightsome people" (2 Ne. 30:7–8). It appears from this statement that the Jews will begin to gather before they fully believe in Christ. This interpretation more closely accords with the facts of recent Jewish history. Although some Jews of the diaspora (dispersion) will be converted to Christ, modern revelation indicates that the majority of Palestinian Jews will not believe in him until he appears at Armageddon (see D&C 45:41–52).

As previously noted, the spiritual and geographical restoration of Israel will be aided by the Gentiles. Jesus said this to his Nephite disciples:

> These sayings which ye shall write shall be kept and shall be manifested unto the Gentiles, that through the fulness of the Gentiles [the phrase refers to the latter-day period when the Gentile nations embrace the gospel], the remnant of their seed [the Jews], who shall be scattered forth upon the face of the earth because of their unbelief, may be brought in, or may be brought to a knowledge of me, their Redeemer.
>
> And then will I gather them in from the four quarters of the earth; and then will I fulfil the covenant which the Father hath made unto all the people of the house of Israel. (3 Ne. 16:4–5.)

Book of Mormon prophets liked Isaiah's phrase that the Gentiles would be like "nursing fathers" and "nursing mothers" to Israel (see 1 Ne. 21:1, 13–14, 22–23; 2 Ne. 10:9, 18). This prophecy has partially been fulfilled through the extraordinary efforts by Great Britain and the United States to establish Palestine as the Jewish homeland, to help Jewish people return, and to provide necessary military and financial support to keep them there. Once restored to their lands, they "should no more be confounded, neither should they be scattered again" (1 Ne. 15:20).

The Lamanites in Book of Mormon Prophecy

The Lamanites are singled out as being one of the special groups for whom the Book of Mormon was written: "Wherefore, it is an abridgment of the record of the people of Nephi, and also of the Lamanites—Written to the Lamanites, who are a remnant of the house of Israel; and also to Jew and Gentile" (Title Page). The book, therefore, has important information for modern Lamanites.

We should begin by defining the term *Lamanite*. To most Latter-day Saints the term refers to American Indians, a conclusion that is probably only partly true. Originally a Lamanite was one in the party of Lehi who followed the leadership of his eldest son, Laman. Almost from the beginning the people of the Book of Mormon polarized into two opposing groups—Lamanites and Nephites. The political basis for this division was that Laman and Lemuel opposed the leadership of righteous Nephi: "Our younger brother thinks to rule over us. . . . We will not have him to be our ruler; for it belongs unto us, who are the elder brethren, to rule over this people." (2 Ne. 5:3.) The Lamanites disintegrated into a "wild, and ferocious, and a blood-thirsty people" (Mosiah 10:12), and taught their children "an eternal hatred towards the children of Nephi" (Mosiah 10:17).

The term *Lamanite* took on a more general meaning by the time of Nephi's death. Although there were many different tribal groups with particular names among the people, Jacob writes: "I . . . shall not hereafter distinguish them by these names, but I shall call them Lamanites that seek to destroy the people of Nephi, and those who are friendly to Nephi I shall call Nephites, or the people of Nephi, according to the reigns of the kings" (Jacob 1:14).

Because of their wickedness the Lamanites were cursed, and, said Nephi, "that they might not be enticing unto my people the Lord God did cause a skin of blackness to come upon them" (2 Ne. 5:21). "This was done," we read elsewhere in the record, "that their seed might be distinguished from the seed of their brethren, that thereby the Lord God might preserve his people, that they might not mix and believe in incorrect traditions which would prove their destruction" (Alma 3:8). There were times in Book of Mormon history when Lamanites were more righteous than the Nephites. Notable examples are Samuel the Lamanite and "the people of Ammon" (Lamanite converts to the gospel).

Following Christ's ministry to America, all distinctions became lost, so that there were no "Lamanites, nor any manner of -ites; but they were in one, the children of Christ, and heirs to the kingdom of God" (4 Ne. 1:17). This classless society began to collapse when "a small part of the people who had revolted from the church and taken upon them the name of Lamanites; therefore there began to be Lamanites again in the land" (4 Ne. 1:20). Later, those "who rejected the gospel were called Lamanites, and Lemuelites, and Ishmaelites" (4 Ne. 1:38), and the society once more split into two warring factions. This later meaning of the term *Lamanites* suggests that it was a designation for unrighteousness and had little or no ethnic or racial connotations. Today's Lamanites, therefore, would be an ethnic mixture of Nephites and Lamanites, and their geographical location largely in Central America, with additional remnants in North and South America.[2]

At the end of Nephite history the Lamanites sank to such depths of wickedness that the Lord's judgments came upon them. Some of their punishments were that they lost exclusive claim to the promised land of America, their blessings were transferred to the Gentiles, and they would reap destruction and scattering from the Gentiles (see 1 Ne. 13:14; 2 Ne. 1:10–11; Hel. 15:12).

Despite these harrowing trials, Book of Mormon prophets foresaw a day when the Lord would preserve and bless the Lamanites, a day when they would "blossom as the rose" (D&C 49:24). Samuel, the great Lamanite prophet, declared:

In the latter times the promises of the Lord have been extended to our brethren, the Lamanites; and notwithstanding the many afflictions which they shall have, and notwithstanding they shall be driven to and fro upon the face of the earth, and be hunted, and shall be smitten and scattered abroad, having no place for refuge, the Lord shall be merciful unto them.

. . . They shall again be brought to the true knowledge, which is the knowledge of their Redeemer, and their great and true shepherd, and be numbered among his sheep. . . .

Therefore, saith the Lord: I will not utterly destroy them, but I will cause that in the day of my wisdom they shall return again unto me, saith the Lord.

And now behold, saith the Lord, concerning the people of the Nephites: If they will not repent, and observe to do my will, I will utterly destroy them, saith the Lord. (Hel. 15:12–13, 16–17.)

One of the interesting ideas from Samuel's prediction is the common Book of Mormon promise that the Lamanites will not be utterly destroyed. Notice that the same promise is not extended to the Nephites. Nephi also predicted the acceptance of the gospel by the latter-day Lamanites:

> Many generations after the Messiah shall be manifested . . . shall the fulness of the gospel of the Messiah come unto the Gentiles, and from the Gentiles unto the remnant of our seed—
> And at that day shall the remnant of our seed know that they are of the house of Israel, and that they are the covenant people of the Lord; and then shall they know and come to the knowledge of their forefathers, and also to the knowledge of the gospel of their Redeemer. . . .
> . . . Yea, will they not come unto the true fold of God?
> Behold, I say unto you, Yea. (1 Ne. 15:13–16.)

After driving and scattering the Lamanites, the Gentiles will nourish them and carry them in their arms and upon their shoulders" (see 1 Ne. 22:6–8), will bring them to the gospel (see 2 Ne. 30:3), and will even participate with them in the building of the New Jerusalem upon the land of America (see 3 Ne. 21:23). This will be a "holy city unto the Lord, like unto the Jerusalem of old," built up for the seed of Joseph (see Ether 13:6–8; also 3 Ne. 20:22; 21:22–23). "And then," exults Nephi, "shall they [the Lamanites] rejoice; for they shall know that it is a blessing unto them from the hand of God; and their scales of darkness shall begin to fall from their eyes; and many generations shall not pass away among them, save they shall be a pure and a delightsome people" (2 Ne. 30:6).

There exists a curious prophecy about the "remnant of Jacob" (usually thought to mean the Lamanites) to the effect that they will be God's instrument to punish the Gentiles unless the latter repent. The language used in the scripture describes them as being like a lion among the flocks of sheep, who "treadeth down and teareth in pieces." (See 3 Ne. 16:14–15; 20:15–19; 21:12–14.) It was Elder Bruce R. McConkie's opinion that these statements are prophetic imagery referring to Israel's final victory over its enemies when the Savior returns in glory.[3]

The Lamanites of the last days will again be a blessed people. Some have suggested that we live in the "day of the Lamanite," and that the amazing growth of the Church in Central and South America is evidence that the appointed time has arrived.

The Savior's Visit to the Lost Tribes

Jesus' personal visit to the people of Israel seems to be part of his ancient covenant. After his Palestinian ministry Jesus came to America to establish his church among a remnant of Joseph's descendants. During his American ministry he announced his intention to visit the lost tribes of Israel:

> And verily, verily, I say unto you that I have other sheep, which are not of this land [the Americas], neither of the land of Jerusalem, neither in any parts of that land round about whither I have been to minister.
> For they of whom I speak are they who have not as yet heard my voice; neither have I at any time manifested myself unto them.
> But I have received a commandment of the Father that I shall go unto them, and that they shall hear my voice, and shall be numbered among my sheep, that there may be one fold and one shepherd; therefore I go to show myself unto them. (3 Ne. 16:1–3.)

It is assumed that the lost tribes were living together when the Savior visited them, but the geographical location is unknown. Several theories exist concerning their present whereabouts, with the idea that they are dispersed among the nations probably the most common view.[4]

Jesus' message to the lost tribes was the same gospel message he had delivered to the Jews and Nephites. "I speak the same words unto one nation like unto another," the Lord once declared (2 Ne. 29:8). The Lord also said that these tribes would write scripture, and someday, when they return, those scriptures will be available to others (see 2 Ne. 29:12–13). Their eventual return is usually described in dramatic terms as an event even overshadowing the ancient deliverance from Egypt (see Jer. 16:14–15; 23:7–8; D&C 133:26ff).

God's hand is still stretched out to the Israelite people, and the restored Church is the instrument through which his latter-day people will be blessed. These blessings for each branch of this historic family will come to pass if they will but open their eyes and return to him.

Chapter 10

THE GENTILES IN THE PROMISED LAND

The Promised Land and What God Requires of Its Occupants

It must have been with considerable anxiety that Lehi's family began their life in the New World. Would their new environment be hostile or benevolent? How would life be different from what they had known? What new challenges would they face?

Feelings similar to these may partly account for Lehi's reassuring discourse concerning this "chosen land" to which they had come. He told his little colony that their arrival was a great blessing of the Lord (see 2 Ne. 1–3). By vision he learned that Jerusalem was destroyed, and, he said, "had we remained . . . we should also have perished" (2 Ne. 1:4). Lehi then spoke at length about the greatness of the new land:

> We have obtained a land of promise, a land which is choice above all other lands; a land which the Lord God hath covenanted with me should be a land for the inheritance of my seed. Yea, the Lord hath covenanted this land unto me, and to my children forever, and also all those who should be led out of other countries by the hand of the Lord.
>
> Wherefore, I, Lehi, prophesy according to the workings of the Spirit which is in me, that there shall none come into this land save they shall be brought by the hand of the Lord.
>
> Wherefore, this land is consecrated unto him whom he shall bring. (2 Ne. 1:5–7.)

Continuing, Lehi informed his children that "this land should be kept as yet from the knowledge of other nations; for behold, many nations would overrun the land, that there would be no place for an inheritance" (2 Ne. 1:8). What interesting ideas! America is made up of numerous racial and national groups. Were these intentionally

brought here by the Lord? As for the land being kept from the knowledge of other nations, one must admit it is strange that the American
continents came to the awareness of the rest of the world so late in
history.

Lehi also uttered a solemn warning to all future inhabitants of
this land, with particular reference to "those whom the Lord God
shall bring out of the land of Jerusalem" (2 Ne. 1:9). Similar warnings
characterize nearly all Book of Mormon statements about the
promised land.

> Wherefore, this land is consecrated unto him whom he [the
> Lord] shall bring. And if it so be that they shall serve him accord-
> ing to the commandments which he hath given, it shall be a land
> of liberty unto them; . . . if iniquity shall abound cursed shall be
> the land for their sakes. . . .
>
> . . . Behold, I say, if the day shall come that they will reject
> the Holy One of Israel, the true Messiah, their Redeemer and
> their God, behold, the judgments of him that is just shall rest
> upon them.
>
> Yea, he will bring other nations unto them, and he will give
> unto them power, and he will take away from them the lands of
> their possessions, and he will cause them to be scattered and
> smitten. (2 Ne. 1:7, 10–11.)

Students of the Book of Mormon know that the descendants of
Lehi did turn to wickedness and did reject the Holy One of Israel. Did
the prophesied judgments then come upon them? The destruction of
the Nephite nation testifies that the judgments occurred. It is possible
that the European depredations of a later date—Cortés's conquest of
the Aztecs, Pizarro's subjugation of the Incas, the Indian wars in
North America—were also part of the prophetic fulfillment.

There is a second important passage concerning the greatness of
America. This warning was given to the Jaredites as the Lord led
them from the Old World to "a land which is choice above all the
lands of the earth" (Ether 1:42). This was a land that the Lord "had
preserved for a righteous people" (Ether 2:7). Here again we read the
warning: "And he had sworn in his wrath unto the brother of Jared,
that whoso should possess this land of promise, from that time
henceforth and forever, should serve him, the true and only God, or
they should be swept off when the fulness of his wrath should come
upon them. . . . And the fulness of his wrath cometh upon them
when they are ripened in iniquity." (Ether 2:8–9.)

Two great civilizations (the Jaredites and Nephites) have been swept off this land because they became "ripened in iniquity"; and Moroni, commenting on the above verse, issues a direct warning to the future Gentile inhabitants of this land: "And this [the Book of Mormon] cometh unto you, O ye Gentiles, that ye may know the decrees of God—that ye may repent, and not continue in your iniquities until the fulness come, that ye may not bring down the fulness of the wrath of God upon you as the inhabitants of the land have hitherto done" (Ether 2:11).

It is very important to point out that the term *choice* (or *chosen*) *land* refers to all the Americas—North, Central, and South (see Alma 46:17). Some might argue that Central and South America, so often poor and subject to political tyrants, would hardly qualify as a "chosen land." Let us remember that the Book of Mormon teaches that the land would be chosen to whoever served the God of this land and be cursed to any who turned against him. Lehi's posterity could have possessed "this land unto themselves" (2 Ne. 1:9), but when they turned to evil they forfeited their blessings to the Gentiles.[1] Mormon explained this transfer of blessings: "The Lord hath reserved their blessings, which they might have received in the land, for the Gentiles who shall possess the land" (Morm. 5:19). The following quotation indicates how future Lamanites would be excluded from promised land blessing: "But behold, this land, said God, shall be a land of thine inheritance, and the Gentiles shall be blessed upon the land. And this land shall be a land of liberty unto the Gentiles, and there shall be no kings upon the land, who shall raise up unto the Gentiles." (2 Ne. 10:10–11.)

A Great Gentile Nation on the Chosen Land

Book of Mormon prophets foresaw that a "mighty nation" of Gentiles would be established upon this land (see 1 Ne. 22:7; 13:30; 3 Ne. 20:27); they also saw that God would play a major role in bringing it about. His spirit fell upon "a man among the Gentiles," and that man traveled across the "many waters, even unto the seed of my [Nephi's] brethren, who were in the promised land" (1 Ne. 13:12). Of course, we interpret this man to be Columbus. Next, the Spirit "wrought upon other Gentiles [those who would be the early colonists of the United States]; and they went forth out of captivity, upon the many waters" (1 Ne. 13:13). Nephi saw God protecting these Gentiles as they defeated their "mother Gentiles" (that is, Great Britain) in the revolutionary war. The Lord fortified "this land against all other nations"; no king was to rule over them, and they were "delivered by the power of God out of the hands of all other nations" (see 2 Ne. 10:11–16; 1 Ne. 13:17–19). Modern revelation tell us that God even raised up "wise men" for the express purpose of writing a democratically inspired constitution by which the Gentiles would be governed (see D&C 101:79–80). Strengthened and prospered from above, this great nation—a nation "lifted up by the power of God above all other nations, upon the face of the land" (1 Ne. 13:30)—would then turn upon the Israelite remnant (American Indians and possibly Mexicans) in the land and cause them to be smitten and scattered (see 1 Ne. 13:14; 15:17; Morm. 5:20; 3 Ne. 20:27–28).

Why did God so carefully superintend the affairs of this nation? The answer is that he intended this American nation to be the base of operations for his kingdom in the last days, and that its administration of the gospel would influence the latter-day gathering of Israel. Consider the following words of Jesus: "For it is wisdom in the Father that they [the Gentiles] should be established in this land, and be set up as a free people by the power of the Father, that these things [the Nephite records] might come forth from them unto a remnant of your seed, that the covenant of the Father may be fulfilled which he hath covenanted with his people, O house of Israel" (3 Ne. 21:4). This says that the Gentiles need to be established in America so that the Book of Mormon and the gospel might come to the Lamanites and so that the Father will be able to fulfill his covenant with the house of Israel. The Gentile ministry to the Lamanites—bringing them the "fulness of the gospel" (1 Ne. 15:13) and the Book of Mormon (see 3 Ne. 26:8)—will be so helpful that the scriptures liken the Gentiles to "nursing fathers" and "nursing mothers" (see 1 Ne. 21:22–23; 2 Ne. 10:18). Modern Lamanites are not the only recipients of Gentile assistance. The resurrected Christ spoke also of the Jews receiving the gospel through the labors of the Gentiles:

These sayings which ye shall write shall be kept and shall be manifested unto the Gentiles, that through the fulness of the Gentiles, the remnant of their seed [the Jews], who shall be scattered forth upon the face of the earth because of their unbelief, may be brought in, or may be brought to a knowledge of me, their Redeemer.

And then will I gather them in from the four quarters of the earth; and then will I fulfil the covenant which the Father hath made unto all the people of the house of Israel.

And blessed are the Gentiles, because of their belief in me, in and of the Holy Ghost, which witnesses unto them of me and of the Father.

> Behold, because of their belief in me, saith the Father, and because of the unbelief of you, O house of Israel, in the latter day shall the truth come unto the Gentiles, that the fulness of these things shall be made known unto them. (3 Ne. 16:4–7.)

Here we are told that the scriptures (the Book of Mormon) will come to the Gentiles so that the Jews may be brought to a knowledge of the Redeemer and so that the Lord can fulfill his covenant with all the house of Israel.

The "Marvelous Work and a Wonder"

The restoration of gospel truth to the Gentiles (and through them to the house of Israel) is called a "marvelous work and a wonder" (2 Ne. 25:17; see also 2 Ne. 27:26; 3 Ne. 21:9; 1 Ne. 13:34). In the words of Nephi, it would be of "great worth unto our seed" (1 Ne. 22:8), to the Gentiles, and to all Israel (see 1 Ne. 22:9). This "marvelous work" would comprise many aspects of the Lord's latter-day work. Included would be the gathering of Israel to the "lands of their inheritance" (1 Ne. 22:12; see also 2 Ne. 25:17–18), the appearance of a great seer like unto Moses (see 2 Ne. 3:9–13), and the coming forth of the Book of Mormon. This book will play a great role, to those who receive it, in clarifying gospel truth and supporting the Bible (see 2 Ne. 3:11–12; see also chapter 2 herein for a more extensive treatment of the Restoration).

From the foregoing we have learned that Nephite prophets saw the future of America with amazing accuracy. It was a land hidden from the rest of the world until the time was right for God's latter-day work to commence. The United States was singled out as the destined nation to bear the gospel to other peoples of the earth.

The Decline of the Great Gentile Nation

Unfortunately, the spiritual ascendency of the Gentiles will not last. They (and the Jews) will be caught up in the maelstrom of evil that will engulf the world in the last days. "Behold, in the last days, or in the days of the Gentiles," predicted Nephi, ". . . all the nations of the Gentiles and also the Jews . . . will be drunken with iniquity and all manner of abominations" (2 Ne. 27:1). Many "nations of the Gentiles" (not only the United States) will be gathered together by the great and abominable church to "fight against the Lamb of God" (1 Ne. 14:13).

Many will reject the Book of Mormon (see 2 Ne. 29:3; 3 Ne. 21:9), and the majority will turn to wickedness (see 2 Ne. 26:20–23; 28; Morm. 8). Two great sermons speaking of these decadent conditions were mentioned in chapter 1. Because of their importance in describing latter-day conditions, they are summarized here:

Religious Apostasy	Moral Degeneracy
2 Ne. 28: Churches are not built up to the Lord. They contend with each other, teach with their own learning, deny the Holy Ghost, deny miracles, and claim there is "no God today, for the Lord . . . hath done his work." There will be false teachers and doctrines, corrupt churches, fine clothing, and expensive sanctuaries.	2 Ne. 28: There will be sinful indulgence; all are corrupt save a few followers of Christ. People will take sin lightly (God, they will claim, "will justify in committing a little sin"). The devil will rage in the hearts of men, and convince many that there is no hell and no devil.
Morm. 8: Churches deny miracles and the power of God. They are defiled and polluted. They love money, neglect the poor, and build elaborate buildings.	Morm. 8: The Saints are persecuted. Churches love money and neglect the poor. Sin is viewed as not serious; there are secret combinations, works of darkness, wars and rumors of wars, great pollutions, murders, robbing, lying, deceivings, whoredoms, and all manner of abominations.

Among the chaotic political conditions will be "wars and rumors of wars" (1 Ne. 14:15) and secret criminal combinations among the Gentiles (see Ether 8:24, 25). The time will come when a great division will occur between the wicked and the righteous among the Gentiles (see 1 Ne. 14:7; 2 Ne. 30:10; 3 Ne. 16:8). These terrible conditions will cause the Lord to finally remove his gospel from among them (2 Ne. 28:32; D&C 45:28–30). Jesus himself made this doleful prophecy concerning the Gentiles:

> And thus commandeth the Father that I should say unto you: At that day when the Gentiles shall sin against my gospel, and shall reject the fulness of my gospel, and shall be lifted up in the

pride of their hearts above all nations, and above all the people of the whole earth, and shall be filled with all manner of lyings, and of deceits, and of mischiefs, and all manner of hypocrisy, and murders, and priestcrafts, and whoredoms, and of secret abominations; and if they shall do all those things, and shall reject the fulness of my gospel, behold, saith the Father, I will bring the fulness of my gospel from among them (3 Ne. 16:10).

What a tragedy! Is the spiritual fall of the Gentiles inevitable? It is important to realize that the Lord always holds out the possibility of repentance (see 2 Ne. 28:32). These are conditional prophecies. The condemning passage above is followed a little further on by these words: "But if the Gentiles will repent and return unto me, saith the Father, behold they shall be numbered among my people, O house of Israel" (3 Ne. 16:13; see also 3 Ne. 21:14, 22–24). During his ministry, Jesus warned that after the Gentiles had "received the fulness of my gospel," had become "mighty above all," and had been a "scourge unto the people of this land, . . . then if they shall harden their hearts against me I will return their iniquities upon their own heads, saith the Father" (see 3 Ne. 20:27–28).

Prophetic Warnings to the Gentiles

Seeing these evil conditions, ancient American prophets naturally sought to warn us of the serious consequences of our sins. In this chapter it has been shown that righteousness is a necessary condition of occupancy in the promised land, but there are many other warnings that deserve careful attention. Here is Mormon: "O ye Gentiles, how can ye stand before the power of God, except ye shall repent and turn from your evil ways?" (See Morm. 5:22–24.) Listen to Mormon again, this time as he gives the words of the Savior: "Turn, all ye Gentiles, from your wicked ways; and repent of your evil doings, of your lyings and deceivings, and of your whoredoms, . . . and come unto me, and be baptized in my name, that ye may receive a remission of your sins, and be filled with the Holy Ghost, that ye may be numbered with my people who are of the house of Israel" (3 Ne. 30:2).

After enumerating the sins of the last days mentioned earlier, Moroni exhorts: "Behold, the sword of vengeance hangeth over you; and the time soon cometh that he avengeth the blood of the saints upon you, for he will not suffer their cries any longer" (Morm. 8:41). Of particular concern to Moroni was the religious disbelief that he foresaw. He used the last chapter of his own book (see Moro.

10:7–25) and the last one of his father's book (see Morm. 9) to lecture the future Gentiles and Lamanites to beware of denying miracles, revelation, and spiritual gifts: "And again I speak unto you who deny the revelations of God, and say that they are done away, that there are no revelations, nor prophecies, nor gifts, nor healing, nor speaking with tongues, and the interpretation of tongues; behold I say unto you, he that denieth these things knoweth not the gospel of Christ; yea, he has not read the scriptures; if so, he does not understand them" (Morm. 9:7–8). "I will show unto you a God of miracles" (Morm. 9:11), Moroni testifies, while bearing witness of numerous scriptural miracles. The reason why God "ceaseth to do miracles among the children of men," he concludes, "is because that they dwindle in unbelief, and depart from the right way, and know not the God in whom they should trust" (Morm. 9:20).

An often-repeated and unusual warning to the Gentiles is that a "remnant of Jacob," or "house of Israel," will be among them like a "young lion among the flocks of sheep" and will tread them down and teareth them in pieces if they fail to repent (see 3 Ne. 16:14–15; 20:16–19; 21:12; Morm. 5:24; for an interpretation, see p. 115 herein). Jesus declared that this is also a conditional warning: "But if the Gentiles will repent and return unto me, saith the Father. . . . I will not suffer my people, who are of the house of Israel, to go through among them, and tread them down." (3 Ne. 16:13–14.)

The most ominous threat to America is that destruction awaits them if they ever turn away from the God of this land and become "ripe in iniquity." How bad is being "ripe in iniquity"? The scriptures provide a probable answer.

Are We Ripe in Iniquity?

The Book of Mormon clearly teaches that the Lord will destroy any people who become "ripe in iniquity" (see 2 Ne. 28:16; Alma 37:28, 31; 45:16; Ether 2:8–9, 15; 9:20; 1 Ne. 17:35). A list of the peoples to whom this has happened in earth's history would at least include the following: (1) those who lived during the time of Noah and were drowned in the Flood, (2) the Jaredites, (3) the cities of Sodom and Gomorrah, (4) the ancient Canaanites, (5) the wicked Nephites at the time of the Savior's coming to America, (6) the Nephites in the fifth century A.D., and finally (7) the entire wicked world at the second coming of Christ. Examining the scriptural descriptions of these nations may give us insight as to why they were destroyed and what is meant by the phrase "ripe in iniquity."

1. *The people of the Flood:* Regarding these people, the Lord lamented that nowhere in all his creations could he find such evil (see Moses 7:36). They are described as "without affection, and they hate their own blood" (Moses 7:33). "Every man was lifted up in the imagination of the thoughts of his heart, being only evil continually" (Moses 8:22). "The earth . . . was filled with violence" (Moses 8:28).

2. *The Jaredites:* It was the existence of secret combinations (criminal and nefarious political organizations) that brought the Jaredite nation to great wickedness (see Ether 8:20–25). These evil conditions led to the rejection and murder of the prophets (see Ether 11:1–5, 22) until the prophets were withdrawn from among the people (see Ether 11:13).

3. *Sodom and Gomorrah:* Little is known concerning what led to the downfall of the inhabitants of these cities besides the fact that their sins included sexual perversion (see Jude 1:7).

4. *The ancient Canaanites:* Nephi, describing the conquest of Canaan under Joshua, told us that after the children of Israel "had crossed the river Jordan he [God] did make them mighty unto the driving out of the children of the land, yea, unto the scattering them to destruction. . . . Behold, this people had rejected every word of God, and they were ripe in iniquity; and the fulness of the wrath of God was upon them; and the Lord did curse the land against them, and bless it unto our fathers; yea, he did curse it against them unto their destruction." (1 Ne. 17:32, 35.)

5. *The Nephites prior to Christ's American ministry:* Mormon described Nephite society, as it existed approximately thirty years before the birth of Christ, as follows: "They who chose evil were more numerous than they who chose good, therefore they were ripening for destruction, for the laws had become corrupted" (Hel. 5:2). Generations before, King Mosiah had warned that "if the time comes that the voice of the people doth choose iniquity, then is the time that the judgments of God will come upon you; yea, then is the time he will visit you with great destruction even as he has hitherto visited this land" (Mosiah 29:27; see also Alma 10:19). Conditions worsened. About 20 B.C. a prophet named Nephi chastised his people for rejecting the truth, "notwithstanding so many evidences which ye have received" (Hel. 8:24). He further declared that "even at this time ye are ripening, because of your murders and your fornication and wickedness, for everlasting destruction; yea, and except ye repent it will come unto you soon" (Hel. 8:26).

Samuel the Lamanite mentioned a factor that often delays the judgments of God—namely, the presence of righteous people. "Wo unto this great city of Zarahemla," he declared, delivering the words of the Lord; "for behold, it is because of those who are righteous that it is saved. . . . But behold, it is for the righteous' sake that it is spared. But behold, the time cometh, saith the Lord, that when ye shall cast out the righteous from among you, then shall ye be ripe for destruction." (Hel. 13:12, 14; see Amulek's similar words to the people of Ammonihah, Alma 10:22–23.) As the record indicates, by the year 30 B.C. wickedness had increased among the people, laws had been corrupted (see Hel. 4:22), the Church had dwindled in iniquity (see Hel. 4:23), and the Spirit of the Lord had withdrawn (see Hel. 4:24). It was not until the people "cast out the prophets," however, that God unleashed his destructive forces (see 3 Ne. 9:10–11; 2 Ne. 26:3–8).

6. *The Nephite civilization in the fifth century A.D.:* Little is said about the final descent of the Nephites into evil, but Mormon's writing graphically describes atrocities that include cannibalism, rape, murder, and torture (see Moro. 9:8–10). "O the depravity of my people!" he laments. "They are without order and without mercy. . . . They have become strong in their perversion; and they are alike brutal, sparing none, neither old nor young; and they delight in everything save that which is good. . . . They are without principle, and past feeling; and their wickedness doth exceed that of the Lamanites." (Moro. 9:18–20.) For some time Mormon had been forbidden to preach to his people, and because they had "wilfully rebelled against their God," the beloved disciples (that is, the three Nephite disciples) had been taken out of their midst (see Moro. 1:16–17).

7. *The world in the last days before Christ's second coming:* The world prior to the coming of Christ will be in a state of evil. The Savior compared it to the days of Noah (see JS—M 1:41). Jesus specifically mentioned that there would be false Christs, false prophets, great deceptions, wars and rumors of wars, and that "because iniquity shall abound, the love of men shall wax cold" (JS—M 1:30). Earlier in this chapter we considered what the Book of Mormon had to say about the moral degeneracy and religious apostasy of the last days. In an obvious attempt to spare the righteous, and probably leave the wicked unprotected, the former will be gathered from around the earth to places of relative safety. The last thing that happens before destruction seems to be the withdrawal of the Saints, the prophets, and the Spirit of God. Nephi taught, "When the Spirit ceaseth to strive with man then cometh speedy destruction" (2 Ne. 26:11).

From these examples, we have learned the circumstances that bring divine vengeance upon a people: (1) extraordinary wickedness flourishing among the majority of the people; (2) a rejection of Christ and his representatives, including persecuting the righteous and casting them out from society; (3) apparently the continued prevalence of these evil conditions over a long period of time until the Lord has tried every means to save the people.

The question remains, Are we ripe in iniquity? I will leave it to the reader to provide the answer.

Part III

THE BOOK OF MORMON EXPANDS OUR UNDERSTANDING OF THE GOSPEL

Chapter 11

THE FORTUNATE FALL

The Book of Mormon always prefaces discussions of the Atonement with information about the Fall. The Fall brought about man's predicament; the Atonement is God's remedy for that predicament. It is difficult to be excited about the gospel solution unless one understands the problem. Following are a few examples of how Book of Mormon prophets juxtapose these two doctrines.

When Aaron, one of Mosiah's famous missionary sons, began to teach the untutored Lamanite king, he "did expound unto him the scriptures from the creation of Adam, laying the fall of man before him, and their carnal state and also the plan of redemption, which was prepared from the foundation of the world, through Christ. . . . And since man had fallen he could not merit anything of himself; but the sufferings and death of Christ atone for their sins." (Alma 22:13–14.) Lehi taught that "all mankind were in a lost and in a fallen state, and ever would be save they should rely on this Redeemer" (1 Ne. 10:6). Both Alma and Amulek taught the Fall before their great sermons on the Atonement. Here is a verse from Amulek's discourse: "For it is expedient that an atonement should be made; for according to the great plan of the Eternal God there must be an atonement made, or else all mankind must unavoidably perish; yea, all are hardened; yea, all are fallen and are lost, and must perish except it be through the atonement which it is expedient should be made" (Alma 34:9).

Without a real Fall, there is no need for the Atonement. Certainly one of the main reasons why many in the world are indifferent to Christ is that they fail to see why a Savior is needed. On the other hand, the Book of Mormon praises and glorifies the Savior because only he can save us from our serious predicament brought on by the Fall. That is why worship of God and Christ, talk of their unfathomable grace, and hymns of adoration are so much a part of true religion. Jacob truly understood the value of his Savior's work. Without Christ's infinite atonement, he declared,

> this corruption could not put on incorruption. Wherefore, the first judgment [physical and spiritual death] which came upon man must needs have remained to an endless duration. And if so, this flesh must have laid down to rot and to crumble to its mother earth, to rise no more.
>
> O the wisdom of God, his mercy and grace! For behold, if the flesh should rise no more our spirits must become subject to that angel who fell from before the presence of the Eternal God, and became the devil, to rise no more.
>
> And our spirits must have become like unto him, and we become devils, angels to a devil, to be shut out from the presence of our God, and to remain with the father of lies, in misery, like unto himself. . . .
>
> O how great the goodness of our God, who prepareth a way for our escape from the grasp of this awful monster; yea, that monster, death and hell. (2 Ne. 9:7–10.)

Why is God to be loved and honored? Because he has provided the way for us to be saved from death and endless misery. It is the reality of the Fall that makes the Atonement so remarkable.

Before detailing the type of existence that resulted from the Fall, we need to remind ourselves what the Book of Mormon says about the *purpose* of mortality. Then we can see more clearly how the conditions created by the Fall contribute to the fulfillment of this purpose.

The Purpose of Mortality

According to Mormon theology, our earthly existence is designed to be a period of growth and testing. God is helping mortal beings to progress in order that they might realize maximum achievement and happiness. "Men are, that they might have joy," was Lehi's unforgettable declaration (2 Ne. 2:25). Alma referred to the gospel as "the great plan of happiness" (Alma 42:8).

The most common Book of Mormon word to describe this mortal condition is *probation*. To be under probation means to be in a situation of proving, testing, or trial. Consider the following Book of Mormon passages and the use of the term *probation:*

2 Ne. 2:21—"And the days of the children of men were pro-

longed, according to the will of God, that they might repent while in the flesh; wherefore, their state became a state of probation."

2 Ne. 9:27—"But wo unto him that has the law given, yea, that has all the commandments of God, like unto us, and that transgresseth them, and that wasteth the days of his probation, for awful is his state!"

Alma 12:24—"There was a space granted unto man in which he might repent; therefore this life became a probationary state; a time to prepare to meet God; a time to prepare for that endless state which has been spoken of by us, which is after the resurrection of the dead."

Alma 42:4—"And thus we see, that there was a time granted unto man to repent, yea, a probationary time, a time to repent and serve God."

2 Ne. 33:9—"For none of these can I hope except they shall be reconciled unto Christ, and enter into the narrow gate, and walk in the strait path which leads to life, and continue in the path until the end of the day of probation."

Hel. 13:38—"But behold, your days of probation are past; ye have procrastinated the day of your salvation until it is everlastingly too late, and your destruction is made sure; yea, for ye have sought all the days of your lives for that which ye could not obtain; and ye have sought for happiness in doing iniquity, which thing is contrary to the nature of that righteousness which is in our great and Eternal Head."

Alma 34:32–33—(This is the most oft-quoted passage on the subject, although the word *probation* is not used.) "For behold, this life is the time for men to prepare to meet God; yea, behold the day of this life is the day for men to perform their labors. And now, as I said unto you before, as ye have had so many witnesses, therefore, I beseech of you that ye do not procrastinate the day of your repentance until the end; for after this day of life, which is given us to prepare for eternity, behold, if we do not improve our time while in this life, then cometh the night of darkness wherein there can be no labor performed."

These passages teach that the religious life is the aim of our existence, that our behavior is being monitored by God, and that there is a sense of urgency for us to improve and progress while living in mortality. Jacob described as "awful" the state of anyone who "wasteth the days of his probation" (2 Ne. 9:27). We are told that the Lord intentionally "prolonged" our days that we might repent while in the flesh (see 2 Ne. 2:21). We must "improve our time while in this life" or there will come the time when "there can be no labor performed" (Alma 34:33). Little wonder Moroni told us of the latter days to "be wise in the days of your probation" and to be "more wise than we [the Nephite-Lamanite people] have been" (Morm. 9:28, 31).

Now, let's turn to the doctrine of the Fall.

The World's View of the Fall

The truth of the Fall has been eroded by modern skepticism. On the one hand, the theory of evolution (a fundamental proposition of biological science) seems incompatible with the biblical story of Adam and Eve. In addition, the modern study of ancient religion and mythology has uncovered many tales similar to the Adam and Eve story and tends to assign them all to the realm of folklore. This modernist perspective has the effect of undermining the doctrines of the Fall and the Atonement, and the Christian religion itself.

The Traditional Christian View of the Fall

Traditional Christianity has maintained that God placed our first parents in the paradisiacal condition of the Garden of Eden. He intended that they remain there and bring forth offspring, and thus all mankind would dwell in perfect peace and happiness. Adam and Eve thwarted God's plan through their transgression, thus bringing upon themselves and their posterity death, sin, and misery. Not only did their "original sin" bring corruption upon themselves, but all their offspring inherited this evil inclination as well. Our primal parents have, therefore, been considered the worst of sinners.

The Book of Mormon Concept of the Fall

Latter-day Saint scriptures take a quite literal interpretation of the Garden of Eden story. It is clear from the Book of Mormon that Adam and Eve were historical people and that the story of their transgression and fall is factual. Revelation to the Prophet Joseph Smith identifies Adam as Michael, the archangel (see D&C 27:11; 107:54; 128:21). "In the creation of the earth," wrote Elder Bruce R. McConkie, "Michael played a part second only to that of Christ."[1]

When Adam and Eve, our first parents (see 1 Ne. 5:11), were placed in the Garden of Eden they were non-mortal beings, not subject to death. If they had remained in this state, the prophet Lehi tells us, "they would have had no children; wherefore they would have remained in a state of innocence, having no joy, for they knew no misery; doing no good, for they knew no sin" (2 Ne. 2:23). No joy, no goodness, no children—the human race would have never existed! Obviously this was not a desirable state. Lehi explains further, "And now, behold, if Adam had not transgressed he would not have fallen, but he would have remained in the garden of Eden. And all things which were created must have remained in the same state in which they were after they were created; and they must have remained forever, and had no end." (2 Ne. 2:22.) Adam's transgression was therefore essential to bring about the mortal condition—"Adam fell that men might be; and men are, that they might have joy" (2 Ne. 2:25). The Fall, rather than being a terrible catastrophe, was God's way of inaugurating mortal existence. We do not fully understand why it was done this way, but Lehi assures us that "all things have been done in the wisdom of him who knoweth all things" (2 Ne. 2:24). Thus, in LDS theology Adam and Eve are heroes, second in importance only to members of the Godhead.

The Fall was a fortunate thing because mortal existence is necessary for the progress of mankind. Possibly the most intriguing aspect of the Fall is the *kind* of mortality that resulted. What are the conditions resulting from the Fall, and how do they affect our period of mortal probation?

Mortal Conditions Created by the Fall

1. *Spiritual death:* Before the Fall, Adam and Eve had been in close contact with God. Being cast out of the garden, they, in Elder Bruce R. McConkie's words, "no longer had communion with Deity either personally or by means of the Spirit."[2] Jacob taught that "because man became fallen they were cut off from the presence of the Lord" (2 Ne. 9:6). Alma also declared that by transgression "our first parents were cut off both temporally and spiritually from the presence of the Lord" (Alma 42:7; see also Hel. 14:16–17). How is this condition desirable for man's probationary state? We have limited knowledge in these matters, yet we can comprehend that continuing to live in God's presence would minimize the trial aspect of mortality. In God's presence, for instance, the way of truth and goodness would be clear; here in a fallen world it is problematical. Walking by faith rather than by sight is a far greater test. Also, since no evil can exist in the presence of God (see Alma 40:26), it follows that we had to leave his presence to be tested by evil. Like an adolescent leaving a comfortable home to live on his own, we have left our Father's heavenly home to

exercise our own choices. One of our challenges is to regain and maintain spiritual contact with our divine parent.

2. *Death and the acquisition of a physical body:* Adam was told by God in Eden that the consequence of eating the forbidden fruit was death. Alma testified that "the fall had brought upon all mankind . . . a temporal death" (Alma 42:9). Many other Book of Mormon prophets also mentioned this outcome (see 2 Ne. 2:5; 9:4, 6, 7; Alma 11:42–45; 12:12, 16, 24, 27, 31, 36; 42:6–9; Hel. 14:16). We learned earlier of Lehi's teachings that without Adam's transgression the undesirable conditions of the garden would have gone on forever.

A modern revelation indicates that without a body man "cannot receive a fulness of joy" (see D&C 93:33–34). To obtain a body is one of the very purposes of coming to earth. The body, however, can bring a host of difficult challenges. Becoming mortal means experiencing disease, suffering, and ultimately death. Our bodies, I believe, bring with them new depths of emotion and appetite. Noble impulses now compete with temptations to evil. Satan influences us through the body. Lehi pleaded with his sons to choose eternal life rather than "eternal death, according to the will of the flesh and the evil which is therein" (2 Ne. 2:29; see also 2 Ne. 4:17–19, 27; 10:23–24). This body, therefore, seems to be a challenge as well as a blessing. Each of us faces the problem of changing from our "carnal and fallen state, to a state of righteousness" (Mosiah 27:25), or returning to God is unthinkable. All this is not to imply that we should despise the body as Christian ascetics have often done. Elder Erastus Snow once said: "The lusts and desires of the flesh are not of themselves unmitigated evils. On the contrary they are implanted in us as a stimulus to noble deeds, rather than low and beastly deeds. . . . Every instinct in us is for a wise purpose in God when properly regulated and restrained, and guided by the Holy Spirit and kept within its proper legitimate bounds."[3]

3. *Freedom of choice:* One of the major reasons for the Fall was to bring man into an environment where freedom of choice could be maximized. President David O. McKay taught that, next to life itself, freedom is man's most precious possession.[4] Choice requires the existence of alternatives between which we can make a selection. "Wherefore, the Lord God gave unto man that he should act for himself. Wherefore, man could not act for himself save it should be that he was enticed by the one or the other." (2 Ne. 2:16.) The Fall, therefore, brought about an environment where alternatives, or opposites, existed. Lehi is remembered for his great discourse on this subject. "It must needs be, that there is an opposition in all things. If not so . . . righteousness could not be brought to pass, neither wickedness, nei-

ther holiness nor misery, neither good nor bad." (2 Ne. 2:11.) Fallen man acquired the ability to more fully discern between good and evil, an aptitude he did not possess before the Fall (see Alma 42:3). "The Spirit of Christ," taught Mormon, "is given to every man, that he may know good from evil" (Moro. 7:16). Another condition seems to be necessary for full freedom to exist: "And it must needs be that the devil should tempt the children of men, or they could not be agents unto themselves; for if they never should have bitter they could not know the sweet" (D&C 29:39).

Thus we see that all the necessary conditions for full freedom to exist were set up at the beginning of mortal existence. Genuine growth must come as a result of our choosing. A world of opposites can be at times a frightening and ugly place—wars, hostility, death, poverty, and suffering counterbalanced by peace, love, beauty, and abundance. Our greatest test is to live in such a world using our agency to choose good and refuse evil. Through the making of countless choices our character is revealed and molded.

4. *The introduction of sin:* Sin was not an automatic result of the Fall. Children are born into this world in innocence (see Moro. 8:8, 19; D&C 93:38–39; Moses 6:48–49, 55–56), and their early sins are covered by the Atonement (see Mosiah 3:16). But when we mature to the age of accountability—since we live in an evil world, since we possess a body that is attracted to evil, since the devil is enticing us to sin, and since we have free agency—we inevitably sin. It should be emphasized that we become "carnal, sensual, and devilish" by our own transgressions. "By the transgression of these holy laws man became sensual and devilish, and became fallen man" (D&C 20:20).

Following are some Book of Mormon passages describing man's fallen nature:

Abinadi, speaking of the wicked at Judgment Day, says: "For they are carnal and devilish, and the devil has power over them; yea, even that old serpent that did beguile our first parents, which was the cause of their fall; which was the cause of all mankind becoming carnal, sensual, devilish, knowing evil from good, subjecting themselves to the devil. Thus all mankind were lost; and behold, they would have been endlessly lost were it not that God redeemed his people from their lost and fallen state." (Mosiah 16:3–4.)

An angel told King Benjamin, who in turn told his people, that "the natural man is an enemy to God, and has been from the fall of Adam, and will be, forever and ever, unless he yields to the enticings of the Holy Spirit, and putteth off the natural man and becometh a saint through the atonement of Christ the Lord" (Mosiah 3:19).

In his confessional prayer to God, the brother of Jared said, "We are unworthy before thee; because of the fall our natures have become evil continually" (Ether 3:2).

Alma explained to Corianton that "all men that are in a state of nature, or I would say, in a carnal state, are in the gall of bitterness and in the bonds of iniquity; they are without God in the world, and they have gone contrary to the nature of God; therefore, they are in a state contrary to the nature of happiness" (Alma 41:11).

Alma further stated that after the Fall, "man became lost forever, yea, they became fallen man. And now, ye see by this that our first parents were cut off both temporally and spiritually from the presence of the Lord; and thus we see they became subjects to follow after their own will. . . . Therefore, as they had become carnal, sensual, and devilish, by nature, this probationary state became a state for them to prepare; it became a preparatory state." (Alma 42:6–7, 10.)

Benjamin's final sermon contains some negative words about man's nature. He asks his people to remember their "nothingness, and his [God's] goodness and long-suffering towards you, unworthy creatures" (Mosiah 4:11; see also Mosiah 2:25; 4:5).

The above scriptures teach that because of the Fall all mankind has become "carnal, sensual, and devilish" and is now existing in a "lost and fallen state." In this condition fallen man is described as being in the "gall of bitterness," living "contrary to the nature of happiness," and being "without God in the world."

Man's sinful and wayward inclinations were often the subject of prophetic lamentation. Nephi, for example, the Spirit having stopped his utterance, said, "I am left to mourn because of the unbelief, and the wickedness, and the ignorance, and the stiffneckedness of men; for they will not search knowledge, nor understand great knowledge, when it is given unto them in plainness, even as plain as word can be" (2 Ne. 32:7). We assume that a grieving Mormon wrote the following negative evaluation of his people:

> And thus we can behold how false, and also the unsteadiness of the hearts of the children of men. . . .
>
> Yea, and we may see at the very time when he doth prosper his people, yea, in the increase of their fields, their flocks and their herds . . . ; yea, and in fine, doing all things for the welfare and happiness of his people; yea, then is the time that they do harden their hearts, and do forget the Lord their God, and do trample under their feet the Holy One—yea, and this because of their ease, and their exceedingly great prosperity.
>
> And thus we see that except the Lord doth chasten his people

with many afflictions, yea, except he doth visit them with death and with terror, and with famine and with all manner of pestilence, they will not remember him.

O how foolish, and how vain, and how evil, and devilish, and how quick to do iniquity, and how slow to do good, are the children of men; yea, how quick to hearken unto the words of the evil one, and to set their hearts upon the vain things of the world!

Yea, how quick to be lifted up in pride; yea, how quick to boast, and do all manner of that which is iniquity; and how slow are they to remember the Lord their God, and to give ear unto his counsels, yea, how slow to walk in wisdom's paths!

Behold, they do not desire that the Lord their God, who hath created them, should rule and reign over them; notwithstanding his great goodness and his mercy towards them, they do set at naught his counsels, and they will not that he should be their guide.

O how great is the nothingness of the children of men; yea, even they are less than the dust of the earth.

For behold, the dust of the earth moveth hither and thither, to the dividing asunder, at the command of our great and everlasting God. (Hel. 12:1–8.)

If the major purpose for the Book of Mormon is to turn people to their Redeemer, one method of doing that is by clearly portraying him as the only solution to their fallen state. Alma, and other great prophets, emphatically taught that, as the Lord told Alma, "all mankind" must be "born of God, changed from their carnal and fallen state, to a state of righteousness, being redeemed of God, becoming his sons and daughters" (Mosiah 27:25). Abinadi declared that "all mankind were lost; and behold, they would have been endlessly lost were it not that God redeemed his people from their lost and fallen state" (Mosiah 16:4). He explained that man can do much to determine the ultimate outcome; we can choose to remain in our fallen state or to rise toward godliness. God will not condemn us because we have fallen, only if we remain fallen. It is our choice, says Abinadi. "But remember that he that persists in his own carnal nature, and goes on in the ways of sin and rebellion against God, remaineth in his fallen state and the devil hath all power over him. Therefore he is as though there was no redemption made, being an enemy to God; and also is the devil an enemy to God. And now if Christ had not come into the world, . . . there could have been no redemption." (Mosiah 16:5–6.)

This revelation of man's nature probably constitutes the greatest challenge of our mortal existence. I am a free soul in a sinful world, living in a body that is not always cooperative with my will. Knowing that "no unclean thing can inherit the kingdom of God" (Alma 40:26), I must use my freedom wisely to accept Christ and, in concert with him, eradicate evil from my life.

Difficulties Are Necessary for Our Growth

The above results of the Fall make clear that human existence was never meant to be easy. We are, in summary, (1) cut off from God's presence, physically and spiritually; (2) subject to death, disease, and bodily temptations; (3) placed in an environment where greater evil exists and the power of Satan is increased; (4) confronted with greater freedom of choice; (5) and finally, responsible for our choices and accountable to God for the way we live our lives. God, it appears, arranged for our fall and is now testing us to see if we will recover. Are we equal to the task? If the purpose of mortality is for our growth and testing, and if we need challenges and difficulties to accomplish this objective, then there is no question that God has created an effective plan.

A popular psychiatrist and writer, M. Scott Peck, gives this intriguing analysis of the importance of difficulties in the growth process:

> Yet it is in this whole process of meeting and solving problems that life has its meaning. Problems are the cutting edge that distinguishes between success and failure. Problems call forth our courage and our wisdom; indeed, they create our courage and our wisdom. It is only because of problems that we grow mentally and spiritually. When we desire to encourage the growth of the human spirit, we challenge and encourage the human capacity to solve problems, just as in school we deliberately set problems for our children to solve. It is through the pain of confronting and resolving problems that we learn. As Benjamin Franklin said, "Those things that hurt, instruct." It is for this reason that wise people learn not to dread but actually to welcome problems and actually to welcome the pain of problems. . . .
>
> This tendency to avoid problems and the emotional suffering inherent in them is the primary basis of all human mental illness.[5]

Trials and problems, in summary, are essential to our progress. This may be difficult for us to comprehend. That is why we are normally depressed by problems, try our best to avoid them, or pretend that they do not exist. The proper attitude, on the other hand, is to acknowledge the inevitability of problems and willingly tackle their solution as growth opportunities.

Overcoming the Fall

How, then, do we overcome the Fall? It will take the remainder of the book to fully answer that question, but here are the three basic answers:

1. By understanding and accepting Christ's atonement. Nephi recorded Lehi's teaching that "all mankind were in a lost and in a fallen state, and ever would be save they should rely on this Redeemer" (1 Ne. 10:6). Amulek added: "All are hardened: yea, all are fallen and are lost, and must perish except it be through the atonement which it is expedient should be made" (Alma 34:9). There is no way that mortals can by themselves overcome their own death or their sins. The atonement of Christ provides a way to overcome these obstacles.

2. By experiencing true conversion. Alma said that the Lord told him that all "must be born again; yea, born of God, changed from their carnal and fallen state, to a state of righteousness, being redeemed of God, becoming his sons and daughters" (Mosiah 27:25).

3. By a personal determination to overcome one's sins. I repeat the prophet Abinadi's statement that he who "persists in his own carnal nature, and goes on in the ways of sin and rebellion against God, remaineth in his fallen state and the devil hath all power over him. Therefore he is as though there was no redemption made." (Mosiah 16:5.)

Although God assists us powerfully in each of these steps, man must also exert a major effort and commitment. Salvation is a cooperative effort between God and man. *We* must accept Christ, the Savior; *we* must cultivate the transforming power of the Holy Spirit in order to be "reborn" as a Christian; *we* must be strong, endure trials, make right choices, and persevere.

Why Do So Many Remain in Their Fallen State?

To remain or not remain fallen is a matter of personal choice. Christ has opened the way for all people to overcome the consequences of the Fall if they so choose.

There are probably dozens of reasons why people remain fallen; here are a few of the most common:

1. Most people do not like to be told of their failings; consequently, the doctrine of the Fall is not always met with the warmest of receptions. When Alma, for instance, told the people of Ammonihah that they were "a lost and a fallen people" and "a hard-hearted and a stiffnecked people," they reacted with anger and, reported Alma, "sought to lay their hands upon me, that they might cast me into prison" (Alma 9:30–32). The proper attitude, by contrast, was demonstrated by King Benjamin's people, who, after hearing the powerful address of their righteous king, realized that they were in a "carnal state, even less than the dust of the earth. And they all cried aloud with one voice, saying: O have mercy, and apply the atoning blood of Christ that we may receive forgiveness of our sins, and our hearts may be purified; for we believe in Jesus Christ, the Son of God, who created heaven and earth, and all things; who shall come down among the children of men." (Mosiah 4:2.)

2. Among many people there is unbelief in both their fallen condition and the Atonement. We live in a secular age of unbelief. Humanity seems oblivious to their lost situation. Our time, thought, and energies are almost totally taken up with worldly affairs. If the average person were told that he is in a fallen state and in great risk of losing his salvation, he would likely regard the statement as strange and silly.

3. Many people do not understand sin or its seriousness. Nephi described people of the last days as being indulgent and unworried about their sinful attitudes (see 2 Ne. 28:7–8). One can turn on television and see educated people justify serious sin (such as abortion and sexual license) on the basis of freedom of expression. Even the word *sin* is disappearing from our vocabulary; we prefer euphemisms such as "alternative life-style," "social deviation," or "aberrant behavior."

Many modern people do not understand that "no unclean thing can inherit the kingdom of God" (Alma 40:26) or that "the Lord cannot look upon sin with the least degree of allowance" (Alma 45:16); nor do they realize that only the truly penitent will be saved, or else mercy would rob justice and "God would cease to be God" (see Alma 42:24–25).

4. Lastly, most people have chosen to remain in their fallen state because they have not tasted the goodness of the gospel and come to realize that "wickedness never was happiness" (Alma 41:10). To those of us with ears to hear, Jacob's words will be recognized as God's marvelous solution to man's fallen status: "Therefore, cheer up your hearts, and remember that ye are free to act for yourselves—to

choose the way of everlasting death or the way of eternal life. Where-fore, my beloved brethren, reconcile yourselves to the will of God, and not to the will of the devil and the flesh; and remember, after ye are reconciled unto God, that it is only in and through the grace of God that ye are saved." (2 Ne. 10:23–24.)

Summary

An understanding of the doctrine of the Fall is important for at least the following reasons: (1) We cannot appreciate the redemptive work of Christ without understanding the fallen condition we are in. (2) An understanding of the conditions created by the Fall helps us to realize the type of mortal test we are going through. (3) We can see that problems are a part of the mortal plan and, therefore, need to view them as growth opportunities rather than misfortunes. (4) We will see the gospel of Christ, rather than man-made remedies, as the solution to the problems created by the Fall.

Chapter 12

THE ATONEMENT:
THE SAVIOR'S CROWNING WORK

Christians the world over believe that Jesus Christ has saved them from a terrible fate. *Redemption* and *atonement* are the most common words used to describe his saving work. "If Christ had not come into the world," said the prophet Abinadi, ". . . there could have been no redemption" (Mosiah 16:6). No one can enter heaven without this redemption. Lehi is emphatic on this:

> Wherefore, redemption cometh in and through the Holy Messiah; for he is full of grace and truth. . . .
>
> Wherefore, how great the importance to make these things known unto the inhabitants of the earth, that they may know that there is no flesh that can dwell in the presence of God, save it be through the merits, and mercy, and grace of the Holy Messiah, who layeth down his life according to the flesh, and taketh it again by the power of the Spirit, that he may bring to pass the resurrection of the dead, being the first that should rise. (2 Ne. 2:6, 8.)

Few would question that this redemption, or atonement, is the central feature of the gospel of Jesus Christ. Many Latter-day Saints are familiar with Elder Bruce R. McConkie's superlative statement on the Atonement: "It is the most important single thing that has ever occurred in the entire history of created things; it is the rock foundation upon which the gospel and all other things rest."[1] In a real sense, the gospel *is* the Atonement. It is the "good news" that mankind can be saved by the gracious work of Christ: "And this is the gospel, the glad tidings, which the voice out of the heavens bore record unto us—that he came into the world, even Jesus, to be crucified for the world, and to bear the sins of the world, and to sanctify the world, and to cleanse it from all unrighteousness" (D&C 76:40–41; see also 3 Ne. 27:13–15).

Different opinions begin to emerge when we try to understand the precise meaning of the term *atonement;* various views still exist within Christendom. It will be remembered from the opening chapter that part of the modern mission of the Book of Mormon is to clarify doctrine and end confusion. The doctrine of the Atonement, along with numerous other doctrines, is wonderfully clarified by the prophets of ancient America.

Why Is a Savior Needed?

We have emphasized that the need for an atonement can be understood only as we comprehend the doctrine of the Fall. The Fall brought all humanity into a predicament from which we cannot extricate ourselves. That predicament can be summed up in the words *death* and *sin.* Without the Savior's assistance in helping us to overcome these two conditions, we could never return to the presence of God.

Overcoming Death

We obviously have no personal power to overcome our own death. Without the Savior, we would remain dead and under the control of the devil. Here are Jacob's remarks on the subject:

> For as death hath passed upon all men, to fulfil the merciful plan of the great Creator, there must needs be a power of resurrection, and the resurrection must needs come unto man by reason of the fall; and the fall came by reason of transgression; and because man became fallen they were cut off from the presence of the Lord.
>
> Wherefore, it must needs be an infinite atonement—save it should be an infinite atonement this corruption could not put on incorruption. Wherefore, the first judgment [spiritual and physical death] which came upon man must needs have remained to an endless duration. And if so, this flesh must have laid down to rot and to crumble to its mother earth, to rise no more.
>
> O the wisdom of God, his mercy and grace! For behold, if the flesh should rise no more our spirits must become subject to that angel who fell from before the presence of the Eternal God, and became the devil, to rise no more.

And our spirits must have become like unto him, and we become devils, angels to a devil, to be shut out from the presence of our God, and to remain with the father of lies, in misery, like unto himself. (2 Ne. 9:6–9.)

The resurrection itself saves us from death, hell, the devil, and misery. We cannot comprehend how the Savior's resurrection broke the "bands" of death, enabling all to be resurrected, but the scripture is emphatic: "Now, there is a death which is called a temporal death; and the death of Christ shall loose the bands of this temporal death, that all shall be raised from this temporal death" (Alma 11:42; see also 2 Ne. 9:22). It was the "Holy Messiah," explained Lehi, "who layeth down his life according to the flesh, and taketh it again by the power of the Spirit, that he may bring to pass the resurrection of the dead, being the first that should rise" (2 Ne. 2:8; see also Alma 42:23). Why, then, is a Savior needed? One answer is that he might rescue us from eternal death and its attendant consequences.

Overcoming Sin

A second aspect of man's predicament occurred when the Fall brought him into a sinful situation. This was done in the wisdom of God to provide mankind with the necessary conditions for his growth and testing. However, since "no unclean thing can inherit the kingdom of heaven" (Alma 11:37), sin, unless paid for and overcome, will exclude us from heaven. The Book of Mormon assures us that man cannot pay for his own transgressions. Amulek told the Zoramites that "nothing which is short of an infinite atonement . . . will suffice for the sins of the world" (Alma 34:12). Earlier in the same sermon, he expanded this idea:

> For it is expedient that an atonement should be made; for according to the great plan of the Eternal God there must be an atonement made, or else all mankind must unavoidably perish; yea, all are hardened; yea, all are fallen and are lost, and must perish except it be through the atonement which it is expedient should be made.
> For it is expedient that there should be a great and last sacrifice; yea, not a sacrifice of man, neither of beast, neither of any manner of fowl; for it shall not be a human sacrifice; but it must be an infinite and eternal sacrifice. (Alma 34:9–10.)

Again, we do not fully comprehend the reasons why a divine sacrifice is needed for the sins of mankind, but by faith we realize that without the Savior's payment for sins we would be "in the grasp of justice; yea, the justice of God, which consigned them [all mankind] forever to be cut off from his presence" (Alma 42:14).

Why do we need a Savior? A second reason why is that only he can make the infinite payment required for our sins.

What Is Meant by "the Justice of God"?

The last scripture quoted asserted that sinful man was locked in the grasp of God's justice. When teaching the Atonement, Book of Mormon prophets constantly use the terms *justice* and *mercy*. How are these terms used?

One of the most profound discussions of God's justice (and the Atonement itself) was given by Alma to his wayward son, Corianton, when the latter was questioning "the justice of God in the punishment of the sinner" (Alma 42:1). Alma explained that it was "requisite with the justice of God that men should be judged according to their works; and if their works were good . . . [they will] be restored unto that which is good. And if their works are evil they shall be restored unto them for evil." (Alma 41:3–4.) Equating the word *restoration* with justice, Alma further commented: "The meaning of the word restoration is to bring back again evil for evil, or carnal for carnal, or devilish for devilish—good for that which is good; righteous for that which is righteous; just for that which is just; merciful for that which is merciful" (Alma 41:13). Samuel the Lamanite is another prophet who explained this principle: "Ye can do good and be restored unto that which is good . . . ; or ye can do evil, and have that which is evil restored unto you" (Hel. 14:31).

These divine spokesmen are saying that God's justice will give us exactly what we deserve; he will be perfectly fair and equitable. To be less than this would be contrary to his very nature. Abinadi, teaching that the Lord cannot save the wilfully rebellious, said that the Lord "cannot deny himself; for he cannot deny justice when it has its claim" (see Mosiah 15:26–27). Mercy cannot rob justice, or "God would cease to be God" (Alma 42:25). Alma promised that at the final judgment, if we have hardened our hearts against God's word we will be forced to "acknowledge to our everlasting shame that all his judgments are just" (Alma 12:15).

In order for God's justice to become operative there must be laws given to his people; then justice can be determined on the basis of how people respond to the law. God gives laws to all his kingdoms (see D&C 88:36–39), and both reward and punishment are attached to each law. Alma's advice to Corianton contained this complex explanation: "And if there was no law given, if men sinned what could justice do, or mercy either, for they would have no claim upon the creature? But there is a law given, and a punishment affixed, and a repentance granted; which repentance, mercy claimeth; otherwise, justice claimeth the creature and executeth the law, and the law inflicteth the punishment; if not so, the works of justice would be destroyed, and God would cease to be God." (Alma 42:21–22.)

We would be well advised to study the above passage carefully. It seems to be saying that justice or mercy could not exist without law. If a law is broken, repentance will bring God's mercy to the offender. If there is no repentance, "justice claimeth the creature and executeth the law, and the law inflicteth the punishment." And all this is required by the justice of God. All have sinned and are therefore faced with a simple choice—repent or suffer punishment (this was clear in Jesus' words to Joseph Smith in D&C 19:17).

All Must Repent to Make Mercy Available

The following scriptures make the point that repentance is required for mercy to be available:

> Therefore, according to justice, the plan of redemption could not be brought about, only on conditions of repentance of men in this probationary state, yea, this preparatory state; for except it were for these conditions, mercy could not take effect except it should destroy the work of justice (Alma 42:13).

> But God ceaseth not to be God, and mercy claimeth the penitent, and mercy cometh because of the atonement. . . .
> For behold, justice exerciseth all his demands, and also mercy claimeth all which is her own; and thus, none but the truly penitent are saved.
> What, do ye suppose that mercy can rob justice? I say unto you, Nay; not one whit. If so, God would cease to be God. (Alma 42:23–25.)

> He that exercises no faith unto repentance is exposed to the whole law of the demands of justice; therefore only unto him that has faith unto repentance is brought about the great and

eternal plan of redemption (Alma 34:16; see also Alma 12:33–34).

For behold, I, God, have suffered these things for all, that they might not suffer if they would repent; But if they would not repent they must suffer even as I (D&C 19:16–17).

Nephi spoke of self-indulgent sinners in the last days that viewed God as leniently overlooking their sins and saving them despite their evil ways (see 2 Ne. 28:8). If such people understood the prophets, they would know that it is impossible for God to grant mercy without repentance. This is why repentance has been such an urgent message of the servants of God throughout history.

Christ's Suffering Makes Mercy Available

One other thing was necessary before the plan of mercy could be extended to mankind—the atonement of Christ. Alma told us, "The plan of mercy could not be brought about except an atonement should be made; therefore God himself atoneth for the sins of the world, to bring about the plan of mercy, to appease the demands of justice, that God might be a perfect, just God, and a merciful God also" (Alma 42:15). The prophet Amulek taught that the "intent of this last sacrifice [was] to bring about the bowels of mercy, which overpowereth justice, and bringeth about means unto men that they may have faith unto repentance. And thus mercy can satisfy the demands of justice, and encircles them in the arms of safety." (Alma 34:15–16.) Notice how this passage says that Jesus' sacrifice brought about the "means" whereby men could exercise faith unto repentance. Why is that so? Because without the sacrifice of Christ, faith and repentance would be useless by themselves. There would be little motivation to repent if we knew that the effort would still bring no remission of sins.

Jesus' death and suffering somehow appeased and satisfied God's justice. Somehow, beyond our finite understanding, Christ's suffering was done in behalf of humanity. His suffering satisfies God's justice and makes mercy effective for the individual who repents. These concepts are beautifully explained by Abinadi:

[Christ] suffereth himself to be mocked, and scourged, and cast out, and disowned by his people. . . .

. . . He shall be led, crucified, and slain, the flesh becoming subject even unto death, the will of the Son being swallowed up in the will of the Father.

And thus God breaketh the bands of death, having gained the victory over death; giving the Son power to make intercession for the children of men—

Having ascended into heaven, having the bowels of mercy; being filled with compassion towards the children of men; standing betwixt them and justice; having broken the bands of death, taken upon himself their iniquity and their transgressions, having redeemed them, and satisfied the demands of justice. (Mosiah 15:5, 7–9.)

Alma had a glimpse of the Savior's future mission. He said that Jesus would "go forth, suffering pains and afflictions and temptations of every kind; and this that the word might be fulfilled which saith he will take upon him the pains and the sicknesses of his people" (Alma 7:11). And what purpose did Alma see in all this suffering? "The Son of God suffereth according to the flesh that he might take upon him the sins of his people, that he might blot out their transgressions according to the power of his deliverance" (Alma 7:13). King Benjamin was told by an angel that Jesus would suffer much "more than man can suffer," sufferings which would include "pain of body," thirst, hunger, fatigue, bleeding from every pore, and great anguish for the wickedness of his people (Mosiah 3:7). It was Isaiah that poetically predicted that the Savior would be "wounded for our transgressions" and "bruised for our iniquities" (Mosiah 14:5).

Scriptural writers often remind us of the terrible price Jesus paid for our sins. As we come to conceive the grace, the goodness, the sacrifice endured for us, we are naturally pulled toward him in worship and repentance. "It is by grace that we are saved, after all we can do," exclaimed Nephi (2 Ne. 25:23). "O how great the goodness of our God," uttered Jacob, "who prepareth a way for our escape from the grasp of this awful monster; yea, that monster, death and hell, which I call the death of the body, and also the death of the spirit" (2 Ne. 9:10). Nephi declared that the Lord God "loveth the world, even that he layeth down his own life that he may draw all men unto him" (2 Ne. 26:24). To draw all humanity to him is a work of reconciliation. *Reconciliation* and *atonement* are synonymous words. Certainly one way the Atonement works for us is that Christ's redeeming work grips our hearts and pulls us to him.

Those Given Special Help Through the Atonement

We stated earlier that for people to be accountable to God's justice they must be given a law and come to an understanding of it. What of those who have never learned God's law, or those who are incapable of understanding it? Book of Mormon prophets taught that they are unaccountable for their sins because of the payment made in the Atonement. King Benjamin, delivering the words spoken to him by an angel, taught that Christ's "blood atoneth for the sins of those who have fallen by the transgression of Adam, who have died not knowing the will of God concerning them, or who have ignorantly sinned. But," the warning voice states, "wo, wo unto him who knoweth that he rebelleth against God! For salvation cometh to none such except it be through repentance and faith on the Lord Jesus Christ." (Mosiah 3:11–12.) Jacob taught a similar doctrine in this powerful statement:

> Wherefore, he has given a law; and where there is no law given there is no punishment; and where there is no punishment there is no condemnation; and where there is no condemnation the mercies of the Holy One of Israel have claim upon them, because of the atonement; for they are delivered by the power of him.
>
> For the atonement satisfieth the demands of his justice upon all those who have not the law given to them, that they are delivered from that awful monster, death and hell, and the devil. (2 Ne. 9:25–26.)

Jacob, like Benjamin in the above quote, did not hesitate to warn those who possess the law of God: "But wo unto him that has the law given, yea, that has all the commandments of God, like unto us, and that transgresseth them, and that wasteth the days of his probation, for awful is his state!" (2 Ne. 9:27.)

Little children, prior to the maturation of their understanding, are also innocent in the eyes of God. Mormon, in an epistle to his son Moroni, stated emphatically that "little children cannot repent; wherefore, it is awful wickedness to deny the pure mercies of God unto them, for they are all alive in him because of his mercy. And he that saith that little children need baptism denieth the mercies of Christ, and setteth at naught the atonement of him and the power of his redemption." (Moro. 8:19–20.) Possessing the law of God and understanding it are the two factors that make us accountable and subject to God's justice.

Conclusion

This, then, is the basic message of the Book of Mormon on the doctrine of the Atonement. Admittedly, many questions are left unanswered: for example, did Jesus suffer the cumulative punishment that would otherwise have befallen all mankind? Does justice require a precise measure of punishment for every sin committed? Does Jesus' atonement apply to the inhabitants of other worlds? And so on. But is it necessary that we know the answers to such questions? Is it not sufficient to know that through the wonderful grace of the Lord Jesus Christ my sins are paid for on condition of my repentance? That, in a nutshell, is the Atonement. What other explanations do we need? Is there not a sufficiency in such simple and direct words as these of Alma?

> But God did call on men, in the name of his Son, (this being the plan of redemption which was laid) saying: If ye will repent, and harden not your hearts, then will I have mercy upon you, through mine Only Begotten Son;
>
> Therefore, whosoever repenteth, and hardeneth not his heart, he shall have *claim on mercy* through mine Only Begotten Son, unto a remission of his sins; and these shall enter into my rest (Alma 12:33–34, emphasis added).

The great Atonement was prepared from before the foundation of the world (see Ether 3:14 and Mosiah 4:6). Through his courageous and sacrificial life, Jesus not only became the Savior of humanity but also undoubtedly further perfected himself. Alma's words on this point are intriguing in their possible implications: "He will take upon him their infirmities, that his bowels may be filled with mercy, according to the flesh, that he may know according to the flesh how to succor his people according to their infirmities" (Alma 7:12). The resurrected Christ, said Mormon, "hath ascended into heaven, and hath sat down on the right hand of God, to claim of the Father *his rights of mercy* which he hath upon the children of men" (Moro. 7:28, emphasis added).

Let us conclude by listening to one of the great theologians of the Atonement, the prophet Alma the Younger. Finishing his discourse to his son Corianton, he urged: "O my son, I desire that ye should deny the justice of God no more. Do not endeavor to excuse yourself in the least point because of your sins, by denying the justice of God; but do you let the justice of God, and his mercy, and his long-suffering have full sway in your heart; and let it bring you down to the dust in humility. . . . And now, my son, go thy way, declare the word with truth and soberness, that thou mayest bring souls unto repentance, that the great plan of mercy may have claim upon them." (Alma 42:30–31.)

Chapter 13

THE CONCEPT OF CONVERSION IN THE BOOK OF MORMON

Mankind is rescued from the Fall by two things: (1) The atonement of Christ ("According to the great plan of the Eternal God there must be an atonement made, or else all mankind must unavoidably perish "[Alma 34:9]), and (2) conversion, or spiritual rebirth ("And the Lord said unto me: Marvel not that all mankind, yea, men and women, all nations, kindreds, tongues and people, must be born again; yea, born of God, changed from their carnal and fallen state, to a state of righteousness, being redeemed of God, becoming his sons and daughters; and thus they become new creatures; and unless they do this, they can in nowise inherit the kingdom of God "[Mosiah 27:25–26]).

The Atonement automatically rescues us from death and, on condition of repentance, will save us from our sins. So we must repent and overcome our sins. God's transforming Spirit contributes much to the process, but the individual must be actively involved. Of course, a person can choose to remain in his fallen and sinful condition; indeed, to many, sin becomes a way of living, their consciences are dulled, and they are seemingly quite content to "live without God in the world" (Mosiah 27:31). But there is a better choice, and that is to become converted to Christ.

The way to conversion is to apply the first principles of the gospel. As mentioned in chapter 2, these principles are designed to transform a person into a Christian. The Book of Mormon says a great deal about these principles, but before we examine them in detail, let us look at the concept of conversion as a whole. What can we learn from a consideration of prominent Book of Mormon conversion stories? Enos, Alma, the sons of Mosiah, the people of King Benjamin, and other Book of Mormon personalities all experienced conversion.

While the circumstances in their stories differ, the underlying principles are remarkably the same. There seems to be four distinct phases
in each conversion experience: (1) a consciousness of God, (2) an
awareness of sin and one's fallen state, (3) the need for a Savior, and
(4) evidence of a transformed life.[1]

Naturally the Book of Mormon does not detail every step of this
process each time someone is converted. Sometimes one step is highlighted, sometimes another. However, in most cases these four phases
stand out prominently. Following are several of the best-known conversion experiences from the Book of Mormon.

The Conversion of Enos

Background

Enos's father was the prophet Jacob. We do not know the age of
Enos at the time of his conversion, but the impression is given that he
was a mature man, a Church member, not a bad man but one who
had not been truly converted.

A Consciousness of God

Enos had gone to "hunt beasts in the forests; and the words
which [he] had often heard [his] father speak concerning eternal life,
and the joy of the saints, sunk deep into [his] heart" (Enos 1:3). So
powerfully was he affected that he prayed all day and into the night.

An Awareness of Sin and One's Fallen State

Enos was praying for his "own soul" and did not cease until he
heard the Lord's voice say, "Enos, thy sins are forgiven thee" (Enos
1:4–5).

The Need for a Savior

Describing his experience Enos says, "And my soul hungered;
and I kneeled down before my Maker, and I cried unto him in mighty
prayer and supplication for mine own soul; and all the day long did I
cry unto him" (Enos 1:4).

Evidence of a Transformed Life

When Enos heard a divine voice tell him his sins were forgiven, his "guilt was swept away" (Enos 1:6). Immediately following his own cleansing, he "began to feel a desire for the welfare of [his] brethren, the Nephites" (Enos 1:9). The record makes clear that Enos served his people for the remainder of his life. "I have declared it [the word of God]," he tells us, "in all my days, and have rejoiced in it above that of the world" (Enos 1:26). He also had an assurance that he would be saved. He knew that the Lord would one day say to him, "Come unto me, ye blessed, there is a place prepared for you in the mansions of my Father." (Enos 1:27.)

The Conversion of Alma the Younger

Background

Alma and the sons of Mosiah were "very wicked and . . . idolatrous" men (see Mosiah 27:8). They went about with the deliberate intent to "destroy the church of God" (Mosiah 27:10).

A Consciousness of God

An angel appeared unto Alma and the sons of Mosiah and spoke "as it were with a voice of thunder, which caused the earth to shake upon which they stood" (Mosiah 27:11). The angel explained that he had come because of the prayers of Alma's father: "for this purpose have I come to convince thee of the power and authority of God" (Mosiah 27:14). Alma was threatened with destruction if he continued on his present course. In addition, Alma was struck dumb, "became weak" and could not move his limbs, and remained in this state for three days and nights. (See Mosiah 27:16–23; Alma 36:6–11.) It goes without saying that these men had received a mighty demonstration of the power of God and of man's impotence.

An Awareness of Sin and One's Fallen State

During Alma's three days of helplessness following the angel's visit, Alma was undergoing a shaking of his soul's foundations. He describes it in these forceful words: "After wading through much tribulation, repenting nigh unto death, the Lord in mercy hath seen fit to snatch me out of an everlasting burning, and I am born of God. My soul hath been redeemed from the gall of bitterness and bonds of iniquity. I was in the darkest abyss; but now I behold the marvelous light of God. My soul was racked with eternal torment; but I am snatched, and my soul is pained no more." (Mosiah 27:28–29.)

The Need for a Savior

In the midst of his anguish, Alma remembered having heard his father speak about Jesus Christ's coming to atone for the sins of the world. "As my mind caught hold upon this thought," he said, "I cried within my heart: O Jesus, thou Son of God, have mercy on me, who am in the gall of bitterness" (Alma 36:18).

Evidence of a Transformed Life

When Alma turned to Christ there was an immediate transition: "When I thought this, I could remember my pains no more; yea, I was harrowed up by the memory of my sins no more. And oh, what joy, and what marvelous light I did behold; yea, my soul was filled with joy as exceeding as was my pain!" (Alma 36:19–20.)

Like others, conversion awakened in Alma and his associates a desire to serve their fellow human beings: "Alma began from this time forward to teach the people, and those who were with Alma at the time the angel appeared unto them, traveling round about through all the land, publishing to all the people the things which they had heard and seen, and preaching the word of God in much tribulation" (Mosiah 27:32). To his son Helaman, Alma later described the effects of his conversion: "Yea, and from that time even until now, I have labored without ceasing, that I might bring souls unto repentance; that I might bring them to taste of the exceeding joy of which I did taste; that they might also be born of God, and be filled with the Holy Ghost" (Alma 36:24).

The Conversion of King Benjamin's People

Background

Good King Benjamin, at the end of his righteous reign, desired to speak to his people. He went to great preparations, calling them to gather at the temple, building a tower from which to speak, and circulating written copies of his sermon. His people are described as having been at one time stiffnecked and not inclined toward peace (see W of M 1: 17–18).

A Consciousness of God

Benjamin began his discourse by warning his people of his serious intent: "I have not commanded you to come up hither to trifle with the words which I shall speak, but that you should hearken unto me, and open your ears that ye may hear, and your hearts that ye may understand, and your minds that the mysteries of God may be unfolded to your view" (Mosiah 2:9). He said that "the things which I shall tell you are made known unto me by an angel from God" (Mosiah 3:2).

Much of the talk reminded them of God's greatness and power: "If you should render all the thanks and praise which your whole soul has power to possess, to that God who has created you, and has kept and preserved you, . . . I say, if ye should serve him with all your whole souls yet ye would be unprofitable servants" (Mosiah 2:20–21). Benjamin exhorted them to "believe in God; believe that he is, and that he created all things, both in heaven and in earth; believe that he has all wisdom, and all power, both in heaven and in earth; believe that man doth not comprehend all the things which the Lord can comprehend" (Mosiah 4:9).

After delivering the angel's message concerning the Savior's mission and its implications for the people, the king looked on his subjects and they had "fallen to the earth, for the fear of the Lord had come upon them" (Mosiah 4:1).

An Awareness of Sin and One's Fallen State

Benjamin, delivering the words of the angel, told his people that the "natural man is an enemy to God, and has been from the fall of Adam, and will be, forever and ever, unless he yields to the enticings of the Holy Spirit, and putteth off the natural man and becometh a saint through the atonement of Christ the Lord" (Mosiah 3:19).

He thus led the people to view themselves in their own "carnal state, even less than the dust of the earth" (Mosiah 4:2), or, in Benjamin's words, "the knowledge of the goodness of God at this time has awakened you to a sense of your nothingness, and your worthless and fallen state" (Mosiah 4:5).

The Need for a Savior

As a consequence of their new perception, Benjamin's people "all cried aloud with one voice, saying: O have mercy, and apply the atoning blood of Christ that we may receive forgiveness of our sins, and our hearts may be purified" (Mosiah 4:2).

The angel's words that Benjamin had delivered to his people had assured them that the law of Moses could not save them (see Mosiah 3:15). The angel's words had also given them some details concerning Christ's earthly ministry and had included this declaration: "There shall be no other name given nor any other way nor means whereby salvation can come unto the children of men, only in and through the name of Christ, the Lord Omnipotent" (Mosiah 3:17).

Evidence of a Transformed Life

Benjamin's people described their conversion experience by saying that "the Spirit of the Lord Omnipotent . . . has wrought a mighty change in us, or in our hearts, that we have no more disposition to do evil, but to do good continually" (Mosiah 5:2).

King Benjamin's description of their new status is as follows: "Ye shall be called the children of Christ, his sons, and his daughters; for behold, this day he hath spiritually begotten you; for ye say that your hearts are changed through faith on his name; therefore, ye are born of him and have become his sons and his daughters" (Mosiah 5:7).

Peace, joy, a mighty change of heart, no more disposition to do evil—these all bear witness that these people had undergone a powerful transformation.

Benjamin spent a good deal of the talk in describing the ethical life expected of the converted. He spoke some eloquent words regarding charity and service and about retaining a remission of sins, and those words include the following: "And now, for the sake of these things which I have spoken unto you—that is, for the sake of retaining a remission of your sins from day to day, that ye may walk guiltless before God—I would that ye should impart of your substance to the poor, every man according to that which he hath, such as feeding the hungry, clothing the naked, visiting the sick and administering to their relief" (Mosiah 4:26).

The Conversion of Zeezrom

Background

Zeezrom was one of the wicked lawyers living in the land of Ammonihah. He initially opposed the missionaries Alma and Amulek. "Now he was the foremost to accuse Amulek and Alma, he being one of the most expert among them" (Alma 10:31). Zeezrom was an "expert in the devices of the devil" (Alma 11:21) who loved lucre more than God (see Alma 11:24).

A Consciousness of God

A conversation with Amulek about Christ, sin, and judgment caused Zeezrom to "tremble" (Alma 11:46). Alma then grilled him with harsh words: "Now Zeezrom, seeing that thou hast been taken in thy lying and craftiness, for thou hast not lied unto men only but thou hast lied unto God . . ." (Alma 12:3). Alma continued by telling him that the devil had "exercised power in thee" (Alma 12:5). At this juncture, Zeezrom "began to tremble more exceedingly, for he was convinced more and more of the power of God" (Alma 12:7).

An Awareness of Sin and One's Fallen State

Zeezrom "began to tremble under a consciousness of his guilt" (Alma 12:1). After Alma and Amulek had spoken, the people were angry and bound them with cords, and Zeezrom realized he had blinded the people "by his lying words; and his soul began to be harrowed up under a consciousness of his own guilt; yea, he began to be encircled about by the pains of hell. And it came to pass that he began to cry unto the people, saying: "Behold, I am guilty, and these men [Alma and Amulek] are spotless before God." (Alma 14:6–7.) Zeezrom began to plead for the missionaries, and the people cast him out of the city. Later, fearing that Alma and Amulek had been killed, Zeezrom blamed himself and became literally sick. "And this great sin, and his many other sins, did harrow up his mind until it did become exceedingly sore, having no deliverance; therefore he began to be scorched with a burning heat" (Alma 15:3).

The Need for a Savior

In Zeezrom's illness, the missionaries visited him and asked if he believed in Christ. He replied, "Yea, I believe all the words that thou hast taught" (Alma 15:7). After being healed in Christ's name he leaped to his feet and was baptized.

Evidence of a Transformed Life

The Book of Mormon simply says that Alma baptized Zeezrom and that Zeezrom "began from that time forth to preach unto the people" (Alma 15:12). Later, he was one of the valiant few chosen to do missionary work among the Zoramites (see Alma 31:6).

The Conversion of Two Lamanite Kings

Background

King Lamoni and his father were converts of the sons of Mosiah—just two of the thousands of Lamanite converts brought into the kingdom during this most successful mission.

These kings were living in spiritual darkness. They believed in a "Great Spirit" but had virtually no knowledge of the gospel of Jesus Christ. After Ammon's exploits in saving Lamoni's flocks from rustlers, the king believed he was the Great Spirit. When Ammon began asking him questions about religion, Lamoni demonstrated an almost complete ignorance of religious matters. For instance, Ammon asked, "Believest thou that there is a God?" The king replied, "I do not know what that meaneth." (Alma 18:24–25.) Ammon explained that "God" was the same as the "Great Spirit" (see Alma 18:26–28). King Lamoni was unfamiliar with the term *heaven* and asked "Is it above the earth?" (Alma 18:31.) So we see that Ammon had to start with the basics.

A Consciousness of God

Ammon was a wise missionary. He went to greath lengths to win the friendship and confidence of King Lamoni before he mentioned his message. This he did by heroically defending the king's flocks, humbly avoiding the glory, and attending to his duties.

When Ammon finally came into the king's presence, Lamoni was so awed by him that he was afraid to speak. Finally Ammon asked if he would hearken to his words if he told him where he obtained his power. The king answered, "Yea, I will believe all thy words" (Alma 18:23). Ammon began patiently to teach him about God, the Creation, and "all the things concerning the fall of man" (Alma 18:36). The king believed everything. In fact, he was so overcome by the Spirit that he fell into a swoon.

An Awareness of Sin and One's Fallen State

Later Aaron, speaking to Lamoni's father, had a similar experience: "And Aaron did expound unto him the scriptures from the creation of Adam, laying the fall of man before him, and their carnal state and also the plan of redemption, which was prepared from the foundation of the world, through Christ" (Alma 22:13).

The sequence of these topics is revealing. We need to comprehend our fallen and sinful state before we can see any need for a Redeemer.

As the missionaries taught these Lamanite kings, the kings both began to feel a sense of their personal guilt. About Lamoni, the scripture says, "Now this was the tradition of Lamoni, which he had received from his father, that there was a Great Spirit. Notwithstanding they believed in a Great Spirit, they supposed that whatsoever they did was right; nevertheless, Lamoni began to fear exceedingly, with fear lest he had done wrong in slaying his servants." (Alma 18:5.) After hearing Aaron teach the plan of salvation, Lamoni's father asked, "What shall I do that I may have this eternal life of which thou hast spoken? Yea, what shall I do that I may be born of God, having this wicked spirit rooted out of my breast, and receive his Spirit, that I may be filled with joy?" (Alma 22:15.) As he prayed to God, the king exclaimed, "I will give away all my sins to know thee" (Alma 22:18).

The Need for a Savior

After hearing Ammon's teachings King Lamoni cried, "O Lord, have mercy; according to thy abundant mercy which thou hast had upon the people of Nephi, have upon me, and my people" (Alma 18:41). After rising from his comatose state Lamoni's first words were, "Blessed be the name of God. . . . I have seen my Redeemer; and he shall come forth, and be born of a woman, and he shall redeem all mankind who believe on his name." (Alma 19:12–13.)

Again, Aaron's experience with Lamoni's father was like that of his brother. After listening to Aaron, the king had an overwhelming desire to obtain eternal life. He said, "I will give up all that I possess, yea, I will forsake my kingdom, that I may receive this great joy" (Alma 22:15). Aaron told him to bow down and call upon God for a remission of his sins. The king proceeded to "prostrate himself upon the earth, and cried mightily, saying: . . . I will give away all my sins to know thee" (Alma 22:17–18).

Evidence of a Transformed Life

After arising out of his spiritual sleep, King Lamoni rejoiced in his knowledge of the Redeemer. So great was his joy that "his heart was swollen within him, and he sunk again with joy . . . being overpowered by the Spirit" (Alma 19:13). When he awakened the second time he went forth and ministered to his own people, "teach[ing] them the words which he had heard from the mouth of Ammon; and as many as heard his words believed, and were converted unto the Lord" (Alma 19:31). The queen and many of the servants arose and "declare[d] unto the people the selfsame thing—that their hearts had been changed; that they had no more desire to do evil" (Alma 19:33).

King Lamoni then aided Ammon and his brothers in every way to promote the spread of the gospel. He accompanied Ammon to the land of Middoni, where he was instrumental in obtaining the release of Ammon's fellow missionaries from prison.

Lamoni's father, after his conversion, also ministered to his household, "insomuch that his whole household were converted unto the Lord" (Alma 22:23). "He caused that Aaron and his brethren should stand forth in the midst of the multitude, and that they should preach the word unto them" (Alma 22:26). He also sent a proclamation throughout the land that no harm should come to the missionaries, and that "they should have free access to their houses, and also their temples, and their sanctuaries. And thus they might go forth and preach the word according to their desires, for the king had been converted unto the Lord, and all his household; therefore he sent his proclamation throughout the land unto his people, that the word of God might have no obstruction." (Alma 23:2–3.)

With this kind of support the missionaries, of course, had enormous success and converted thousands to the Lord.

Conclusion

Dramatic Book of Mormon conversion experiences make one wonder if all such experiences must be similarly outstanding. Most of us were not converted by the appearance of an angel as was Alma, nor did many of us have the emotional wrenching of an Enos. Elder Bruce R. McConkie, Latter-day Saint Apostle and writer, has given us this explanation: "For most members of the Church this spiritual re-birth takes place gradually; it is a process. They become alive to one spiritual reality after another as they keep the commandments and seek to sanctify their souls."[2] In one case, certain Lamanite converts "were baptized with fire and with the Holy Ghost, and they knew it not" (3 Ne. 9:20). Notwithstanding this, it seems that the four basic principles we have studied in this chapter always occur in every con-version story, despite the uniqueness of each conversion. Sometimes one's awareness of these principles comes in an instantaneous flash of insight, and sometimes it comes gradually after years of gospel learning. Likewise, the change in one's actual behavior can be sudden or slow.

We have seen that the Book of Mormon provides us with valu-able insight into this step in gospel progress. Alma once asked some Church members some very pointed questions, including the follow-ing: "And now behold, I ask you, my brethren of the church, have ye spiritually been born of God? Have ye received his image in your countenances? Have ye experienced this mighty change in your hearts?" (Alma 5:14.) On the basis of information presented in this chapter, I would ask four additional questions: (1) Are you daily con-scious of your God—his love for you, his power and his efforts to help you? (2) Are you aware of your sins and your fallen condition? (3) Do you appreciate Jesus Christ and understand your need to rely on him as your Savior? (4) Is your daily conduct evidence that your life has been transformed, that you have been converted?

Chapter 14

THE FIRST PRINCIPLES: GOD'S WAY OF CONVERSION

The purpose of the first principles and ordinances of the gospel is to transform an individual and set him on the path of godly living, to change a person from his "carnal and fallen state, to a state of righteousness" (Mosiah 27:25). A thorough application of these saving principles equips a person with powerful, motivating belief in Christ; new and righteous behavioral patterns; a firm commitment to enter into a new life; and a change of heart generated by the power of the Holy Ghost. Thus prepared, one is ready to live the life of a Christian. So central are these doctrines in the gospel of Jesus Christ, that each step of the process deserves to be considered in detail.

Interrelatedness of the First Principles

Studying the first principles of the gospel separately could lead to a distortion in our understanding of them. We need to see a dynamic continuity in these steps of gospel progress. The Book of Mormon speaks of having "faith unto repentance" (Alma 34:15). Samuel the Lamanite told the Nephites: "And if ye believe on his [Jesus Christ's] name ye will repent of all your sins" (Hel. 14:13). Mormon said that the "first fruits of repentance is baptism" (Moro. 8:25). Hence, if a man truly repents, baptism of the water and of the Spirit will inevitably follow. Thus, the first principles are applied in one's life as a natural unfolding of real faith in the Savior.

Faith in Jesus Christ

Faith cannot exist in isolation; one must have faith in something, and the faith that leads to salvation is faith in the Lord Jesus Christ (see 2 Ne. 25:28, Mosiah 3:18; Alma 5:15, 48).

The Meaning of Faith in Jesus Christ

What is faith? There is a classic sermon on the subject given by Alma the Younger to the Zoramite poor. He spoke of those who would believe in the gospel if only they could see a sign from heaven. "Now I ask, is this faith?" he queried. "Behold, I say unto you, Nay; for if a man knoweth a thing he hath no cause to believe, for he knoweth it." (Alma 32:18.) "Faith," he continued, "is not to have a perfect knowledge of things; therefore if ye have faith ye hope for things which are not seen, which are true" (Alma 32:21). Faith, then, is not to have a certain knowledge that something is true, but is a belief or hope in that something. When one arrives at the point of knowing something to be true, his "faith is dormant" (Alma 32:34). The book of Ether corroborates this definition when speaking about the brother of Jared's experience of seeing the Lord. The record says that after having this privilege the brother of Jared "had faith no longer, for he knew, nothing doubting" (Ether 3:19; see also 12:6, 8).

It must be stressed that faith is a strong, motivating belief. Joseph Smith taught that faith is "the moving cause of all action in [men],"[1] and James E. Talmage taught that the term *faith*, as used in scripture, is a strong conviction that invariably leads to works.[2] The statement of Samuel the Lamanite that "if ye believe on his [Jesus Christ's] name ye will repent" is a good illustration of the point (Hel. 14:13).

Degrees of Faith

It goes without saying that there are degrees of faith, ranging from a vague hope to near certainty. Humanity is admonished to have "perfect faith in the Holy One of Israel, or they cannot be saved" (2 Ne. 9:23). Nephi spoke of the need for "unshaken faith" (2 Ne. 31:19). What kind of faith is this? We probably will not be far from an answer if we use Nephi as an example of one who had "perfect faith."

When commanded to return for the brass plates, Nephi responded with these unforgettable words: "I will go and do the things which the Lord hath commanded, for I know that the Lord giveth no commandments unto the children of men, save he shall prepare a way for them that they may accomplish the thing which he commandeth them" (1 Ne. 3:7). His doubting brothers, Laman and Lemuel, on the other hand, hesitated because "it [was] a hard thing" that their father required of them (1 Ne. 3:5). After two unsuccessful attempts to get the plates, the four brothers were told by an angel to go again to Jerusalem, assuring them that the Lord would provide the way to complete their mission. The older brothers again murmured. "How is it possible that the Lord will deliver Laban into our hands? Behold, he is a mighty man, and he can command fifty, yea, even he can slay fifty; then why not us?" (1 Ne. 3:31.) They were using good logic, but one with perfect faith will sometimes need to trust the Lord more than the dictates of reason. Nephi did this: "Let us go up again unto Jerusalem, and let us be faithful in keeping the commandments of the Lord; for behold he is mightier than all the earth, then why not mightier than Laban and his fifty, yea, or even than his tens of thousands?" (1 Ne. 4:1.) A final example of Nephi's faith occurred when his brothers were ridiculing him for thinking he could build a ship that would carry them to the promised land. Here was Nephi's faithful response: "If God had commanded me to do all things I could do them. If he should command me that I should say unto this water, be thou earth, it should be earth; and if I should say it, it would be done. And now, if the Lord has such great power, and has wrought so many miracles among the children of men, how is it that he cannot instruct me, that I should build a ship?" (1 Ne. 17:50–51.)

It should be pointed out that a person still needs faith even after knowing for certain that the gospel is true. One's faith is dormant and knowledge perfect only "in that thing" (Alma 32:34), but not in all things. Nephi, for example, had communed with the Lord and had seen an angel, yet he knew not how to obtain the brass plates. But his trust in the Lord was unwavering: "I was led by the Spirit, not knowing beforehand the things which I should do" (1 Ne. 4:6).

How to Acquire Faith

Most men in the Book of Mormon acquired faith by hearing the teachings of a servant of the Lord. Mormon taught that the ministry of angels is to declare "the word of Christ unto the chosen vessels of the Lord, that they may bear testimony of him. And by so doing, the Lord God prepareth the way that the residue of men may have faith in Christ." (Moro. 7:31–32.)

The written word, though not as potent as the spoken word, can also awaken faith. Nephi's full intent in writing was to "persuade men to come unto the God of Abraham, and the God of Isaac, and the God of Jacob, and be saved" (1 Ne. 6:4). Still he confessed that he was not "mighty in writing, like unto speaking; for when a man speaketh by the power of the Holy Ghost the power of the Holy Ghost carrieth it unto the hearts of the children of men" (2 Ne. 33:1). The prophet Jacob once observed that his people's "search[ing] the prophets" was a factor in making their faith become "unshaken" (Jacob 4:6).

When we inquire about the ability of parental teaching to engender faith, we have mixed information. Certainly Nephi (see 1 Ne. 1:1) and Enos (see Enos 1:1, 3) were inspired by the example and teachings of their fathers. Yet the faithless Laman and Lemuel had the same parents as Nephi. Alma the Younger and the four sons of Mosiah were sired by the two greatest spiritual men of their time and were still scoundrels in their youth. There must be more than environmental influences involved here. Nephi seemed to have an inherent capacity to believe, whereas his older brothers were just the opposite. Though the Book of Mormon is silent on the issue, modern revelation suggests that much of our personality is carried over from abilities and attitudes developed in our premortal life.

We are also taught that faith is, to some extent, a gift of God, although recipients qualify for this gift by their righteous living. In response to Nephi's "great desires to know of the mysteries of God," the Lord "did soften" his heart so that he believed all that his father had spoken (1 Ne. 2:16). The Lord told a later Nephi that he would make him mighty in faith (see Hel. 10:5). Moroni lists faith as one of the "gifts" of the Spirit (see Moro. 10:11). The record tells us that at the time that Alma and Amulek and others were preaching among the Nephites, "the Lord did pour out his Spirit on all the face of the land to prepare the minds of the children of men, or to prepare their hearts to receive the word which should be taught among them at the time of his coming—that they might not be hardened against the word, that they might not be unbelieving, . . . but that they might receive the word with joy" (Alma 16:16–17).

From Skepticism to Testimony

Alma's marvelous sermon to the Zoramites is the best scriptural formula for increasing one's faith. Because "faith is not to have a perfect knowledge" (Alma 32:21), he admitted that his listeners could not know at first if his words were true (see Alma 32:26). "But behold," he continued, "if ye will awake and arouse your faculties, even to an experiment upon my words, and exercise a particle of faith, yea, even if ye can no more than desire to believe, let this desire work in you, even until ye believe in a manner that ye can give place for a portion of my words" (Alma 32:27). In comparing the word of God to a seed, Alma directed the people to first allow it to be planted in their hearts. Then, if it were a true seed and they did not cast it out (prematurely) by their unbelief or resistance to the Spirit of the Lord (see Alma 32:28), and if they would "nourish the word, yea, nourish the tree as it beginneth to grow, by [their] faith with great diligence, and with patience, looking forward to the fruit thereof, it shall take root; and behold it shall be a tree springing up unto everlasting life" (Alma 32:41). How do these words translate into the modern vernacular? Surely to "nourish" the word of God means to study, pray about, and ponder the scriptures. If we are not too skeptical; if we do not resist the Spirit of the Lord but prayerfully encourage its influence; and if we do all this with "great diligence" and "patience," then we will reap the results. What results should we expect? Alma says we will begin to feel swelling motions in our bosom and begin to say within ourselves that "the word is good, for it beginneth to enlarge my soul; yea, it beginneth to enlighten my understanding, yea, it beginneth to be delicious to me" (Alma 32:28). Alma is describing an inner, subjective experience with the word of God. Nevertheless he testifies that it is "real" (Alma 32:35) and that our knowledge is "perfect in that thing" (Alma 32:34). You then know, says Alma, for "ye know that the word hath swelled your souls, and ye also know that it hath sprouted up, that your understanding doth begin to be enlightened, and your mind doth begin to expand" (Alma 32:34).

Alma was probably describing elements of his own experience. In an earlier statement, he testified: "And how do ye suppose that I know of their [gospel principles'] surety? Behold, I say unto you they are made known unto me by the Holy Spirit of God. Behold, I have fasted and prayed many days that I might know these things of myself. And now I do know of myself that they are true." (Alma 5:45–46.)

Notice that the acquisition of a testimony is not an instantaneous happening. Only after an "experiment" with the word, only after spiritual effort, and only after the "trial of your faith" (Ether 12:6) is this precious blessing received. This latter phrase comes from the prophet Moroni. After decrying the unbelief of the Jaredites because they "saw . . . not" (Ether 12:5), he launched into a lengthy discourse, giving examples of how God works mighty miracles only after people demonstrate that they have faith. In strong words he assured his readers "that faith is things which are hoped for and not seen; wherefore, dispute not because ye see not, for ye receive no witness until after the trial of your faith" (Ether 12:6).

Why is the process so difficult? Why isn't a testimony available for the asking? One reason why lies in the fact that accountability for sin becomes greater in proportion to the knowledge that one has of the truth; therefore, the Lord mercifully withholds knowledge until we are ready to accept the responsibilities that accompany it. Alma said this on the subject: "How much more cursed is he that knoweth the will of God and doeth it not, than he that only believeth, or only hath cause to believe, and falleth into transgression?" (Alma 32:19.) Surely another reason why has to do with this life being a time of testing, as discussed in an earlier chapter. If everyone knew the gospel was true, it would be obvious that dire consequences awaited the disobedient and great rewards followed the faithful. Consequently, many would live the gospel for opportunistic reasons rather than for the love of righteousness, and the testing aspect of mortality would be minimized. So, to try our faith, the Lord often withholds knowledge and testimony (see 3 Ne. 26:9–11; Alma 12:9–11).

The Fruits of Faith

Many times Jesus tried to tell his Jerusalem disciples that great blessings followed faith—"All things are possible to him that believeth" (Mark 9:23); faith the size of a mustard seed could move mountains (see Mark 11:20–26). So abundant are the scriptures cataloging the blessings that follow great faith that a brief list may be helpful in demonstrating the point:

1 Ne. 10:17—Lehi received the power of the Holy Ghost by faith.

1 Ne. 2:19—Nephi was commended by God because of faith.

1 Ne. 11:6—Faith opens up the visions of God.

1 Ne. 12:10—Twelve Nephite disciples' "garments [were] made white" (sanctification) because of faith.

1 Ne. 16:27–28—Liahona worked by faith.

2 Ne. 2:9—They who believe in Christ shall be saved. There is no salvation without faith (see Mosiah 3:9; Moro. 7:38, 10:20–21).

2 Ne. 25:25—The Nephites were "made alive in Christ" because of faith.

2 Ne. 26:13—Miracles cannot be performed except by faith (see also Mosiah 8:18; Ether 12:12; Moro. 7:37).

2 Ne. 26:13—Holy Ghost is given to all who believe (see also Jarom 1:4).

2 Ne. 27:23—God does not work among men save by faith.

Enos 1:6–8—Sins are forgiven because of faith.

Enos 1:15—Enos could receive anything if he would ask in faith.

Mosiah 5:4—Great knowledge comes by faith.

Mosiah 5:7—The hearts of King Benjamin's people were changed by faith.

Mosiah 23:22—One with faith will be lifted up at the last day.

Mosiah 24:16—Alma's people were delivered from bondage because of faith.

Alma 7:24—If one has faith, hope, and charity he'll abound in good works.

Alma 11:40—Christ takes upon himself the transgressions of those who have faith.

Alma 33:20—People were not healed, because they lacked faith.

3 Ne. 7:18–19—Angels ministered to the disciples daily because of great faith.

Ether 3:9—The brother of Jared saw God because of faith.

Ether 12:21—Because of his faith the brother of Jared could not be kept without the veil.

Ether 12:30—Mount Zerin was moved by faith.

Moro. 7:26—We become sons of God by faith.

Moro. 7:33—By faith one gets power to do God's work.

Moro. 7:25—"By faith, they did lay hold upon every good thing."

In summary, saving faith is a strong belief and trust in the Savior. It is the motivating power that produces repentance (see Hel. 11:4, 7; 14:13), righteous works, perseverance in hardships, and, in the words of Moroni, power to "lay hold upon every good thing." Every real Saint must endure to the end in manifesting true faith in Christ (see Mosiah 4:6, 11).

The Doctrine of Repentance

The second saving principle that we will examine in detail here is repentance, which, as stated earlier, is motivated by and grows out of faith in Jesus Christ.

Remission of Sins

The purpose of the first principles of the gospel includes leading a person to gain a remission of his sins and thus to be cleansed and purified. God cannot save us in our sins (see Alma 11:36–37). "No unclean thing can enter into his kingdom" is the consistent testimony of the prophets (3 Ne. 27:19; see also Alma 13:16; 12:34). A few scriptures illustrate this topic:

Mosiah 3:13—". . . whosoever should believe that Christ should come, the same might receive remission of their sins." (See also 2 Ne. 25:26; Mosiah 12:11; Alma 13:16.)

2 Ne. 31:17—Remission of sins comes by fire and the Holy Ghost.

Enos 1:1–9—Enos obtained forgiveness by faith and mighty prayer.

Mosiah 4:3, 11, 20, 23—Benjamin's people obtained a remission of their sins by faith, repentance, and prayer.

Mosiah 26:29–31—Forgiveness requires confession and repentance "in the sincerity of [one's] heart."

Alma 38:8—Alma received a remission of his sins by repentance and crying unto the Lord for mercy.

Hel. 14:13—Remission of sins comes by repentance.

3 Ne. 12:2—"Blessed are they who shall believe in your words, and come down into the depths of humility and be baptized, for they shall be visited with fire and with the Holy Ghost, and shall receive a remission of their sins."

Alma 12:34—"Whosoever repenteth, and hardeneth not his heart, he shall have claim on mercy . . . , unto a remission of his sins."

Though none of the foregoing scriptures say exactly the same thing, there is no conflict of ideas. Prophets often state the same principle in slightly different ways and a brief statement often presupposes a more complete statement. We conclude that a remission of sins comes because of Christ's atonement and by man's application of the first principles.

What Constitutes Sin?

Since it is from sin that one repents, we need to know what constitutes sin. Many fail to repent because they define sin in a way that excludes them from guilt. Nephi predicted that a very lenient attitude toward sin would characterize the last days (see 2 Ne. 28:7–8). Corianton had this same inclination but was corrected by his father: "Do not endeavor to excuse yourself in the least point because of your sins" (Alma 42:30). God's strictness in the matter is indicated by the statement, "The Lord cannot look upon sin with the least degree of allowance" (Alma 45:16).

The Bible tells us that sin is the transgression of God's law (see 1 Jn. 3:4). God's law includes all of Christ's teachings—the Sermon on the Mount as well as the Ten Commandments. The writer of the book of James (see James 4:17) plus numerous teachings of Jesus make it clear that sins of omission are as real as sins of commission. King Benjamin gave one of the most comprehensive definitions: "And finally, I cannot tell you all the things whereby ye may commit sin; for there are divers ways and means, even so many that I cannot number them. But this much I can tell you, that if ye do not watch yourselves, and your thoughts, and your words, and your deeds, and observe the commandments of God, and continue in the faith of what ye have heard concerning the coming of the Lord, even unto the end of your lives, ye must perish." (Mosiah 4:29–30; see also Alma 12:13–15.)

Jacob taught that "to be carnally-minded is death" (2 Ne. 9:39), and Alma warned that if one's desires were evil he would receive his reward of evil when the judgment comes (see Alma 41:3, 5). Mormon spoke of the necessity of a person's having pure motives, or else that person's deeds are not accounted unto him for righteousness. For instance, if one gave a gift grudgingly or prayed without real intent of heart, it would profit him nothing and he would be "counted evil before God." (See Moro. 7:6–9.) Another dimension of this topic is the Book of Mormon teaching that the magnitude of a sin increases as one's knowledge of the truth increases (see 2 Ne. 31:14; Hel. 7:23–24).

The following definition of sin condemns everyone: "All have sinned, and come short of the glory of God" (Rom. 3:23). All need repentance; all must rely on the Savior's atonement. This is undoubtedly why repentance is given such emphasis in the scriptures, why it is the burden of every prophet's message, and why it is sometimes stated as the purpose of life itself (see Alma 12:24; 2 Ne. 2:21; Alma 34:31–35). "Preach nothing but repentance" was the Lord's counsel to the Nephites and to our own generation (see Mosiah 18:20; 25:22; D&C 6:9; 11:9; 19:21).

Steps of Repentance

How does one repent?

First, we acknowledge that repentance would not bring forgiveness of sins without Christ. Samuel the Lamanite said that the Atonement brought "to pass the condition of repentance" (Hel. 14:18). In our discussion of the Atonement, we saw that the Savior paid the debt of justice for all those who repent. God cannot forgive the unrepentant, "for he cannot deny himself; for he cannot deny justice when it has its claim" (Mosiah 15:27; see also Alma 12:34). Remember the somber words of Alma, "Justice exerciseth all his demands, and also mercy claimeth all which is her own; and thus, none but the truly penitent are saved" (Alma 42:24).

Recognition of sins: Those who would repent must initially admit that they have sins. This is not as easy as it sounds. Prophets have always had a difficult time convincing people of their sins. There are many reasons for this, including the devil's efforts to make us feel secure in our carnality (see 2 Ne. 28:21). The devil's disciples, like Korihor, tried to convince people that "whatsoever a man did was no crime" and that they should even rejoice in their wickedness (see Alma 30:17–18). Because we live in the world, we have a tendency to judge our behavior by its standards rather than the Lord's, and as a consequence, we often judge our actions to be better than they really are.

In the Book of Mormon, most people recognized their sins when they were taught the gospel. "If men come unto me," said the Lord to Moroni, "I will show unto them their weakness" (Ether 12:27). King Benjamin's final discourse had a powerful impact on his people, who were described as being, at one point in their history, stiffnecked (see W of M 1:17). When King Benjamin told them the words of the angel, they fell to the earth, "for the fear of the Lord had come upon them. And they had viewed themselves in their own carnal state, even less than the dust of the earth. And they all cried aloud with one voice, saying: O have mercy, and apply the atoning blood of Christ that we may receive forgiveness of our sins, and our hearts may be purified." (Mosiah 4:1–2.)

Zeezrom, the wicked lawyer from Ammonihah, is another example of one who came to a full recognition of his sins by hearing the preaching of God's servants. After a period of doubt and criticism toward Alma and Amulek, he became "astonished at the words which had been spoken; and he also knew concerning the blindness of the minds, which he had caused among the people by his lying words; and his soul began to be harrowed up under a consciousness of his own guilt; yea, he began to be encircled about by the pains of hell" (Alma 14:6). So poignant were his feelings that he "lay sick at Sidom, with a burning fever, which was caused by the great tribulations of his mind on account of his wickedness, for he supposed that Alma and Amulek were no more; and he supposed that they had been slain because of his iniquity. And this great sin, and his many other sins, did harrow up his mind until it did become exceedingly sore, having no deliverance; therefore he began to be scorched with a burning heat." (Alma 15:3.)

To see other samples, one might read Alma's graphic description of his sinful anguish in Alma 36, or the repentance of the people of Ammon in Alma 24:9.

Sorrow for sins: Recognition of sin is naturally accompanied with regret—that one has brought injury to others and upon oneself, and has lived contrary to God's will. The scriptures call it "godly sorrow," or "a broken heart and a contrite spirit." Lehi told his son Jacob that Christ "offereth himself a sacrifice for sin, to answer the ends of the law, unto all those who have a broken heart and contrite spirit; and unto none else can the ends of the law be answered" (2 Ne. 2:7; see also 3 Ne. 9:20; 12:19–20; Ether 4:15; Moro. 6:2).

According to Alma's instructions to his son Helaman, reading scripture can convince "many of the error of their ways" (see Alma 37:8–9). At another time, when counseling his son Corianton, Alma spoke of the "law" bringing "remorse of conscience unto man" (Alma 42:18). Alma admonished Corianton to contemplate God's goodness, suffering, justice, and mercy as a means of bringing himself to a recognition of sin. "Let your sins trouble you," counseled this loving father, "with that trouble which shall bring you down unto repentance" (Alma 42:29). The key to this step of repentance is to come unto Christ and he will show us our weaknesses (see Ether 12:27).

Confession of sins: When one sees his sins in their true light and feels sorrow for his wayward behavior, his next inclination is to confess and pray for forgiveness. This is the pattern seen again and again in the Book of Mormon. The Lord spoke these words to Alma the Elder about confession: "And whosoever transgresseth against me, him shall ye judge according to the sins which he has committed; and if he confess his sins before thee and me, and repenteth in the sincerity of his heart, him shall ye forgive, and I will forgive him also" (Mosiah 26:29). Those who did confess their sins, we are told, were "number[ed] among the people of the church; and those that would not confess their sins and repent of their iniquity, the same were not numbered among the people of the church, and their names were blotted out" (Mosiah 26:35–36).

Prayer for forgiveness: For many in the Book of Mormon, repentance was not an easy thing. Some achieved success only after a tremendous spiritual struggle. The powerful words used by scriptural writers to describe these experiences are moving and quite revealing. The elder Alma, a wicked priest under King Noah, said that his former sins "caused me sore repentance; nevertheless, after much tribulation, the Lord did hear my cries, and did answer my prayers" (Mosiah 23:9–10). The most dramatic conversion in the Book of Mormon happened to this man's son, Alma the Younger. He was "a very wicked and an idolatrous man" (Mosiah 27:8) and with the sons of Mosiah sought to destroy the Church. Then, in answer to the prayers of Alma the Elder and others, an angel appeared to these wayward souls, an experience that was such a shock to Alma the Younger's system that he was seized by some type of paralytic state for three days. During this period he was undergoing a soul-shaking experience: "I was thus racked with torment, while I was harrowed up by the memory of my many sins" (Alma 36:17). He spoke of it as "wading through much tribulation, repenting nigh unto death" (Mosiah 27:28). He told his son later that he was in "the most bitter pain and anguish of soul; and never, until I did cry out unto the Lord Jesus Christ for mercy, did I receive a remission of my sins" (Alma 38:8).

King Benjamin exhorted his people to pray "in sincerity of heart" for forgiveness (Mosiah 4:10), and at one point described them as even "begging for a remission of [their] sins" (Mosiah 4:20). Enos pleaded unto the Lord through an entire day and into the evening before he became cleansed from his sins (see Enos 1:4–5). He described his struggle to receive a remission of sins as "the wrestle which I had before God" (Enos 1:2).

It is interesting to note that all the people mentioned above apparently were members of the Church long before their conversion experiences. Repentance often comes more easily to those who sin before receiving a knowledge of the truth and the ordinances of initiation into the Church. Even the converted Lamanites (Anti-Nephi-Lehies) who had committed "many sins and murders" (Alma 24:10) were granted a remission of sins, but only after hard repentance. "And now behold, my brethren," their king said to them, "since it has been all that we could do, (as we were the most lost of all mankind) to repent of all our sins and the many murders which we have committed, and to get God to take them away from our hearts, for it was all we could do to repent sufficiently before God that he would take away our stain—now, my best beloved brethren, since God hath taken away our stains, . . . let us stain our swords no more with the blood of our brethren" (Alma 24:11–12).

It is heartening to know that repentance is possible to virtually all.

Restoration for harm done: Any sincere penitent will seek to heal the wounds or restore the damage he has caused through his transgressions. It is not always possible to make restitution for past wrongs, but it must be done where possible. After their conversion the gallant sons of Mosiah "traveled throughout all the land of Zarahemla, . . . zealously striving to repair all the injuries which they had done to the church, confessing all their sins, and publishing all the things which they had seen" (Mosiah 27:35). Not long after this they embarked on a fourteen-year mission to the Lamanites.

Willingness to forgive others: Since the repentant person seeks forgiveness for his sins, he should be quick to forgive others. Jesus taught that forgiveness will be extended to the forgiving (see 3 Ne. 13:11–15). It was revealed to Alma that "ye shall also forgive one another your trespasses; for verily I say unto you, he that forgiveth not his neighbor's trespasses when he says that he repents, the same hath brought himself under condemnation" (Mosiah 26:31).

When Should We Repent?

Every reader of the Book of Mormon is familiar with the impassioned plea of Amulek to the Zoramites that they not procrastinate their repentance:

> For behold, this life is the time for men to prepare to meet God; yea, behold the day of this life is the day for men to perform their labors.
> . . . I beseech of you that ye do not procrastinate the day of your repentance until the end; for after this day of life, which is given us to prepare for eternity, behold, if we do not improve our time while in this life, then cometh the night of darkness wherein there can be no labor performed.
> Ye cannot say, when ye are brought to that awful crisis, that I will repent, that I will return to my God. Nay, ye cannot say this; for that same spirit which doth possess your bodies at the time that ye go out of this life, that same spirit will have power to possess your body in that eternal world.
> For behold, if ye have procrastinated the day of your repentance even until death, behold, ye have become subjected to the spirit of the devil, and he doth seal you his; therefore, the Spirit of the Lord hath withdrawn from you, and hath no place in you, and the devil hath all power over you; and this is the final state of the wicked. (Alma 34:32–35.)

Repentance should not be procrastinated, says Amulek, for these reasons: (1) This life is the time given us to repent. (2) Prolonged procrastination brings us to a time when repentance is virtually impossible. Why? Because the same sinfully trained spirit at death will be the same spirit that one will have in the eternal world. The more wicked that spirit is, the less capable it is of change. (3) In fact, the sinful person eventually becomes captive (and "sealed") to the devil. This is a state that obviously renders repentance nearly impossible.

There are many Book of Mormon scriptures that threaten grave eternal consequences for those who understand the gospel and yet "die in their sins" (see Mosiah 2:33, 38; 3:11–12; 1 Ne. 15:32–35; 2 Ne. 9:38; Alma 12:16; 20:17; Moro. 10:26). The prophet Abinadi taught that "the Lord redeemeth none such that rebel against him and die in their sins; yea, even all those that have perished in their sins ever since the world began, that have wilfully rebelled against God . . . ; these are they that have no part in the first resurrection" (Mosiah 15:26). Lehi said that the days of men have been "prolonged . . . that they might repent while in the flesh" (2 Ne. 2:21). There is an urgency here to make the most of our brief mortal existence.

Many prophets have warned us of the consequences of not repenting. This we will treat more fully in chapter 18. One sampling will give us the flavor. These are the words of Samuel the Lamanite: "Whosoever repenteth not is hewn down and cast into the fire; and there cometh upon them again a spiritual death, yea, a second death, for they are cut off again as to things pertaining to righteousness. Therefore repent ye, repent ye, lest by knowing these things and not doing them ye shall suffer yourselves to come under condemnation, and ye are brought down unto this second death." (Hel. 14:18–19.)

Thank God for the principle of repentance. Even if we repent and subsequently fall back into sin, we can repent again, if our hearts are right: "As often as my people repent will I forgive them their trespasses against me" (Mosiah 26:30). Moroni wrote that as often as people "repented and sought forgiveness, with real intent, they were forgiven" (Moro. 6:8).

The Covenant of Baptism

Baptism is symbolic of a new birth into the kingdom of God and the commencement of a new life. When one emerges from the watery grave, he leaves behind the "old man of sin" and steps into the Lord's kingdom. Possibly the most significant aspect of this ordinance is the making of a solemn covenant to live as a true disciple of Christ. Having spoken of the qualifications for the ordinance, Alma the Elder said to those at the Waters of Mormon: "What have you against being baptized in the name of the Lord, as a witness before him that ye have entered into a covenant with him, that ye will serve him and keep his commandments, that he may pour out his Spirit more abundantly upon you?" (Mosiah 18:10.) The people of Limhi were spoken of as being "desirous to be baptized as a witness and a testimony that they were willing to serve God with all their hearts" (Mosiah 21:35). One further example comes from Alma the Younger's counsel to the people of Gideon:

Yea, I say unto you come and fear not, and lay aside every sin, which easily doth beset you, which doth bind you down to destruction, yea, come and go forth, and show unto your God that ye are willing to repent of your sins and enter into a covenant with him to keep his commandments, and witness it unto him this day by going into the waters of baptism.

And whosoever doeth this, and keepeth the commandments of God from thenceforth, . . . he shall have eternal life, according to the testimony of the Holy Spirit, which testifieth in me. (Alma 7:15–16; see also 2 Ne. 31:14; 3 Ne. 7:25.)

The prophet Nephi sermonized that by submitting to baptism, even Christ "witnesseth unto the Father that he would be obedient unto him in keeping his commandments" (2 Ne. 31:7). By doing this, Nephi continued, Jesus "showeth unto the children of men the straitness of the path, and the narrowness of the gate, by which they should enter, he having set the example before them" (2 Ne. 31:9).

Baptism, then, is a serious step in the Christian life and, according to Moroni, should not be done unworthily (see Morm. 9:29). This is why Book of Mormon prophets so often lay out the necessary prerequisites to the ordinance. Alma addressed his converts at the Waters of Mormon in these words:

And now, as ye are desirous to come into the fold of God, and to be called his people, and are willing to bear one another's burdens, that they may be light;

Yea, and are willing to mourn with those that mourn; yea, and comfort those that stand in need of comfort, and to stand as witnesses of God at all times and in all things, and in all places that ye may be in, even until death, that ye may be redeemed of God, and be numbered with those of the first resurrection, that ye may have eternal life—

Now I say unto you, if this be the desire of your hearts, what have you against being baptized? (Mosiah 18:8–10.)

Moroni lists the following qualifications: "They were not baptized save they brought forth fruit meet that they were worthy of it. Neither did they receive any unto baptism save they came forth with a broken heart and a contrite spirit, and witnessed unto the church that they truly repented of all their sins. And none were received unto baptism save they took upon them the name of Christ, having a determination to serve him to the end." (Moro. 6:1–3.)

The Book of Mormon clarifies several controversial elements that have surrounded this ordinance. For instance, while here upon the American continent the Savior not only indicated that the ordinance must be by immersion but also gave the prayer to be used by the administrator (see 3 Ne. 11:23–28). The book of Moroni also contains a forceful letter from Mormon condemning infant baptism (see Moro. 8). In that letter, Mormon wrote: "Behold I say unto you that this thing shall ye teach—repentance and baptism unto those who are accountable and capable of committing sin" (Moro. 8:10). Little children are innocent, therefore "it is solemn mockery before God, that ye should baptize little children" (Moro. 8:9).

Baptism of Fire and the Holy Ghost

Involved in this noble goal of becoming a Christian, we often fall short of our aspirations. We begin to sense the enormity of the task of transforming human nature. The faith is there, the enthusiasm, but the power? In seeking to live righteously, one may find himself acting contrary to strong appetites within his being. He may sense an inner resistance, the diminished yet downward pull of his lower nature. "Man's natural powers are unequal to this task . . . ," wrote Latter-day Saint theologian B. H. Roberts. "Mankind stand in some need of a strength superior to any they possess of themselves, to accomplish this work of rendering pure our fallen nature. Such strength, such power, such a sanctifying grace is conferred on man in being born of the Spirit—in receiving the Holy Ghost."[3] The angel's words that King Benjamin delivered to his people corroborate this idea: "The natural man is an enemy to God, and has been from the fall of Adam, and will be, forever and ever, unless he yields to the enticings of the Holy Spirit, and putteth off the natural man and becometh a saint" (Mosiah 3:19).

The role of the Holy Ghost is often explained by the words "mighty change of heart" (see Alma 5:14; also Alma 5:7; 22:15; Mosiah 5:7). This seems to mean a radical change of attitude toward sin and righteousness. One's love of righteousness is powerfully increased while the lure of sin is greatly weakened. King Benjamin's people testified, "The Spirit of the Lord Omnipotent . . . has wrought a mighty change in us, or in our hearts, that we have no more disposition to do evil, but to do good continually" (Mosiah 5:2). When King Lamoni and his people were converted by Ammon, they likewise remarked "that their hearts had been changed; that they had no more desire to do evil" (Alma 19:33). We cannot help but wonder how long this feeling remained with these converts. Their hearts may have undergone a permanent change, but the intensity of their desires for righteousness probably did not remain constant as they continued to live their lives in the world. Keeping the Spirit as a continual influence in one's life is therefore of critical importance.

This "born again" status is the culmination of the conversion experience. It is a step that is not only desirable but essential for salvation. Here are Alma's important words on the topic:

I have repented of my sins, and have been redeemed of the Lord; behold I am born of the Spirit.

And the Lord said unto me: Marvel not that all mankind, yea, men and women, all nations, kindreds, tongues and people, must be born again; yea, born of God, changed from their carnal and fallen state, to a state of righteousness, being redeemed of God, becoming his sons and daughters;

And thus they become new creatures; and unless they do this, they can in nowise inherit the kingdom of God. (Mosiah 27:24–26.)

By searching the Book of Mormon, we see little variation in the method of receiving this gift. Faith, repentance, baptism, and mighty prayer seem to be essential. When Lamoni's father asked Aaron what he must do to have the "wicked spirit rooted out" of his breast, he was told: "If thou desirest this thing, if thou wilt bow down before God, yea, if thou wilt repent of all thy sins, and will bow down before God, and call on his name in faith, believing that ye shall receive, then shalt thou receive the hope which thou desirest" (Alma 22:15–16). Samuel the Lamanite said that one needs to be brought to a knowledge of the truth, then faith and repentance will bring "a change of heart" to the individual (see Hel. 15:7). Benjamin's people were awakened to an awareness of the greatness of the gospel and their own sinfulness by the preaching of an inspired man. They repented and pleaded for mercy and as a consequence were born of God. Enos, in a moment of insight, perceived as never before the importance of the gospel. This motivated him to pray until he experienced this mighty change. In Alma the Younger's case, it was a combination of his father's prayers, the appearance of an angel, and his own profound repentance that led to the new birth.

To transform us from our fallen condition into Saints is the great purpose of the first principles of the gospel. To become a new creature, converted, born again, a Christian—that is the great achievement. In an argument over circumcision, the Apostle Paul once wrote, "Neither circumcision nor uncircumcision means anything; what counts is a new creation" (Gal. 6:15, New International Version). Still, Nephi tells us that all is not done (see 2 Ne. 31:19). We are still in our Christian infancy; we have yet to mature in gospel living. That is the task that lies ahead.

Chapter 15

THE VIRTUOUS CHRISTIAN

The process of conversion, described in the last two chapters, transforms a person's beliefs, behavior, commitment, and attitude. The born-again person is a "new creature," capable of living the "Christian life. What manner of life is that? How am I to live? It is impossible to avoid this question, since moral issues confront us at every turn—in business, in politics, in sex, in the rearing of children, and in the mundane affairs of our daily existence: Is it immoral, for instance, for one billion persons on this planet to live in absolute poverty while we in the affluent nations scramble for bigger homes, expensive cars, and stylish clothes? Is it immoral to bring more people into an already overcrowded world? Is abortion immoral or just another method of population control? If it is evil to take unborn life, what about crime, what about wars that kill thousands? What about countries that manufacture and sell arms to the nations of the world? Is it immoral to believe and behave as if my race, religion, or national identity makes me superior to someone who is different in these matters? What of alcoholism, rampant drug abuse, divorce, pornography, and sexual promiscuity? Does my behavior matter? Why should I refrain from stealing, taking advantage of others, lying, breaking promises, if these behaviors can bring me advantage in a competitive world?

Where can I find guidance on these issues? The contemporary world offers little help. Many of our best-educated people are moral relativists—morals are only a matter of cultural preference or taste. Many are hedonists—living to get all the pleasure they can from their existence. Even many churches are confused and seem to manifest the same relativism about right and wrong as the man in the street. Debates about clerical celibacy, homosexuality, chastity, and divorce fill the world's chapels as well as the media. Scandals among some high-profile televangelists add to the problem by weakening the moral leadership of the churches.

We live in a time when traditional values are challenged and often ridiculed as outmoded standards of a Victorian era. This is evident in our literature, music, movies, and television. A 1992 report by the American Psychological Association's Task Force on Television and Society, for example, voiced concern about the negative impact of television on children, whose viewing time at age twelve averaged four hours daily. Young people saw constant portrayals of sexual activity, "negative stereotypes of ethnic minorities," and a great deal of violence. The report said that the average child "witnessed more than 8,000 TV murders before finishing elementary school."[1] Another study by the American Family Association estimated that in 1991 "the three networks displayed more than 10,000 sexual incidents during prime time; for every scene depicting sexual intercourse between married partners, the networks showed 14 scenes of sex outside of marriage."[2] "What are the real American values?" asks one writer. This is her insightful answer:

> Look who our heroes are. They aren't the people who volunteer in the soup kitchens; they aren't struggling writers and artists; they aren't the librarians or the nurses or the social workers. Mainly they are the rich and the famous and the successful and the beautiful, the film and sports stars, the Wall Street barons, even the articulate convicts who charm us on talk shows once they've done their time. Perhaps the best indicator of what we really are is what we spend our money on or what we watch on television. Look at what we read. Look at what we choose to do with our spare time. That's what we value.[3]

In a world such as this, how important is a book of scripture filled with divine direction concerning the proper living of life? No message is clearer in the Book of Mormon than that God expects of us a life of moral excellence; the most obvious instruction we receive from the book is that our lives must be lived in a particular way.

Upon each of us rests the responsibility of determining what will be done with his or her life. We live with ourselves twenty-four hours of every day; we know ourselves better than we know anything in the world. Most of us do the normal things that nearly all people do—go to school, date the opposite sex, become married, rear a family, work at a job, and recreate. Is that the sum total of our existence? As soon as we acknowledge a belief in God and the prophets, we are confronted with a higher purpose. "This life is the time for men to prepare to meet God," preached Amulek, the time to "perform [our] labors" (Alma 34:32). Furthermore there is an urgency to get going; procrastination will bring the forfeiture of eternal blessings (see Alma 34:33–35). As I read the word of God, I am, therefore, simultaneously undergoing self-analysis. The scriptures are like a mirror held up to examine life. This was Nephi's method of studying the scriptures: "I did liken all scriptures unto us, that it might be for our profit and learning" (1 Ne. 19:23). I might, for instance, be reading Alma's discourse to Church members but hear his questions addressed to me:

> And now behold, I ask of you, my brethren of the church, have ye spiritually been born of God? Have ye received his image in your countenances? Have ye experienced this mighty change in your hearts?
>
> Do ye exercise faith in the redemption of him who created you? . . .
>
> I say unto you, can you imagine to yourselves that ye hear the voice of the Lord, saying unto you, in that day: Come unto me ye blessed, for behold, your works have been the works of righteousness upon the face of the earth?
>
> Or do ye imagine to yourselves that ye can lie unto the Lord in that day, and say—Lord, our works have been righteous works upon the face of the earth—and that he will save you? . . .
>
> Have ye walked, keeping yourselves blameless before God? Could ye say, if ye were called to die at this time, within yourselves, that ye have been sufficiently humble? . . .
>
> Behold, are ye stripped of pride? I say unto you, if ye are not ye are not prepared to meet God. . . .
>
> Behold, I say, is there one among you who is not stripped of envy? I say unto you that such an one is not prepared; and I would that he should prepare quickly. . . . (Alma 5:14–17, 27–29.)

When I couple statements like this with reminders of my agency ("For behold, ye are free; ye are permitted to act for yourselves" [Hel. 14:30]), I begin to sense the seriousness of my daily decisions. I do not want to minimize the grace of God; I know that I have not come thus far without "relying wholly upon the merits of him who is mighty to save" (2 Ne. 31:19). Nevertheless, I must bear the responsibility for my own growth.

How, then, shall I live? The Book of Mormon is filled with prophetic guidance on this question—the Ten Commandments, the Sermon at the Temple, and the exhortations of countless prophets. I will return to Nephi's wonderful summary of the gospel (see chapter 2 of this book) as a useful format for studying the Christian way of life. Here we learn that there is still much to do after one has entered through the "gate" of conversion: "And now, my beloved brethren, after ye have gotten into this strait and narrow path, I would ask if all is done? Behold, I say unto you, Nay. . . . Ye must press forward with a steadfastness in Christ, having a perfect brightness of hope, and a love of God and of all men. Wherefore, if ye shall press forward, feasting upon the word of Christ, and endure to the end, behold, thus saith the Father: Ye shall have eternal life." (2 Ne. 31:18–20.)

Here are six summary statements of what we have earlier called the second phase of the Christian life: (1) One must "press forward with a steadfastness in Christ." (2) We must do so with a "perfect brightness of hope," (3) a love of God, (4) and a love of "all men." (5) Finally, as one "endure[s] to the end," he must (6) feast "upon the word of Christ." This chapter, plus the two that follow, will deal with these topics. Our present objective is to treat those gospel ideas that pertain to our personal character. The following chapters will deal with our relationship with God and with other people. There is obviously some overlapping among these categories, as is the case with the following topic of love. Love, the dominant characteristic of a Christian personality, is both a personal virtue and a way of reacting to God and others. Some portion of it will therefore be discussed in all three chapters on Christian living.

"The Pure Love of Christ"

Nephi mentioned the two great commandments, the love of God and the love of man. The ideal life is not merely an abstention from certain vices nor a mechanical performance of formal duties, but a whole life of service motivated by a love of God and people. In Palestine, Jesus taught that by the quality of love "shall all men know that ye are my disciples" (John 13:35). Paul and Mormon taught us that there are three cardinal virtues—faith, hope, and charity—and the most important of the three is charity, or love (see 1 Cor. 13; Moro. 7). We have discussed faith and will, in this chapter, consider hope and love. Paul and Mormon saw love as encompassing the other virtues. One who possesses it is kind, not envious or conceited, unselfish, slow to anger, pure of mind, steadfast in hardships, full of hope and rejoicing (see Moro. 7:45; 1 Cor. 13:4–7). The Lord told Moroni, Mormon's son, that "faith, hope and charity bringeth unto me—the fountain of all righteousness" (Ether 12:28).

Mormon called this love "charity," or the "pure love of Christ" (Moro. 7:47). It is the kind of love the Savior has for mankind. Moroni was speaking of how Christ "loved the world, even unto the laying down of [his] life for the world," when in a flash of insight he declared, "And now I know that this love which thou hast had for the children of men is charity; wherefore, except men shall have charity they cannot inherit that place which thou hast prepared in the mansions of thy Father" (Ether 12:33–34; see also 2 Nephi 26:30). Mormon called charity the greatest of all the virtues; we are "nothing" without it (Moro. 7:46), and if we are "found possessed of it at the last day, it shall be well with [us]" (Moro. 7:47).

It is clear that this "pure love of Christ" transcends normal and conventional goodwill. In the Savior's famous Sermon on the Mount, delivered also in America, we are struck by the lofty and difficult nature of this standard. Disciples are asked to refrain from anger and name-calling (see 3 Ne. 12:22). (Indeed, as the Savior indicated to the twelve Nephite disciples prior to delivering the well-known sermon, his followers are to avoid "disputations," even over "points of my doctrine." "The spirit of contention," said Jesus, "is not of me, but is of the devil." [3 Ne. 11:28, 29.]) A disciple will go to great lengths to reconcile differences with others (see 3 Ne. 12:24–26), tolerate a degree of abuse and ill will rather than retaliate in kind (see 3 Ne. 12:39–42), pray for and do good to his enemies (see 3 Ne. 12:43–45), refrain from criticism of another's faults (see 3 Ne. 14:1–6), and treat others as he would like to be treated (see 3 Ne. 14:12). As Moroni later wrote, our love for God should be with all our "might, mind and strength" (Moro. 10:32). Such an elevated ethical standard, all must admit, is a rarity among mortals.

Since love is the greatest of all Christian virtues, it becomes a major objective of every sincere Christian to grow in his ability to love. How is it possible to acquire the high degree of love asked of us? Surely it is within the power of human beings to act lovingly even when not feeling disposed to do so, to engage in helpful acts, and to be friendly and caring by the power of our own will. However, Mormon tells us that we can only obtain the "pure love of Christ" in its fullest extent as a gift from God. "Wherefore, my beloved brethren," he says, "pray unto the Father with all the energy of heart, that ye may be filled with this love, which he hath bestowed upon all who are true followers of his Son, Jesus Christ" (Moro. 7:48). Notice that persons qualify for this gift by praying with all "the energy of heart" and by being "true followers" of Jesus Christ. Mormon wrote a letter that contained information on how "perfect love" is acquired. He explained that the "first fruits of repentance is baptism" and that "the remission of sins bringeth meekness, and lowliness of heart; and because of meekness and lowliness of heart cometh the visitation of the Holy Ghost, which Comforter filleth with hope and perfect love, which love endureth by diligence unto prayer" (Moro. 8:25–26). The "pure love of Christ" is beyond human capacity to generate on its own; only supernatural power can fully bestow this preeminent gift.

The Process of Sanctification

I suggested earlier that spiritual rebirth makes one an infant Christian with the need to continue growing. When will this growing process be completed? I once spoke to my son about Sabbath observance. He wanted to know if he could watch television, play baseball, etc., on Sundays. It became clear that his desire was to do only the absolute minimum. I asked him how good he wanted to be. To do the minimum at this point in his life might be an acceptable beginning, I explained, but the Lord expected us to keep improving. The real question is: How can I use the Sabbath in a maximum way to serve God and for my own spiritual growth? There are many "minimal Mormons" in the kingdom, while the scriptures teach that spiritual growth is ongoing. Jesus taught his disciples, "I would that ye should be perfect even as I, or your Father who is in heaven is perfect" (3 Ne. 12:48). It is apparent that the process of growth will not be completed in a short while, certainly not in this life.

Returning to Nephi's summary of the gospel, we notice that he mentions this idea of continued progression three times in one verse: "Ye must press forward with a steadfastness in Christ. . . . Wherefore, if ye shall press forward, feasting upon the word of Christ, and endure to the end, behold, thus saith the Father: Ye shall have eternal life." (2 Ne. 31:20.) "Enduring to the end" is a phrase often used by Book of Mormon prophets (for example, see 1 Ne. 13:37; 22:31; 2 Ne. 9:24; Mosiah 2:41; and 3 Ne. 15:9). This process of enduring and becoming increasingly holy is called sanctification. We must eventually be sanctified to return to the presence of God, for "no unclean thing can dwell" in his presence (1 Ne. 10:21).

The Book of Mormon tells us that sanctification begins when we are cleansed of our sins by the power of the Atonement; it continues through a combination of our personal efforts and the workings of the Holy Ghost. Jesus told all to repent, come unto him, and be baptized, "that ye may be sanctified by the reception of the Holy Ghost, that ye may stand spotless before me at the last day" (3 Ne. 27:20). Alma, speaking of certain high priests who exercised "exceeding faith and repentance," wrote: "They were called after this holy order, and were sanctified, and their garments were washed white through the blood of the Lamb. Now they, after being sanctified by the Holy Ghost, having their garments made white, being pure and spotless before God, could not look upon sin save it were with abhorrence; and there were many, exceedingly great many, who were made pure and entered into the rest of the Lord their God." (Alma 13:10–12; see also Alma 5:54.)

Final sanctification requires a high level of righteousness. The Lord told Moroni that the Gentiles would become sanctified when they exercised faith as the brother of Jared did; then "they may become sanctified in me, then will I manifest unto them the things which the brother of Jared saw, even to the unfolding unto them all my revelations, saith Jesus Christ" (Ether 4:7). A beautiful description of some who became sanctified is found in the account of those righteous people living in the Americas about forty years prior to the coming of the Savior to this continent. It was said that they "did fast and pray oft, and did wax stronger and stronger in their humility, and firmer and firmer in the faith of Christ, unto the filling their souls with joy and consolation, yea, even to the purifying and the sanctification of their hearts, which sanctification cometh because of their yielding their hearts unto God" (Hel. 3:35).

As the lonely Moroni neared the end of his days, he left this eloquent plea for perfection:

> Come unto Christ, and be perfected in him, and deny yourselves of all ungodliness; and if ye shall deny yourselves of all ungodliness, and love God with all your might, mind and strength, then is his grace sufficient for you, that by his grace ye may be perfect in Christ; and if by the grace of God ye are perfect in Christ, ye can in nowise deny the power of God.
>
> And again, if ye by the grace of God are perfect in Christ, and deny not his power, then are ye sanctified in Christ by the grace of God, through the shedding of the blood of Christ, which is in the covenant of the Father unto the remission of your sins, that ye become holy, without spot. (Moro. 10:32–33.)

According to this beautiful passage, if we come to Christ, become perfected in him, deny ourselves of "all ungodliness," love God with all our hearts, and do not deny the power of God, we will become "sanctified in Christ," or, in other words, "become holy, without spot." In summary, as we endure to the end in doing what Moroni counseled, the Lord will bestow the Spirit upon us in such fulness that we will become purified and sanctified by its power.

The sanctification process includes the need to, in Mormon's words, "lay hold upon every good thing" (Moro. 7:19). "I will tell you the way whereby ye may lay hold on every good thing," Mormon advises. "For behold, God knoweth all things, being from everlasting to everlasting, behold, he sent angels to minister unto the children of men, to make manifest concerning the coming of Christ; and in Christ there should come every good thing." (Moro. 7:21–22.) Nephi's was a similar emphasis. We must "feast upon the words of Christ" and they will tell us "all things what [we] should do" (2 Ne. 32:3). He also taught that "unless a man shall endure to the end, in following the example of the Son of the living God, he cannot be saved" (2 Ne. 31:16). Christ is the exemplar, the teacher. No one can "lay hold upon every good thing" unless he places Christ at the focal point of his life.

It is possible for the sanctified person to be sealed up to salvation even before he leaves this mortal existence. King Benjamin told his people that they "should be steadfast and immovable, always abounding in good works, that Christ, the Lord God Omnipotent, may seal you his, that you may be brought to heaven" (Mosiah 5:15). Several Book of Mormon greats were sealed up to salvation, among whom were Alma (see Mosiah 26:20), Mormon (see Morm. 2:19), the brother of Jared (see Ether 3:13), and Moroni (see Ether 12:37). Another phrase used by the prophets to express the same thing is to say that someone had entered into the "Lord's rest" (see Alma 12:36; 13:12, 16; 60:13; Moro. 7:3).

The Continuing Need of the Spirit

The Spirit of God (or the Holy Ghost) has a vital role to play in assisting us to live the Christian life. The Spirit enlarges our ability to love, aids us in the sanctification process, and guides our actions as we traverse the strait and narrow path to salvation. At the time of conversion, the Spirit worked on us in a powerful manner; but it is unlikely that the same degree of spiritual power can be maintained. There is, therefore, a crucial need to cultivate that divine energy. The following is an overview of the Spirit's role in the total salvation experience.

A limited bestowal of the Spirit is given to every person born into the world. Mormon taught that the "Spirit of Christ is given to every man, that he may know good from evil" (Moro. 7:16). The gift of discernment between right and wrong, equated with conscience, provides a person with the basic means to live a good life. If one gives heed to his inner impressions, he will be led to the Savior and the Church, where a higher spiritual endowment is available through the laying on of hands for the gift of the Holy Ghost. Moroni said that the Holy Ghost was the power that would tell a person if the Book of Mormon was true (see Moro. 10:4); and not only is this the case with regard to the Book of Mormon, but "by the power of the Holy Ghost ye may know the truth of all things" (Moro. 10:5). On the other hand, if one repeatedly transgresses against the spiritual light he receives, the Spirit of the Lord will "cease to strive" with him (see 2 Ne. 26:11; Ether 2:15; 15:19; 1 Ne. 7:14; Moro. 3:28; 9:4).

Spiritual rebirth changes a person's heart, gives him the right to the constant companionship of the Holy Ghost, and gives him access to valuable spiritual gifts, such as inspired teaching, healing, working of miracles, and interpretation of languages (see Moro. 10:7–18). Again using Nephi's phrase, the Holy Ghost will show a person "all things" that he should do as he lives out the days of his life. Since celestial beings are always described as beings of radiance and glory, it is possible that celestialization is, in part, a higher grant of spiritual power.

A catalogue of the gifts and blessings of the Spirit would probably fill pages. The following list, though incomplete, will illustrate the valuable role the Holy Ghost can play in the life of a Christian:

1 Ne. 4:6—Nephi was led by the spirit from moment to moment because he personally did not know what to do.

1 Ne. 10:17–19—Nephi desired to see the vision his father saw, having faith that the "mysteries of God" are revealed by the Holy Ghost to all those "who diligently seek him."

1 Ne. 13:12–16—The Spirit of God led Columbus, pilgrims, and others to the New World.

1 Ne. 22:2—"By the Spirit are all things made known unto the prophets."

2 Ne. 28:1; 32:7—Nephi was "constrained" to speak by the Spirit, and later his utterance was stopped by the Spirit.

2 Ne. 28:26—Wo unto him that denieth the power of the Spirit!

2 Ne. 32:8—The Spirit teaches a person that he must pray.

2 Ne. 33:1–2—When one speaks by the power of the Spirit, that same power carries it with impact to the heart of the listener.

Jacob 4:13—"The Spirit speaketh the truth and lieth not. Wherefore, it speaketh of things as they really are, and of things as they really will be."

Jarom 1:4—"And as many as are not stiffnecked and have faith, have communion with the Holy Spirit."

Mosiah 3:19—We put off the natural man by yielding to the Spirit.

Mosiah 13:5—Abinadi glowed with spiritual power.

Alma 5:45–46—Alma's testimony came by the Spirit after many days of fasting and prayer (see also Ether 4:11).

Alma 8:31—Alma and Amulek were filled with the Holy Ghost and had such power that they could not be slain or confined in dungeons.

Alma 12:3–7—Zeezrom's thoughts were made known to Alma and Amulek by the Spirit.

Alma 17:3, 9, 10—By "much prayer, and fasting" the sons of Mosiah had great spiritual power on their mission.

Alma 18:16—"Ammon, being filled with the Spirit of God, therefore he perceived the thoughts of the king."

Alma 40:13—Evil people "have no part nor portion of the Spirit of the Lord."

Hel. 5:45—"The Holy Spirit of God did come down from heaven, and did enter into their hearts, and they were filled as if with fire, and they could speak forth marvelous words."

Hel. 10:15–17—Nephi was conveyed by the Spirit away from his enemies.

Hel. 16:2—Stones could not hit Samuel because of the protecting power of the Spirit.

3 Ne. 18:7, 1; 20:9—People received the Spirit by properly partaking of the sacrament.

3 Ne. 19:9—Jesus' twelve disciples "did pray for that which they most desired; and they desired that the Holy Ghost should be given unto them."

3 Ne. 19:25, 30—The disciples were "white" when filled with the Spirit.

3 Ne. 28:11; 16:6—The Spirit bears witness of the Father and the Son.

Moro. 6:9—Their meetings were led by the Spirit.

Moro. 10:4–5—The Spirit will reveal all truth.

The Nature of Hope

In the list of supreme virtues no one would dispute the inclusion of charity (love) or faith (which is the principle that motivates us to righteous actions), but hope? Is it that important? Both Paul and Mormon taught it to be among the three greatest virtues. Hope can be defined as a happy expectation of desirable results in the future.

When we realize that life's difficulties often discourage and defeat people, thus stifling their progress, and when we admit that progress is the very essence of gospel living, we begin to see the necessity of hope. Hope—"a perfect brightness of hope" is Nephi's charming phrase (2 Ne. 31:20)—is that positive affirmation of life, that optimism we must possess to keep moving upward despite the trials of living.

What do we hope for in the future? We hope that death is not the end of existence; we hope for a life where justice and righteousness reign; we hope for loving relationships to continue; we hope, in a word, for eternal happiness. This the gospel promises, and because of our faith in the gospel we have hope that it will become real. Mormon said that "without faith there cannot be any hope" (Moro. 7:42). "Behold I say unto you that ye shall have hope through the atonement of Christ and the power of his resurrection, to be raised unto life eternal, and this because of your faith in him according to the promise" (Moro. 7:41). In his Jaredite record, Moroni wrote impressive words about hope: "Wherefore, whoso believeth in God might with surety hope for a better world, yea, even a place at the right hand of God, which hope cometh of faith, maketh an anchor to the souls of men, which would make them sure and steadfast, always abounding in good works, being led to glorify God" (Ether 12:4).

Therefore, the Christian person, anchored in hope, walks the path to salvation with happiness, enthusiasm, and a positive attitude. Burdens cannot defeat him, sickness cannot, occasional failures cannot. Only sin can destroy his hope. If one leaves the path and turns again to sin he will lose the basis upon which his hope is grounded. Moroni put it succinctly: "Despair cometh because of iniquity" (Moro. 10:22).

Humility Is Necessary for Growth

A quality of character necessary for the growing life is humility. Humility and its antonym, pride, are mentioned constantly in the Book of Mormon. It was pride, Mormon declared, that caused the downfall of the Nephite nation (see Moro. 8:27). Nephi and Moroni saw pride as one of our problems in the latter days (see 2 Ne. 28:14–15; Morm. 8:27–28, 36–37). The Lord has therefore instructed the modern Church to "beware of pride, lest ye become as the Nephites of old" (D&C 38:39).

Nephite prophets often mention a recurring cycle of righteousness and wickedness among their people. Nearly always, it seems, pride was the cause of the people's descent into wickedness. The Nephite golden age, for example, was destroyed when the people began to be "lifted up in pride, such as the wearing of costly apparel, and all manner of fine pearls, and of the fine things of the world" (4 Ne. 1:24). Pride led them to abandon their economic cooperation, divided them into classes, and distorted their values (see 4 Ne. 1:25–26). Some who had acquired wealth in the days of the prophet Jacob were warned, "Because some of you have obtained more abundantly than that of your brethren ye are lifted up in the pride of your hearts, and wear stiff necks and high heads because of the costliness of your apparel, and persecute your brethren because ye suppose that ye are better than they" (Jacob 2:13). The same thing happened again and again in the Book of Mormon (see Alma 4:6–10; 31:24–28; Hel. 3:33–36; 7:20–28; 3 Ne. 6:10–16; 4 Ne. 1).

The most serious aspect of pride is illustrated in the foregoing verses. In the words of President Ezra Taft Benson, it is enmity or hatred. "The proud make every man their adversary by pitting their intellects, opinions, works, wealth, talents, or any other worldly measuring device against others."[4]

Another great danger of pride is that it inhibits or stops progression. During the time of Jesus' earthly ministry, the pride of the Pharisees prevented their repentance because they could not see their own deficiencies. Their intellectual arrogance prevented their listening to Jesus, because their pride would not admit that he had anything to teach them. Said President Benson: "The proud are not easily taught. (See 1 Ne. 15:3, 7–11.) They won't change their minds to accept truths, because to do so implies they have been wrong."[5] I used to think that Elder Bruce R. McConkie's statement that "all progress in spiritual things is conditioned upon the prior attainment of *humility*"[6] was an exaggeration. I have changed my mind. A healthy sense of inadequacy and a consciousness of achievements yet to be accomplished are essential for growth. This is undoubtedly the reason why Mormon said that "none is acceptable before God, save the meek and lowly in heart" (Moro. 7:44). This is why the prophet Jacob said: "And the wise, and the learned, and they that are rich, who are puffed up because of their learning, and their wisdom, and their riches—yea, they are they whom he despiseth; and save they shall cast these things away, and consider themselves fools before God, and come down in the depths of humility, he will not open unto them" (2 Ne. 9:42).

The Zoramite poor who were despised and cast out of their synagogues were told by Alma that this was a fortunate occurrence, "that ye may be humble, and that ye may learn wisdom." Their circumstances, he explained, "compelled" them to be humble, and "a man sometimes, if he is compelled to be humble, seeketh repentance; and now surely, whosoever repenteth shall find mercy; and he that findeth mercy and endureth to the end the same shall be saved." (Alma 32:12–13.) Nevertheless, Alma continued, "do ye not suppose that they are more blessed who truly humble themselves because of the word? Yea. . . . Blessed is he that believeth in the word of God, and is baptized without stubbornness of heart, yea, without being brought to know the word, or even compelled to know, before they will believe." (Alma 32:14–16.)

A final argument for humility is that when we comprehend our weaknesses we depend on Christ's power to save and not our own. The prophet Jacob said that "the Lord God showeth us our weakness that we may know that it is by his grace, and his great condescensions unto the children of men, that we have power to do these things [i.e., accomplish great things by faith]" (Jacob 4:7).

In the light of what has been said, we can see the wisdom in this exhortation by the prophet Alma:

> And now, my brethren, I wish from the inmost part of my heart, yea, with great anxiety even unto pain, that ye would hearken unto my words, and cast off your sins, and not procrastinate the day of your repentance;
>
> But that ye would humble yourselves before the Lord, and call on his holy name, and watch and pray continually, that ye may not be tempted above that which ye can bear, and thus be led by the Holy Spirit, becoming humble, meek, submissive, patient, full of love and all long-suffering;
>
> Having faith on the Lord; having a hope that ye shall receive eternal life; having the love of God always in your hearts, that ye may be lifted up at the last day and enter into his rest (Alma 13:27–29).

And these beautiful words given by an angel to King Benjamin, who in turn delivered them to his people: "For the natural man is an enemy to God, and has been from the fall of Adam, and will be, forever and ever, unless he yields to the enticings of the Holy Spirit, and putteth off the natural man and becometh a saint through the atonement of Christ the Lord, and becometh as a child, submissive, meek, humble, patient, full of love, willing to submit to all things which the Lord seeth fit to inflict upon him, even as a child doth submit to his father" (Mosiah 3:19).

God has told us that he will "make weak things become strong" for us. When Moroni was worried that the "Gentiles shall mock at our words" because of the Nephite record keepers' imperfect writing ability, the Lord replied with a powerful message about humility: "And if men come unto me I will show unto them their weakness. I give unto men weakness that they may be humble; and my grace is sufficient for all men that humble themselves before me; for if they humble themselves before me, and have faith in me, then will I make weak things become strong unto them." (Ether 12:25, 27.)

Conclusion

We have emphasized, because the Book of Mormon emphasizes, the continued growth required of a Christian, a growth that, if humbly and diligently pursued, will bring us a crown of immortal glory. A fitting summation of this chapter is the message of Alma to the people in Gideon:

> And now my beloved brethren, I have said these things unto you that I might awaken you to a sense of your duty to God, that ye may walk blameless before him, that ye may walk after the holy order of God, after which ye have been received.
>
> And now I would that ye should be humble, and be submissive and gentle; easy to be entreated; full of patience and long-suffering; being temperate in all things; being diligent in keeping the commandments of God at all times; asking for whatsoever things ye stand in need, both spiritual and temporal; always returning thanks unto God for whatsoever things ye do receive.
>
> And see that ye have faith, hope, and charity, and then ye will always abound in good works.
>
> And may the Lord bless you, and keep your garments spotless, that ye may at last be brought to sit down with Abraham, Isaac, and Jacob, and the holy prophets who have been ever since the world began, having your garments spotless even as their garments are spotless, in the kingdom of heaven to go no more out. (Alma 7:22–25.)

Chapter 16

THE SPIRITUAL CHRISTIAN

How can finite mortals relate to the Almighty God? Should we burn animals on an altar, construct formalized ritual, offer endless petitions, travel to holy places, participate in physical asceticism or transcendental meditation? Modern secular man is likely to have no experience with the divine, no inner urgency to pray or worship, no feelings of intimacy with God; he lives, in the words of Alma, "without God in the world" (Alma 41:11). Contrast this with the prophet Nephi's experiences with God:

> My God hath been my support; he hath led me through mine afflictions in the wilderness; and he hath preserved me upon the waters of the great deep.
>
> He hath filled me with his love, even unto the consuming of my flesh.
>
> He hath confounded mine enemies. . . .
>
> Behold, he hath heard my cry by day, and he hath given me knowledge by visions in the nighttime.
>
> And by day have I waxed bold in mighty prayer before him; yea, my voice have I sent up on high; and angels came down and ministered unto me. . . .
>
> Rejoice, O my heart, and cry unto the Lord, and say: O Lord, I will praise thee forever; yea, my soul will rejoice in thee, my God, and the rock of my salvation. (2 Nephi 4:20–24, 30.)

God had supported Nephi in his wilderness afflictions, preserved his life during their transoceanic voyage, filled him with divine love, confounded his enemies, heard his prayers, and sent him visions and ministrations of angels. Nephi's life was filled with divine influences.

In the last chapter we spoke of the Christian's need of the Holy

Spirit. This Spirit can teach the things of God, give guidance and inner impressions, cause a "mighty change of heart," impart numerous spiritual gifts, and fill us with exalted feelings of blessedness and closeness to God, our beloved Father. Spiritual people have often spoken of this divine power in words of intimate spiritual connectedness. The Apostle Paul described his relationship with Christ in these beautiful words: "I am crucified with Christ: nevertheless I live; yet not I, but Christ liveth in me: and the life which I now live in the flesh I live by the faith of the Son of God, who loved me, and gave himself for me" (Gal. 2:20). Paul used the descriptive phrase "in Christ" 164 times to express this spiritual union between himself and the Savior. Jesus himself used interesting metaphors to describe this bond with the Father and his disciples. "Abide in me, and I in you," he said to his Apostles just prior to Gethsemane. "As the branch cannot bear fruit of itself, except it abide in the vine; no more can ye, except ye abide in me. I am the vine, ye are the branches." (John 15:4–5.) On the same occasion he prayed that all disciples "may be one; as thou, Father, art in me, and I in thee, that they also may be one in us" (John 17:21).

King Benjamin, another American prophet, was one who had "known of [God's] goodness and [had] tasted of his love" (see Mosiah 4:11). He appealed to his people to show gratitude to their divine Father. If I deserve your thanks for spending my life in your service, he explained, how much more "you ought to thank your heavenly King!" He continued:

> I say unto you, my brethren, that if you should render all the thanks and praise which your whole soul has power to possess, to that God who has created you, and has kept and preserved you, and has caused that ye should rejoice, and has granted that ye should live in peace one with another—
>
> I say unto you that if ye should serve him who has created you from the beginning, and is preserving you from day to day, by lending you breath, that ye may live and move and do according to your own will, and even supporting you from one moment to another—I say, if ye should serve him with all your whole souls yet ye would be unprofitable servants.
>
> And behold, all that he requires of you is to keep his commandments; and he has promised you that if ye would keep his commandments ye should prosper in the land. . . .
>
> And now, in the first place, he hath created you, and granted unto you your lives, for which ye are indebted unto him.
>
> And secondly, he doth require that ye should do as he hath

commanded you; for which if ye do, he doth immediately bless you; and therefore he hath paid you. And ye are still indebted unto him, and are, and will be, forever and ever; therefore, of what have ye to boast? (Mosiah 2:19–24.)

Like Nephi, Benjamin emphasized our indebtedness to God and our reasonable response—thanks, praise, service, and an eagerness to keep his commandments.

One more example, this from Christ's appearance on the American continent, undoubtedly the greatest demonstration of divine power ever witnessed on this hemisphere. The events preceding his coming were sufficient to strike awe, if not terror, into the hearts of any people—physical destruction ("the whole face of the land was changed" [3 Nephi 8:12]) followed by three days of total darkness; then the mild yet piercing voice of Christ calling the people to repentance; next was heard the voice of the Father introducing the Son; and finally all witnessed the Savior's descent from heaven (see 3 Nephi 8–11).

How did the people react to this display of divine power? "They did cry out with one accord, saying: Hosanna! Blessed be the name of the Most High God! And they did fall down at the feet of Jesus, and did worship him." (3 Nephi 11:16–17.) In the days that followed, the people prayed often and attentively listened to Jesus' teachings. When he announced his departure to visit the lost tribes, he saw the intent, tear-filled eyes of the multitude and decided to stay (see 3 Nephi 17:4–5). Jesus not only stayed but also asked them to bring forth their sick and afflicted and proceeded to heal them all (see 3 Nephi 17:9). Afterwards they knelt with him as he prayed to the Father. So great was the prayer that they recorded that "eye hath never seen, neither hath the ear heard, before, so great and marvelous things as we saw and heard Jesus speak unto the Father" (3 Nephi 17:16).

In the above examples, we learn that the converted disciple lives in close spiritual communion with his Maker and uses worship, prayer, and service to cultivate and maintain that relationship. In these ways man applies the great commandment to love God with all his heart and strength (see Matt. 22:36–37). Nephi's summary of the gospel urged disciples to walk the "strait and narrow" path, having a "love of God and of all men" (2 Nephi 31:19–20). Love and loyalty to God are, therefore, the highest priorities for a Christian.

How is this love acquired? Surely the first step is to understand God's true nature. How could someone have loved the capricious gods of the ancient pagan, or "the first great cause" or "ground of being" of the philosopher, or the absentee god of the Deist, or even the triune, spiritual essence worshipped by traditional Christians? Only the omnipotent, loving Father of prophetic teaching is truly lovable. "We love him," said John the Beloved Apostle, "because he first loved us" (1 Jn. 4:19). How much does God love us? As the Lord of the vineyard and his workers labor tirelessly to produce a fruitful vineyard, so does God strive to save his fallen children. That is the message of the allegory of the prophet Zenos. (See Jacob 5 and chapter 5 in this book.) God's great desire to save his children is beautifully communicated in the following passage: when efforts to save the vineyard had failed, "the Lord of the vineyard wept, and said unto the servant: What could I have done more for my vineyard? . . . Have I slackened mine hand, that I have not nourished it? Nay, I have nourished it, and I have digged about it, and I have pruned it, and I have dunged it; and I have stretched forth mine hand almost all the day long, and the end draweth nigh." (Jacob 5:41, 47.)

As we come to comprehend the nature of God, his majesty, his love and concern, we are naturally drawn to him in love and adoration, which in turn find expression in worshipful prayer and service. This chapter will focus on these activities as our principal means of loving God.

Prayer: Humanity's Link with the Divine

Prayer was an important part of Jesus' brief American ministry. In the magnificent Sermon at the Temple, Jesus instructed the multitude: "Ask, and it shall be given unto you; seek, and ye shall find; knock, and it shall be opened unto you. For every one that asketh, receiveth; and he that seeketh, findeth; and to him that knocketh, it shall be opened." (3 Ne. 14:7–8.) At one point during his first day's ministry, Jesus perceived that the people were not fully comprehending his words. Go to your homes, he told them, "and ponder upon the things which I have said, and ask of the Father, in my name, that ye may understand, and prepare your minds for the morrow" (3 Ne. 17:3). The thought of his leaving brought them to tears, so Jesus continued to minister to them. He healed their sick and prayed with them. Never, says the record, had anyone heard such marvelous words as Jesus spoke to his Father. They were overcome with joy. The Savior blessed their children, and angels descended and encircled the children with celestial fire.

After introducing the sacrament, Jesus gave instructions on prayer:

Verily, verily, I say unto you, ye must watch and pray always, lest ye be tempted by the devil, and ye be led away captive by him.

And as I have prayed among you even so shall ye pray in my church. . . . Behold I am the light; I have set an example for you. . . .

Behold, verily, verily, I say unto you, ye must watch and pray always lest ye enter into temptation; for Satan desireth to have you, that he may sift you as wheat.

Therefore ye must always pray unto the Father in my name;

And whatsoever ye shall ask the Father in my name, which is right, believing that ye shall receive, behold it shall be given unto you.

Pray in your families unto the Father, always in my name, that your wives and your children may be blessed. (3 Ne. 18:15–16, 18–21.)

When Jesus appeared on the second day he commanded his disciples to again kneel and pray (see 3 Ne. 19:16–17). He then separated himself a little distance and conversed with the Father (see 3 Ne. 19:18, 22). Ending his prayer, he returned to find that "they did still continue, without ceasing, to pray unto him; and they did not multiply many words, for it was given unto them what they should pray, and they were filled with desire" (3 Ne. 19:24). After Jesus blessed his disciples, his countenance shone upon them until they glowed with divine whiteness (see 3 Ne. 19:25). He told them to "pray on" and departed to continue with his own prayers. He finally commanded the multitude to cease praying verbally, but added "that they should not cease to pray in their hearts" (3 Ne. 20:1).

It is rare that one glimpses in scripture (or anywhere) such an exalted spiritual state. Mighty prayer was undoubtedly both a cause and a result of this outpouring of divine power.

Great Things Accomplished by Prayer

It was the biblical James who said, "The effectual fervent prayer of a righteous man availeth much" (James 5:16). Jesus taught that "every one that asketh, receiveth; and he that seeketh, findeth; and to him that knocketh, it shall be opened" (3 Ne. 14:8). And again, "Whatsoever ye shall ask the Father in my name, which is right, believing that ye shall receive, behold it shall be given unto you" (3 Ne. 18:20). Nephi said that "God will give liberally to him that asketh"

(2 Ne. 4:35). These are great promises, but they are promises often realized many times by those who prayed faithfully:

1. Enos experienced a forgiveness of sins and a powerful conversion to Christ as a result of "mighty prayer" (see Enos 1:1–12).

2. Nephi wrote: "And I, Nephi, did go into the mount oft, and I did pray oft unto the Lord; wherefore the Lord showed unto me great things" (1 Ne. 18:3). These great things included the directions to build a ship in addition to great spiritual manifestations.

3. Alma the Younger was converted because of the prayers of his father: "And again, the angel said: Behold, the Lord hath heard the prayers of his people, and also the prayers of his servant, Alma, who is thy father; for he has prayed with much faith concerning thee that thou mightest be brought to the knowledge of the truth; therefore, for this purpose have I come to convince thee of the power and authority of God, that the prayers of his servants might be answered according to their faith" (Mosiah 27:14).

4. After two days of fasting and prayer by the priests, Alma was revived from his dumb and motionless condition (see Mosiah 27:23).

5. Amulek warned the wicked people of Ammonihah "that if it were not for the prayers of the righteous, who are now in the land, that ye would even now be visited with utter destruction" (Alma 10:22).

6. Alma prayed earnestly for missionary success among the Zoramites: "Behold, O Lord, their souls are precious, and many of them are our brethren; therefore, give unto us, O Lord, power and wisdom that we may bring these, our brethren, again unto thee" (Alma 31:32). The Lord responded by blessing them with great success.

The Varieties of Prayer

Prayer is used not only as an expression of praise and gratitude (see 1 Ne. 16:32; Mosiah 2:20ff.; 24:22; Alma 45:1, 3 Ne. 4:31) but also for a variety of other purposes. The following is a sampling from the Book of Mormon:

Prayers for Understanding the Things of God

1 Ne 2:16—Nephi had "great desires to know of the mysteries of God, wherefore [he] did cry unto the Lord." The resultant revelations are well known.

1 Ne. 15:3, 7–8—Lehi spoke great things to Laman and Lemuel,

"which were hard to be understood, save a man should inquire of the Lord." When they complained, "We cannot understand the words which our father hath spoken," Nephi asked, "Have ye inquired of the Lord?"

Alma 5:46—Explaining how he received a testimony of the gospel, Alma declared, "Behold, I have fasted and prayed many days that I might know these things of myself."

3 Ne. 17:1–3—When Jesus perceived that the multitude was "weak" and could not understand all his words, he told them to return to their homes and "ponder upon the things which I have said, and ask of the Father, in my name, that ye may understand, and prepare your minds for the morrow, and I come unto you again."

Moro. 10:4–5—Moroni challenged people to read the Book of Mormon and then pray with a "sincere heart, with real intent, having faith in Christ, [and] he will manifest the truth of it unto you, by the power of the Holy Ghost. And by the power of the Holy Ghost ye may know the truth of all things."

Prayers for the Welfare of Others

2 Ne. 33:3—So great was Nephi's concern for his people that he said: "For I pray continually for them by day, and mine eyes water my pillow by night, because of them; and I cry unto my God in faith, and I know that he will hear my cry."

Enos 1:9—Enos writes that, following his conversion, "I began to feel a desire for the welfare of my brethren, the Nephites; wherefore, I did pour out my whole soul unto God for them."

Mosiah 27:14—Alma the Younger's miraculous conversion came as a consequence of his father's prayers. Alma the Elder had prayed with "much faith" that his son might "be brought to the knowledge of the truth."

Alma 8:10—"Alma labored much in the spirit, wrestling with God in mighty prayer, that he would pour out his Spirit upon the people who were in the city."

Prayers for Protection and Deliverance from Hardships

Mosiah 21:14—Limhi's people "did cry mightily to God . . . that he would deliver them out of their afflictions."

Alma 2:30—Alma prayed, saying: "O Lord, have mercy and spare my life, that I may be an instrument in thy hands to save and preserve this people."

Alma 31:30–35—Alma uttered these beautiful words as he labored with the Zoramites: "O Lord, wilt thou give me strength, that I may bear with mine infirmities. . . . O Lord, my heart is exceedingly sorrowful; wilt thou comfort my soul in Christ. O Lord, wilt thou grant unto me that I may have strength, that I may suffer with patience these afflictions which shall come upon me. . . ."

Prayers for Guidance in Difficult Problems

Mosiah 28:6—"And King Mosiah went and inquired of the Lord if he should let his sons go up among the Lamanites to preach the word."

Alma 17:9—The sons of Mosiah "fasted much and prayed much that the Lord would grant unto them a portion of his Spirit to go with them . . . that they might be an instrument in the hands of God to bring, if it were possible, . . . the Lamanites, to the knowledge of the truth."

Alma 28:6—After a tremendous battle in which many were killed, the scripture says: "And now surely this was a sorrowful day; yea, a time of solemnity, and a time of much fasting and prayer."

Alma 43:23—General Moroni sought military information through prayer. He sent certain men to Alma, asking him to "inquire of the Lord whither the armies of the Nephites should go to defend themselves against the Lamanites."

Alma 46:16—"Moroni prayed that the cause of the Christians, and the freedom of the land might be favored."

Hel. 11:4—Nephi (son of Helaman) was granted great powers by the Lord because of his unwearying service and because, the Lord said, "thou shalt not ask that which is contrary to my will" (Hel. 10:5). Nephi asked that the Lord send a famine "to stir [the people] up in remembrance of the Lord their God, and perhaps they will repent and turn unto thee."

Ether 1, 2, 3—The brother of Jared prayed that his people's language would not be confounded at the Tower of Babel, and that the Lord would guide him in building their barges and providing a source of interior lighting.

Prayers for Greater Virtue and Godliness

> Mor. 7:48—After expounding on the supremacy of charity, Mormon tells us to "pray unto the Father with all the energy of heart, that ye may be filled with this love, which he hath bestowed upon all who are true followers of his Son, Jesus Christ."
>
> 2 Ne. 4:31ff.—Nephi pleads for greater righteousness: "O Lord, wilt thou redeem my soul? . . . Wilt thou make me that I may shake at the appearance of sin? May the gates of hell be shut continually before me. . . . O Lord, wilt thou encircle me around in the robe of thy righteousness! . . . Wilt thou make my path straight before me!"
>
> 3 Ne. 19:23—Jesus prayed for oneness among his disciples.

How to Pray

The phrase "mighty prayer" is frequently used in the Book of Mormon. This seems to be perfect prayer, accompanied by great faith and effort. We will consider five ingredients of mighty prayer found in the Book of Mormon: faith, sincerity, perseverance, righteousness, and receptivity.

Faith

Nephi reminded his wayward brothers of the Lord's promise: "If ye will not harden your hearts, and ask me in faith, believing that ye shall receive, with diligence in keeping my commandments, surely these things shall be made known unto you" (1 Ne. 15:11). The Lord said to Enos: "Whatsoever thing ye shall ask in faith, believing that ye shall receive in the name of Christ, ye shall receive it" (Enos 1:15; see also v. 12). Jesus, during his Nephite ministry, and Moroni are among others who taught the same principle (see 3 Ne. 18:20; Morm. 9:21).

Sincerity

For good examples of sincerity (and persistence) consider the experiences of Enos (see Enos 1:1–16) and Nephi (see 3 Ne. 1:11–12). They both prayed all the day long. Notice the descriptive phrases used by Enos: "I will tell you of the wrestle which I had before God"; "my soul hungered"; "I cried unto him in mighty prayer and supplication for mine own soul"; "while I was thus struggling in the spirit"; "I prayed unto him with many long strugglings for my brethren, the Lamanites"; "after I had prayed and labored with all diligence, the Lord said unto me: I will grant unto thee according to thy desires, because of thy faith." These phrases breathe with earnestness and sincerity. Jesus' criticism of the prayers of the hypocrites—praying publicly to be seen of men and using "vain repetitions"—focused on their lack of sincerity (see 3 Ne. 13:5, 7). The prophet Moroni counseled that we pray "with a sincere heart, with real intent" (Moro. 10:4), and "with a firmness unshaken" (Morm. 9:28). His father, Mormon, used the phrase "with all the energy of heart" (Moro. 7:48) and in the same discourse used probably the most forceful words in scripture concerning sincerity: "And likewise also is it counted evil unto a man, if he shall pray and not with real intent of heart; yea, and it profiteth him nothing, for God receiveth none such" (Moro. 7:9).

Perseverance

The important quality of perseverance is taught throughout the Book of Mormon. Nephi told us to "pray always, and not faint; . . . ye must not perform any thing unto the Lord save in the first place ye shall pray unto the Father in the name of Christ, that he will consecrate thy performance unto thee, that thy performance may be for the welfare of thy soul" (2 Ne. 32:9). Amulek suggested that we pray in our houses "both morning, mid-day, and evening" (Alma 34:21), and when not praying audibly, "let your hearts be full, drawn out in prayer unto him continually for your welfare, and also for the welfare of those who are around you" (Alma 34:27). Jesus reiterated this concept when he told his disciples to cease praying vocally but that they "not cease to pray in their hearts" (3 Ne. 20:1). We hear echoes of the "Shema," Israel's ancient confession of faith, in Alma's counsel that his son Helaman live in constant communion with God:

> Yea, and cry unto God for all thy support; yea, let all thy doings be unto the Lord, and whithersoever thou goest let it be in the Lord; yea, let all thy thoughts be directed unto the Lord; yea, let the affections of thy heart be placed upon the Lord forever.
> Counsel with the Lord in all thy doings, and he will direct thee for good; yea, when thou liest down at night lie down unto the Lord, that he may watch over you in your sleep; and when

thou risest in the morning let thy heart be full of thanks unto God; and if ye do these things, ye shall be lifted up at the last day. (Alma 37:36–37.)

The Lord promised the brother of Jared, "There shall be none greater than the nation which I will raise up unto me of thy seed, upon all the face of the earth," because, the Lord said, "this long time ye have cried unto me" (Ether 1:43). After their long and arduous journey the Jaredites camped by the sea preparatory to their oceanic crossing. Maybe in the press of other concerns, the brother of Jared neglected his prayers. The Lord therefore came to him in a cloud, "and for the space of three hours did the Lord talk with the brother of Jared, and chastened him because he remembered not to call upon the name of the Lord. And the brother of Jared repented of the evil which he had done, and did call upon the name of the Lord." (Ether 2:14–15.) Without constant prayer, Jesus taught we are in danger of the devil's power (see 3 Ne. 18:15); that's undoubtedly why the devil tries mightily to keep men from prayer (see 2 Ne. 32:8–9).

Righteousness

This criterion has at least two dimensions: first, compassionate relations with our brothers. Amulek had these eloquent words on the idea:

> And now behold, my beloved brethren, I say unto you, do not suppose that this is all; for after ye have done all these things, if ye turn away the needy, and the naked, and visit not the sick and afflicted, and impart of your substance, if ye have, to those who stand in need—I say unto you, if ye do not any of these things, behold, your prayer is vain, and availeth you nothing, and ye are as hypocrites who do deny the faith.
>
> Therefore, if ye do not remember to be charitable, ye are as dross, which the refiners do cast out, [it being of no worth] and is trodden under foot of men. (Alma 34:28–29.)

Second, proper prayer must ask for righteous outcomes. Jesus taught that "whatsoever ye shall ask the Father in my name, which is right, believing that ye shall receive, behold it shall be given unto you" (3 Ne. 18:20). Here are Nephi's words on the subject: "God will give liberally to him that asketh. Yea, my God will give me, if I ask not amiss."

(2 Ne. 4:35.) One final statement, this by Moroni: he advised that we should "ask not, that ye may consume it on your lusts" (Morm. 9:28).

Based on the criteria we have discussed, it is interesting to compare the apostate prayer of the Zoramites with Alma's prayer, mentioned in the same chapter (see Alma 31). Whereas Alma's prayer contains most of the proper ingredients that we have mentioned, the prayer of the Zoramites was a (1) mechanical and memorized prayer, lacking sincerity. (2) It was infrequent, offered only once a week from their "holy stand" (Alma 31:21). (3) It was arrogant, since they repeatedly praised themselves as "a chosen and a holy people" (Alma 31:18). (4) There was no faith in Christ, since part of the prayer was a denial of the Savior (see Alma 31:16). (5) It falls under the category of "vain repetitions," since "every man did go forth and offer up these same prayers" (Alma 31:20).

Receptivity

With regard to prayer, receptivity means a willingness to receive whatever the Lord gives in answer to prayer. No righteous person will demand that the Lord conform to his will but will humbly acknowledge the superior wisdom of the Lord and ask that His will be done. Jacob's advice on this matter was profound: "Wherefore, brethren, seek not to counsel the Lord, but to take counsel from his hand. For behold, ye yourselves know that he counseleth in wisdom, and in justice, and in great mercy, over all his works." (Jacob 4:10.) Our Heavenly Father is eager to bless us with those things that are for our best good and not necessarily with those things we would request from our limited perspective. Jesus asked of the multitude gathered in Bountiful: "If ye then, being evil, know how to give good gifts unto your children, how much more shall your Father who is in heaven give good things to them that ask him?" (3 Ne. 14:11.)

Other components of righteous prayer mentioned in scripture are humility (see Mosiah 4:11; 21:14; Alma 13:28); fasting (see Alma 5:46; 17:9); and repeated mention of the Father as the one to whom we should address our prayers, an idea that Jesus personally expressed many times (see 3 Ne. 17:3; 18:19, 21, 23, 30; 20:31; 27:28; Moro. 2:2).[1]

The Book of Mormon teaches of God as a devoted Father who desires the well-being of his children above all else. We can petition him for any need; nothing is too trivial to take sincerely to our

Father. We must ask sincerely, not with hollow, repetitive words. Prayer must be unselfish and righteous; its highest expression is not acquisitiveness but cooperation with the divine will—"not my will, but thine, be done." (Luke 22:42). Prayer cannot be an occasional thing but needs to be a constant attitude of the heart. Nephi's advice to "pray always" (2 Ne. 32:9) and Alma's to "counsel with the Lord in all thy doings" (Alma 37:37), to "let all thy thoughts be directed unto the Lord," and to "let the affections of thy heart be placed upon the Lord forever" (Alma 37:36) speak not of an infrequent or distant relationship, but a relationship so intimate that one's daily walk is to live in the awareness of God's presence.

Prayer can be a mighty power, and some of our scriptural heroes were granted incredible power through the fervent use of prayer. The brother of Jared was allowed to see the Savior's spirit body (see Ether 3:13); Nephi was given great visions that were too marvelous for him to record (see 2 Ne. 4:23–25); so faithful was a later Nephi in giving unwearying service that the Lord promised to grant him anything that he asked: "All things shall be done unto thee according to thy word, for thou shalt not ask that which is contrary to my will" (Hel. 10:5). Like their exemplar, Jesus Christ, their will became "swallowed up in the will of the Father" (Mosiah 15:7), so that it became like food and drink to them to participate in his work (see John 4:34).

Service to God

As mentioned earlier, service is also an important expression of our love of God. Think of the many examples the Book of Mormon gives us: Nephi's constancy, Abinadi's death-defying courage, the incredible exertions of Alma and the sons of Mosiah, and the unwearying service of Nephi (son of Helaman). Who could match the devotion to duty exhibited by Mormon? In a poignant letter to his son he expressed his fear that the Nephites would be destroyed. "I am laboring with them continually," he wrote; "and when I speak the word of God with sharpness they tremble and anger against me; and when I use no sharpness they harden their hearts against it; wherefore, I fear lest the Spirit of the Lord hath ceased striving with them" (Moro. 9:4). So degenerate had they become that they had "lost their love, one towards another; and they thirst after blood and revenge continually" (Moro. 9:5). Why not give up on them? Why not flee for one's own safety? Not Mormon. His words to Moroni were: "My beloved son, notwithstanding their hardness, let us labor diligently; for if we should cease to labor, we should be brought under condemnation; for we have a labor to perform whilst in this tabernacle of clay, that we may conquer the enemy of all righteousness, and rest our souls in the kingdom of God" (Moro. 9:6).

This stringent concept of duty is not uncommon in the Book of Mormon. Read these impressive words of Jacob: "And we did magnify our office unto the Lord, taking upon us the responsibility, answering the sins of the people upon our own heads if we did not teach them the word of God with all diligence; wherefore, by laboring with our might their blood might not come upon our garments; otherwise their blood would come upon our garments, and we would not be found spotless at the last day" (Jacob 1:19).

King Benjamin did not deliver his final discourse simply for the benefit of his people, but also to completely fulfill his duty to God: "I at this time have caused that ye should assemble yourselves together, that I might be found blameless, and that your blood should not come upon me, when I shall stand to be judged of God of the things whereof he hath commanded me concerning you. I say unto you that I have caused that ye should assemble yourselves together that I might rid my garments of your blood, at this period of time when I am about to go down to my grave, that I might go down in peace." (Mosiah 2:27–28.)

These statements convey a most sobering thought: those called to God's service must discharge their responsibilities with the utmost diligence in order to maintain personal worthiness in his sight!

One of the most oft-quoted statements in the Book of Mormon is the following by King Benjamin: "When ye are in the service of your fellow beings ye are only in the service of your God" (Mosiah 2:17). As parents feel gratitude to anyone who assists their beloved children, so does God consider a service to any of his children a service to him—"Inasmuch as ye have done it unto one of the least of these my brethren, ye have done it unto me" (Matt. 25:40). In the next chapter we will more fully explore service to others as another way of expressing our love of God.

Chapter 17

THE SERVING CHRISTIAN

The purpose of the first principles of the gospel is to change the individual; the emphasis is on "me." Yet once a person is converted his attention turns toward serving; the emphasis is on "others." One way of looking at the Christian life is to see it as the accomplishment of two major goals: first, to get my own life in order so that, second, I might more effectively serve God and my fellowman. This chapter will focus on the second of those goals.

Retaining a Remission of Sins

Since "no unclean thing can dwell with God" (1 Ne. 10:21), and since the converted person has become clean of his past sins, he will naturally want to take a course in life that will secure for him a retention of this holy condition. King Benjamin declared that this requires that a person become involved in the service of others:

> And now, for the sake of . . . retaining a remission of your sins from day to day, that ye may walk guiltless before God—I would that ye should impart of your substance to the poor, every man according to that which he hath, such as feeding the hungry, clothing the naked, visiting the sick and administering to their relief, both spiritually and temporally, according to their wants.
>
> And see that all these things are done in wisdom and order; for it is not requisite that a man should run faster than he has strength. And again, it is expedient that he should be diligent, that thereby he might win the prize; therefore, all things must be done in order. (Mosiah 4:26–27.)

Concerning their relationship with God, King Benjamin also said to his people:

> I would that ye should remember, and always retain in remembrance, the greatness of God, and your own nothingness, and his goodness and long-suffering towards you, unworthy creatures, and humble yourselves even in the depths of humility, calling on the name of the Lord daily, and standing steadfastly in the faith of that which is to come, which was spoken by the mouth of the angel.
>
> And behold, I say unto you that if ye do this ye shall always rejoice, and be filled with the love of God, and always retain a remission of your sins. (Mosiah 4:11–12.)

If they would do these things, he promised, they would not only retain a remission of sins but also grow in the knowledge of the glory of God, "or in the knowledge of that which is just and true" (Mosiah 4:12).

Alma concurred with Benjamin on this topic. About eighty years before the birth of Christ, Alma saw that wickedness was growing among his people. He saw that there were some who turned "their backs upon the needy and the naked and those who were hungry, and those who were athirst, and those who were sick and afflicted: (Alma 4:12). He also saw that, by contrast, there were others who were "abasing themselves, succoring those who stood in need of their succor, such as imparting their substance to the poor and the needy, feeding the hungry, and suffering all manner of afflictions, for Christ's sake, who should come according to the spirit of prophecy; looking forward to that day, thus retaining a remission of their sins" (Alma 4:13–14).

Real service, spiritual and temporal, is the key, therefore, to retaining this blessed gift of holiness in the sight of God.

Love: The Indispensable Virtue

In chapter 15 we discussed love as the fundamental virtue of a Christian. Love not only produces social harmony among people but also generates a desire to be of service. Love is more than sentiment, it is action. I heartily agreed with the writer who said: "The desire to love is not itself love. Love is as love does. Love is an act of will— namely, both an intention and an action."[1] Jesus declared that one could recognize true and false prophets—and by extension, we might say, genuine Christians—by their "fruits" (see 3 Ne. 14:16–20). The unmistakable evidence of Christian living, therefore, is what one actually *does* about his beliefs.

Amulek taught that our prayers are "vain" if our lives are bereft of service: "If ye turn away the needy, and the naked, and visit not the sick and afflicted, and impart of your substance, if ye have, to those who stand in need—I say unto you, if ye do not any of these things, behold, your prayer is vain, and availeth you nothing" (Alma 34:28). Some of the best scriptural advice on service comes from old King Benjamin, who spent his days ruling justly and laboring with his hands for his own support. He told his people to remain "steadfastly in the faith" (Mosiah 4:11), to live peaceably and have no mind to injure one another, to "render to every man according to that which is his due" (Mosiah 4:13). He advised that they provide materially for and teach their children (see Mosiah 4:14–15) and "administer of [their] substance unto him that standeth in need" without asking if the petitioner is worthy (see Mosiah 4:16–19). "For behold, are we not all beggars?" he asks. (Mosiah 4:19.) If charity is withheld with the thought that the individual deserves what he is suffering, then one has "great cause to repent" and, if he does not repent, has "no interest in the kingdom of God" (Mosiah 4:18). Benjamin said he was speaking primarily to the rich, but adds that the poor must have a giving attitude or they too were guilty (see Mosiah 4:23–25). After teaching these principles, Benjamin appended a wise condition: "See that all these things are done in wisdom and order; for it is not requisite that a man should run faster than he has strength." Yet, it was "expedient that he should be diligent, that thereby he might win the prize." (Mosiah 4:27.) Overzealousness is not required, rather a consistent and reasonable caring.

A Zion Society

Loving treatment of our neighbors practiced on a large scale would transform society. This is indeed what happened as a result of Jesus' American ministry. All were sincerely converted to the Lord, and "there was no contention in the land, because of the love of God which did dwell in the hearts of the people" (4 Ne. 1:15). Some of the conditions that prevailed were: (1) complete social harmony—there were no "strifes, nor tumults," nor "disputations," and "every man did deal justly one with another" (4 Ne. 1:16, 2); (2) no crime—there were no "whoredoms, nor lyings, nor murders, nor any manner of lasciviousness," and "no robbers" (4 Ne. 1:16–17); (3) no class structure—there were no Nephites, "Lamanites, nor any manner of -ites; but they were in one, the children of Christ, and heirs to the kingdom of God" (4 Ne. 1:17); (4) economic cooperation and material prosperity—they rebuilt cities and prospered "exceedingly" (4 Ne. 1:7), and "had all things common among them; therefore there were not rich and poor, bond and free, but they were all made free, and partakers of the heavenly gift" (4 Ne. 1:3). The end result of these conditions was happiness. In fact, we are told that "there could not be a happier people among all the people who had been created by the hand of God" (4 Ne. 1:16).

These ideal conditions began to disintegrate when materialism returned as the primary goal of many (see 4 Ne. 1:24–26). Pride, contention, division, class status, and religious apostasy soon resulted.

Temporal Service

It is important to notice, in all the foregoing, the stress on temporal service, such as care for the poor and needy. To the true disciple there is no separation between his religious and economic affairs. Having "all things common," thus eliminating poor-rich distinctions, was a prominent feature of the Nephite Zion.

While the most conspicuous example of economic sharing was during the "golden age" of Nephite history that followed the ministry of Jesus, still there were a few times when the Nephite Church rose to similar heights of justice and generosity. Alma the Elder taught his little group of Church members in the wilderness to "impart of their substance" to those in need. Those blessed with more possessions were to "impart more abundantly"; those who had little were to give little; and those who had nothing would receive from others. (Mosiah 18:27.) "And thus they should impart of their substance of their own free will and good desires towards God, and to those priests that stood in need, yea, and to every needy, naked soul" (Mosiah 18:28). And thus "they did walk uprightly before God, imparting to one another both temporally and spiritually according to their needs and their wants" (Mosiah 18:29). In the early years of Alma the Younger's judgeship there was continued success among Church members in practicing a program of economic justice. The priests and teachers considered themselves equal with those to whom they ministered, and they all shared their material possessions. (See Alma 1:26–27.) "And thus, in their prosperous circumstances, they did not send away any who were naked, or that were hungry, or that were athirst, or that were sick, or that had not been nourished; and they did not set their hearts upon riches; therefore they were liberal to all, both old and young, both bond and free, both male and female, whether out of the church or in the church, having no respect to persons as to those who stood in need" (Alma 1:30).

Perhaps one of the clearest messages in the Book of Mormon is that riches nearly always lead to pride and evil. Nephite writers were fond of recording this repeating cycle of prosperity, wickedness, collapse, humility, righteousness, and return to prosperity (see examples in Hel. 12:1–2 and Alma 4:6–13). Numerous Book of Mormon passages show that almost always the possessions of the rich set them apart from the poor, whom they neglected and despised. This happened during the ministry of the prophet Jacob: "And the hand of providence hath smiled upon you most pleasingly, that you have obtained many riches; and because some of you have obtained more abundantly than that of your brethren ye are lifted up in the pride of your hearts, and wear stiff necks and high heads because of the costliness of your apparel, and persecute your brethren because ye suppose that ye are better than they" (Jacob 2:13).

Reminding them of God's displeasure, Jacob counseled his people to "think of your brethren like unto yourselves, and be familiar with all and free with your substance, that they may be rich like unto you" (Jacob 2:17). He then outlined a remarkable formula for obtaining wealth! "But before ye seek for riches," he said, "seek ye for the kingdom of God. And after ye have obtained a hope in Christ ye shall obtain riches, if ye seek them; and ye will seek them for the intent to do good—to clothe the naked, and to feed the hungry, and to liberate the captive, and administer relief to the sick and the afflicted." (Jacob 2:18–19.)

So, riches are not evil per se; if one seeks them for "the intent to do good" they can contribute to righteous living. This righteous use of wealth, we repeat, has always been exceptional behavior. President Brigham Young, a latter-day prophet who lived through several attempts of the Church to establish a gospel economic program, had these comments on the subject: "I observed then, and I now think, that it [the law of consecration] will be one of the last revelations which the people will receive into their hearts and understandings, of their own free will and choice, and esteem it as a pleasure, a privilege, and a blessing unto them to observe and keep most holy."[2]

Normally wealth is used for personal gratification, and the less fortunate are disregarded in the process. That is why we often read blanket statements against the rich as if they all fit into one category. Condemning a list of sins such as intellectual pride, lying, and murder, the prophet Jacob says this about the rich: "But wo unto the rich, who are rich as to the things of the world. For because they are rich they despise the poor, and they persecute the meek, and their hearts are upon their treasures; wherefore, their treasure is their god." (2 Ne. 9:30.)

Moroni predicted that materialism would be a problem in our day. After saying, "I speak unto you as if ye were present, and yet ye are not," he proceeded to condemn us for the "pride" of our hearts, the wearing of fine apparel, strife, malice, and persecution. "For behold," he warned, "ye do love money, and your substance, and your fine apparel, and the adorning of your churches, more than ye love the poor and the needy, the sick and the afflicted." (Morm. 8:35–37.) Because of these conditions, the "sword of vengeance" hangs over us (Morm. 8:41).

A disciple of Christ is, therefore, a socially conscious individual, aware of the injustices in society and aware of human suffering. Motivated by love he reaches out to ameliorate these conditions. "The Lord God hath given a commandment," writes Nephi, "that all men should have charity, which charity is love. And except they should have charity they were nothing. Wherefore, if they should have charity they would not suffer the laborer in Zion to perish. But the laborer in Zion shall labor for Zion; for if they labor for money they shall perish." (2 Ne. 26:30–31.)

Missionary Work: A Priority Service

Love seeks expression in service, and as one reads the Book of Mormon it becomes apparent that missionary work is one of the most significant ways to render service in the kingdom of God. People must hear and live the gospel of Christ to be saved, and God relies on his disciples to disseminate that saving message. Without missionaries the world would remain in darkness. Therefore, Jesus commanded the twelve Nephite disciples to "go forth unto this people, and declare the words which I have spoken, unto the ends of the earth" (3 Ne. 11:41). And he made it clear that rejecting his authorized representatives was equivalent to rejecting him (see 3 Ne. 28:34).

All the great personalities of the Book of Mormon were missionaries to some degree. The prophet Alma said that if he were an angel and could have the wish of his heart, he would "go forth and speak with the trump of God, with a voice to shake the earth, and cry repentance unto every people!" (Alma 29:1.) The first thought of the newly converted sons of Mosiah was to serve through missionary work. "They could not bear that any human soul should perish; yea, even the very thoughts that any soul should endure endless torment did cause them to quake and tremble" (Mosiah 28:3). This concern led them to sacrifice fourteen years of their lives among the ferocious Lamanites, enduring "all manner of afflictions" that they "might be the means of saving some soul" (Alma 26:30). What a contrast with the attitude of the Nephite majority, who said concerning the Lamanites: "Let us take up arms against them, that we destroy them and their iniquity out of the land, lest they overrun us and destroy us" (Alma 26:25). The caring Nephi, who prayed continually for his people by day and watered his pillow by night with his tears (see 2 Ne. 33:3), desired above all to bring people to Christ. His whole intent in writing was to "persuade" people to come to the Savior (see 1 Ne. 6:4).

Writing is an effective way to persuade people to come to Christ; after all, the major purpose for the production of the Book of Mormon was the "convincing of the Jew and Gentile that Jesus is the Christ, the Eternal God" (Title Page). Still, Nephi knew that the power of inspired speaking carried a much greater impact (see 2 Ne. 33:1). Alma knew this also. Chosen to be the first chief judge among the Nephites, he resigned that office to "go forth among his people . . . that he might preach the word of God unto them, to stir them up in remembrance of their duty, and that he might pull down, by the word of God, all the pride and craftiness and all the contentions which were among his people, seeing no way that he might reclaim them save it were in bearing down in pure testimony against them" (Alma 4:19).

Alma knew the power of the word. Making preparations for his mission to the apostate Zoramites, he knew the inspired preaching of God's word had the highest probability of turning them from evil: "And now, as the preaching of the word had a great tendency to lead the people to do that which was just—yea, it had had more powerful effect upon the minds of the people than the sword, or anything else, which had happened unto them—therefore Alma thought it was expedient that they should try the virtue of the word of God" (Alma 31:5).

Enos declared that during his ministry nothing could keep his people from destruction except "exceeding harshness, preaching and prophesying of wars, and contentions, and destructions, and continually reminding them of death, and the duration of eternity, and the judgments and the power of God, and all these things—stirring them up continually to keep them in the fear of the Lord. I say there was nothing short of these things, and exceedingly great plainness of speech, would keep them from going down speedily to destruction." (Enos 1:23.)

The Book of Alma: A Great Missionary Record

How can disciples of Christ be effective missionaries? The book of Alma particularly can help us with an answer to that question. This book tells of three great missions performed in the first century before Christ: (1) Alma and Amulek's "local" mission to Zarahemla and its environs, (2) the "foreign" mission of the sons of Mosiah to the Lamanites in the land of Nephi, and finally (3) the mission to the apostate Zoramites.

What Makes Successful Missionaries?

By studying the book of Alma let us try to ascertain the contributing factors that lead to missionary success.

First must come personal worthiness. At the conclusion of the marvelous mission of the sons of Mosiah, Ammon, speaking to his brothers and the others who accompanied them, uttered these words: "Yea, he that repenteth and exerciseth faith, and bringeth forth good works, and prayeth continually without ceasing—unto such it is given to know the mysteries of God; yea, unto such it shall be given to reveal things which never have been revealed; yea, and it shall be given unto such to bring thousands of souls to repentance, even as it has been given unto us to bring these our brethren to repentance" (Alma 26:22).

It appears that all the missionaries mentioned in the record of Alma were converted (several are mentioned in chapter 13 herein). Indeed, it was because of their conversion that they desired to bring others to "taste of the exceeding joy of which [they] did taste; that they might also be born of God, and be filled with the Holy Ghost" (Alma 36:24).

Describing Alma's reunion with the sons of Mosiah after their fourteen-year mission to the Lamanites, the record says that these sons of Mosiah "had given themselves to much prayer, and fasting; therefore they had the spirit of prophecy, and the spirit of revelation, and when they taught, they taught with power and authority of God" (Alma 17:3). Alma told the people of Zarahemla that he had "fasted and prayed many days" for his testimony. "And now I do know of myself," he testified, "that they are true: for the Lord God hath made them manifest unto me by his Holy Spirit." (Alma 5:46.)

A second key to successful missionary work is to know the word of God. The missionaries in the book of Alma were students of scripture. Mosiah's sons were described as men of "sound understanding and they had searched the scriptures diligently, that they might know the word of God" (Alma 17:2). In a modern revelation the Lord told the eager Hyrum Smith, "Seek not to declare my word, but first seek to obtain my word" by diligent study (see D&C 11:21–22). The missionaries in the book of Alma also used the scriptures in their preaching (see Alma 37:8–9).

A third important prerequisite for missionary work is a willingness to make sacrifices. The sons of Mosiah gave up important political careers. They labored among a dangerous people and even chose to split up when they came to Lamanite country (see Alma 17:13). The Lamanites were described as a "wild and a hardened and a ferocious people; a people who delighted in murdering the Nephites, and robbing and plundering them; and their hearts were set upon riches. . . . They were a very indolent people, many of whom did worship idols." (Alma 17:14–15.) They knew nothing about the gospel, nor did they have any conception of right and wrong (see Alma 18:5).

The missionaries hunted for food as they journeyed (see Alma 17:7), and "they had many afflictions; they did suffer much, both in body and in mind, such as hunger, thirst and fatigue, and also much labor in the spirit" (Alma 17:5). Aaron "and a certain number of his brethren" (Alma 21:13) were thrown into prison for a lengthy period and when finally released "were naked, and their skins were worn exceedingly because of being bound with strong cords. And they also had suffered hunger, thirst, and all kinds of afflictions; nevertheless they were patient in all their sufferings." (Alma 20:29.) Ammon was given a dangerous job of defending the king's flocks but was more than equal to the task and performed heroic deeds. The assurance that the Lord was with these missionaries buoyed them up and gave them courage. In a later reminiscence Ammon said, "Now when our hearts were depressed, and we were about to turn back, behold, the Lord comforted us, and said: Go amongst thy brethren, the Lamanites, and bear with patience thine afflictions, and I will give unto you success" (Alma 26:27). "We have suffered all manner of afflictions," Ammon also said, "and all this, that perhaps we might be the means of saving some soul; and we supposed that our joy would be full if perhaps we could be the means of saving some" (Alma 26:30).

Alma's labors in the city of Ammonihah brought him jeers, rejection, and reviling; he was spat upon and driven out of the city (see Alma 8:12–13). He departed, "being weighed down with sorrow, wading through much tribulation and anguish of soul" (Alma 8:14), when an angel appeared and told him to rejoice! "Blessed art thou, Alma; therefore, lift up thy head and rejoice, for thou hast great cause to rejoice; for thou hast been faithful in keeping the commandments of God from the time which thou receivedst thy first message from him" (Alma 8:15). How different is the divine perspective from the human! The Lord sympathizes with our hardships but expects us to be courageous in his service.

A fourth factor in successful missionary work, particularly in the case of the sons of Mosiah, was their friendly efforts to win the confidence of their investigators prior to preaching their message. Both Ammon and Aaron impressed the Lamanite kings by their humble attitudes and their willingness to serve. After his initial capture and during his interrogation, Ammon was asked if he desired to dwell in the land of the Lamanites. He answered in the affirmative and added "perhaps until the day I die (Alma 17:23). The king was pleased with Ammon and offered his daughter. Ammon said he would like to be the king's servant. He was given the hazardous job of defending the king's flocks. When the flocks were scattered and the other servants were expecting the king's vengeance, Ammon said within himself, "I will show forth my power . . . in restoring these flocks unto the king, that I may win the hearts of these my fellow-servants, that I may lead them to believe in my words" (Alma 17:29). And what power! His bravery and fighting ability were nothing short of miraculous. Others took the story of Ammon's heroics to the king while Ammon was attending to duties. Finally, in an interview with Ammon, King Lamoni had become so impressed that he was willing to believe anything Ammon said.

Later, through the efforts of Ammon and Aaron, the head king, Lamoni's father, was converted, and he issued a proclamation that the missionaries could go anywhere they wanted to preach without molestation. Thousands were converted; they laid down their weapons and "never did fall away" from the truth (see Alma 23:6–7). These were the "Anti-Nephi-Lehies," the most impressive mass conversion in Book of Mormon history.

A fifth key to successful missionary work is member participation. Church members were often involved in the missionary effort as recorded in the book of Alma. At one point the Saints gathered often to fast and pray "in behalf of the welfare of the souls of those who knew not God" (Alma 6:6).

A father's advice, like that given by Alma to his sons, is a sixth factor that can contribute to missionary success. Alma gave some wonderful advice to his son Shiblon, useful advice for all missionaries: (1) "I would that ye would be diligent and temperate in all things." (2) "See that ye are not lifted up unto pride; yea, see that ye do not boast in your own wisdom, nor of your much strength." (3) "Use boldness, but not overbearance." (4) "Bridle all your passions, that ye may be filled with love." (5) "Refrain from idleness." (6) "Do not pray as the Zoramites. . . . "Do not say: O God, I thank thee that we are better than our brethren; but rather say: O Lord, forgive my unworthiness, and remember my brethren in mercy—yea, acknowledge your unworthiness before God at all times." (Alma 38:10–14.)

One final thing might be said about missionary work. We have been discussing tremendously successful missions, but what of those millions of missionaries that have labored without success? Surely, we sometimes think, the Lord in his wisdom could devise a more effective way of bringing souls to his kingdom. Look at the outpouring of supernatural power preceding the coming of Christ to America, for example. After experiencing earthquakes, tempest, darkness, and voices coming from the darkness bearing testimony, the people were in a very receptive mood to receive the gospel! But instead of using such methods generally, God has resorted to the simple method of one individual teaching another. This technique is slow and often ineffective, depending much on the skill of the preacher and the readiness of the learner. How can God allow such an important thing as one's eternal salvation to depend on such a fallible method? Undoubtedly part of the answer is to preserve faith and freedom of choice. A powerful display of divine power not only would make the choice obvious (thus negating faith), but also would have a coercive effect upon the mind (minimizing free agency). Every missionary, frustrated at his own limitations, can identify with Alma's outcry: "O that I were an angel, and could have the wish of mine heart, that I might go forth and speak with the trump of God, with a voice to shake the earth, and cry repentance unto every people!" (Alma 29:1.) But, after reflection, Alma realized that he did "sin in [his] wish" and that he ought to be content with what the Lord had allotted him (Alma 29:3), because God gives to people only that amount of truth that they are ready for (see Alma 29:8). Therefore, Alma said, "why should I desire more than to perform the work to which I have been called?" (Alma 29:6.) We conclude that the traditional method of winning souls for the kingdom of God is indeed the best method, the divine way.

The Joy of Missionary Success

No one can read Ammon's and Alma's glowing mission reports without sensing the unequaled joy that comes to the faithful servants of the Lord. Ammon was so enthusiastic in talking to his brethren that Aaron "rebuked him, saying: Ammon, I fear that thy joy doth carry thee away unto boasting." Here was Ammon's reply:

I do not boast in my own strength, not in my own wisdom; but behold, my joy is full, yea, my heart is brim with joy, and I will rejoice in my God. . . .

Behold, how many thousands of our brethren has he loosed from the pains of hell; and they are brought to sing redeeming love, and this because of the power of his word which is in us, therefore have we not great reason to rejoice? . . .

Therefore, let us glory, yea, we will glory in the Lord; yea, we will rejoice, for our joy is full; yea, we will praise our God forever. Behold, who can glory too much in the Lord? Yea, who can say too much of his great power, and of his mercy, and of his long-suffering towards the children of men? Behold, I say unto you, I cannot say the smallest part which I feel. (Alma 26:10–11, 13, 16.)

What a reunion occurred when Ammon and his brethren met their old friend Alma! Ammon was so overcome with joy that he fell to the earth. "Behold," says the Book of Mormon writer, "this is joy which none receiveth save it be the truly penitent and humble seeker of happiness" (Alma 27:18). A little later in the record is this touching statement by Alma: "This is my glory, that perhaps I may be an instrument in the hands of God to bring some soul to repentance; and this is my joy. And behold, when I see many of my brethren truly penitent, and coming to the Lord their God, then is my soul filled with joy; then do I remember what the Lord has done for me, yea, even that he hath heard my prayer; yea, then do I remember his merciful arm which he extended towards me." (Alma 29:9–10.)

Surely this is what Lehi meant when he uttered those immortal words: "Men are, that they might have joy" (2 Ne. 2:25).

Family Service

To Latter-day Saints, no service is higher, no duty more paramount, than the rearing of a righteous family. The family is regarded as a divine institution, the cornerstone of civilization, the fundamental unit of a righteous society. These teachings, constantly emphasized by Church leaders, should help us see the need to search the prophets of ancient America for their counsel on this most important topic. Authors E. Douglas Clark and Robert S. Clark, in a 1991 publication entitled *Fathers and Sons in the Book of Mormon*, argue that the Nephite scripture is "structured around fathers and sons" and that the record's main compiler, Mormon, "ushers onto center stage a consecutive train of father-son pairs."[3] According to the Clarks, little is said about mothers in the Book of Mormon because the Nephites belonged to a patriarchal society where women are rarely mentioned, plus the fact that in the record gospel teaching on parenting is nearly always a part of the historical narrative, which deals exclusively with male leaders.[4] Despite this limitation, Mormon filled his record with wonderful advice on the role of parents. Perhaps he saw the modern disintegration of the family—couples living together without marriage, rampant promiscuity, a 50-percent divorce rate, single-parent families, working mothers seeking careers often at the expense of stable homes—and consequently sought to raise our awareness to this societal danger.

At the outset, we see that the Lord's commandments seek to protect children and the family institution. Because life is so precious in God's eyes, he restricts the use of the power of procreation to married couples so that children will be born into a nurturing family. To assure that the nurturing will not be disrupted, the Lord prohibits divorce to prevent the family's dissolution (see 3 Ne. 12:31–32). Jesus forbade not only adultery but also adulterous thinking—"Behold, I give unto you a commandment, that ye suffer none of these things [adulterous thoughts] to enter into your heart; for it is better that ye should deny yourselves of these things . . . than that ye should be cast into hell" (see 3 Ne. 12:27–30). Alma spoke frankly to his wayward son, Corianton, about abandoning his ministry and committing sexual sin with the harlot Isabel: "Know ye not, my son, that these things are an abomination in the sight of the Lord; yea, most abominable above all sins save it be the shedding of innocent blood or denying the Holy Ghost?" (Alma 39:5.)

In the early days of Nephite history the prophet Jacob spoke harshly against what he called the "grosser crimes" of his people. Because their scripture mentioned the "many wives and concubines" of David and Solomon, many Nephites were justifying their whoredoms and calling them biblically sanctioned practices (see Jacob 2:23–24). The Lord, through Jacob, declared such behavior (that is, unlawful cohabitation) abominable. He commanded each Nephite man to have only one wife and no concubines, "for I, the Lord God, delight in the chastity of women. And whoredoms are an abomination before me." (See Jacob 2:26–28.) If the practice of having multiple wives was ever allowed, added the Lord, he would give a specific commandment; otherwise monogamy was to be the rule (see Jacob 2:30).

Once children are born and the family unit secure, the major task of parents is to teach and guide their offspring in the ways of righteousness. We see many loving fathers within the pages of the Book of Mormon. Lehi taught his children from their youth (see 1 Ne.

2:9–14); and despite the insolence of his eldest sons, he persisted in his attempts to reform them. Having seen in his dream their refusal to partake of the fruit, he "did exhort them . . . with all the feeling of a tender parent, that they would hearken to his words, that perhaps the Lord would be merciful to them, and not cast them off" (1 Ne. 8:37). At the end of his life, after all the abuse he had taken, Lehi still promised his "first blessing" to Laman and Lemuel if they would hearken unto Nephi; otherwise the blessing would fall to Nephi (see 2 Ne. 1:28–29). "Awake, my sons," he pleaded; "put on the armor of righteousness. Shake off the chains with which ye are bound, and come forth out of obscurity, and arise from the dust." (2 Ne. 1:23.)

We learn that Jacob "often" taught his son Enos about eternal life and the joy of the Saints, teachings that later were the key element in his son's conversion. Perhaps Enos had not fully heeded his father's advice until that day in the forest when "the words which I had often heard my father speak . . . sunk deep into my heart." (See Enos 1:1–3.)

King Benjamin, another exemplary father, caused that his sons "should be taught in all the language of his fathers, that thereby they might become men of understanding; and that they might know concerning the prophecies" (Mosiah 1:2). He told them of the value of the scriptures and admonished them "to search them diligently, that ye may profit thereby; and I would that ye should keep the commandments of God, that ye may prosper in the land" (Mosiah 1:7). In his final discourse, King Benjamin summed up the responsibility of parents in these words: "And ye will not suffer your children that they go hungry, or naked; neither will ye suffer that they transgress the laws of God, and fight and quarrel one with another, and serve the devil, who is the master of sin. . . . But ye will teach them to walk in the ways of truth and soberness; ye will teach them to love one another, and to serve one another." (Mosiah 4:14–15.)

It was the fervent prayers of the elder Alma that sent the angel to turn his son, Alma, from his evil ways (see Mosiah 27:14). Alma's memory of his loving father undoubtedly acted as a model for his own parenting. Nowhere in the Book of Mormon do we hear such inspired advice as that from Alma the Younger to his three sons (see Alma 36–42). To his eldest son, Helaman, Alma recited his conversion in vivid detail and counseled him as the new custodian of the plates and as a spiritual leader of the people. "Preach unto them repentance, and faith on the Lord Jesus Christ; teach them to humble themselves and to be meek and lowly in heart. . . . Teach them to never be weary of good works, but to be meek and lowly in heart; for such shall find rest to their souls." (Alma 37:33–34.) With regard to

Helaman's personal life, Alma instructed: "O, remember, my son, and learn wisdom in thy youth; yea, learn in thy youth to keep the commandments of God. Yea, and cry unto God for all thy support; yea, let all thy doings be unto the Lord, and whithersoever thou goest let it be in the Lord; yea, let all thy thoughts be directed unto the Lord; yea, let the affections of thy heart be placed upon the Lord forever." (Alma 37:35–36.)

To Shiblon went commendation for his courage and patience in bearing ill treatment from the Zoramites: "I say unto you, my son, that I have had great joy in thee already, because of thy faithfulness and thy diligence, and thy patience . . . among the people of the Zoramites" (Alma 38:3). "As much as ye shall put your trust in God," he counseled, "even so much ye shall be delivered out of your trials, and your troubles, and your afflictions, and ye shall be lifted up at the last day" (Alma 38:5).

To Corianton, who had forsaken his mission and committed sexual sin, Alma spoke forcefully: "Ye cannot hide your crimes from God; and except ye repent they will stand as a testimony against you at the last day" (Alma 39:8). Possibly because of his sins, Corianton had questions about the justice of God in the punishment of the sinner (see Alma 42:1) and concerning the resurrection (see Alma 40:1). Alma patiently and profoundly explained these doctrines and then urged his son to repentance: "O my son, I desire that ye should deny the justice of God no more. Do not endeavor to excuse yourself in the least point because of your sins, by denying the justice of God." (Alma 42:30.) Alma's counsel to Corianton also included these words: "Do not suppose . . . that ye shall be restored from sin to happiness. Behold, I say unto you, wickedness never was happiness. . . . Therefore, my son, see that you are merciful unto your brethren; deal justly, judge righteously, and do good continually; and if ye do all these things then shall ye receive your reward; yea, ye shall have mercy restored unto you again." (Alma 41:10, 14.)

We could talk of noble sons. What a contrast greets Book of Mormon readers between the saintly Nephi and the rebellious Laman and Lemuel! The latter, always cantankerous, always negative, must have been a constant irritation to the family. Nephi, on the other hand, although he may have suppressed his anger at times (see 2 Ne. 4:28–29), sought only their "eternal welfare" (see 2 Ne. 1:24–25). Nephi always showed respect for his father and mother, even beginning his record with a tribute to his "goodly parents" (1 Ne. 1:1). His obedience must have been put to the test during their wilderness struggles. While many in their group thought of Lehi as a "visionary man" and at one time some of them sought to take his life, Nephi persisted in his filial loyalty. During the crisis brought on by Nephi's broken bow, food became scarce, and even Lehi "murmured" along with the others; but Nephi went ahead and made a new bow and then respectfully asked his father where he should go to hunt for food (see 1 Ne. 16:18–23). Rather than think his father a victim of hallucinations, he had profound respect for him as a prophet of God.

We must not forget Helaman's strippling warriors, for they are one of the only specifically mentioned examples in the Book of Mormon of mighty heroes being the result of motherly training. Their courage in battle, their righteousness, and their unwavering faith in God's protecting care were all attributed to the testimonies and training of their mothers (see Alma 56:47–48; 57:21).

There are many lessons to be gained from these Book of Mormon examples. We see over and over as the primary duty of parents the religious training of their children. The book shows us parents with confidence and patience, even when their offspring have strayed from the path of righteousness. Their counsel is always frank, helpful, and solidly grounded in gospel truth.

Conclusion

Love is the great commandment, and service is the evidence of love. Christians are admonished to show concern for temporal needs (primarily manifested in economic sharing), spiritual needs (manifested most importantly in the preaching of the gospel of Jesus Christ), and family needs (demonstrated in the proper training of our children). True service, however, will never have limits. Love will find expression in hundreds of different ways. Probably the one who said it best was the Prophet Joseph Smith: "A man filled with the love of God, is not content with blessing his family alone, but ranges through the whole world, anxious to bless the whole human race."[5]

Chapter 18

ON RESURRECTION, JUDGMENT, AND THE LIFE TO COME

I had my first experience with death as a young boy in southern Idaho. I was with my beloved grandfather in the barn and saw him topple from his milking stool. Unable to obtain any response from him, I ran to the house to herald the terrible news. In the ensuing days, Grandfather's absence left a sorrowful void in our family circle. I found myself wondering if I would ever see him again, if he was really still living.

Most of us have some kind of encounter with death that brings on similar questions and longings. One of the reasons for the enduring strength of Christianity is the hope it imparts that death was conquered by the resurrected Christ. The Book of Mormon testifies of a living Christ, a Christ who appeared to the Nephites and allowed each of them to touch his wounds that they might know of the reality of the Resurrection (see 3 Ne. 11:14–15). Death is not the end of human existence but a transition to another state of living.

Although it appears that the Nephite Church had less knowledge concerning the afterlife than the restored Church does, Book of Mormon prophets often spoke of the status of good and evil people in the afterlife. That future existence, they taught, can be a "state of never-ending happiness" in the presence of God (Mosiah 2:41; Alma 28:12) or a life of misery with the devil and his angels (see 2 Ne. 2:27–29). All depends on how one lives in mortality. "Therefore remember, O man," said Nephi, "for all thy doings thou shalt be brought into judgment. Wherefore, if ye have sought to do wickedly in the days of your probation, then ye are found unclean before the judgment-seat of God; and no unclean thing can dwell with God; wherefore, ye must be cast off forever." (1 Ne. 10:20–21.) Death can be "sweet" to the righteous (D&C 42:46; see also Alma 27:28); God's judgment can be "pleasing" (Moro. 10:34) or "dreadful" (3 Ne. 25:5) to those who come under his "all-searching eye" (2 Ne. 9:44).

The World of Spirits

The first stage of the afterlife begins at death. There was no death in the world when Adam and Eve were placed in the Garden of Eden; it was their transgression that introduced death—"Adam fell that men might be" (see 2 Ne. 2:22–25). The mortal condition was necessary for our earthly probation, thus "death hath passed upon all men, to fulfil the merciful plan of the great Creator" (2 Ne. 9:6). Death separates a person's eternal spirit from his temporary body and transfers him into a world of spirits. Alma the Younger describes the contrasting conditions that will be experienced by the righteous and the wicked in the spirit world:

> Therefore, there is a time appointed unto men that they shall rise from the dead; and there is a space between the time of death and the resurrection. . . .
>
> Now, concerning the state of the soul between death and the resurrection—Behold, it has been made known unto me by an angel, that the spirits of all men, as soon as they are departed from this mortal body, yea, the spirits of all men, whether they be good or evil, are taken home to that God who gave them life.
>
> And then shall it come to pass, that the spirits of those who are righteous are received into a state of happiness, which is called paradise, a state of rest, a state of peace, where they shall rest from all their troubles and from all care, and sorrow.
>
> And then shall it come to pass, that the spirits of the wicked, yea, who are evil—for behold, they have no part nor portion of the Spirit of the Lord; for behold, they chose evil works rather than good; therefore the spirit of the devil did enter into them, and take possession of their house—and these shall be cast out into outer darkness; there shall be weeping, and wailing, and gnashing of teeth, and this because of their own iniquity, being led captive by the will of the devil.
>
> Now this is the state of the souls of the wicked, yea, in darkness, and a state of awful, fearful looking for the fiery indignation of the wrath of God upon them; thus they remain in this state, as well as the righteous in paradise, until the time of their resurrection. (Alma 40:9, 11–14.)

The Torments of Hell

The enlightening passage quoted above from the book of Alma makes a clear distinction between the paradise of the righteous and the torment of the wicked. The Book of Mormon uses the term *hell* (see, for example, 2 Ne. 9:12) to describe this period of suffering for sinners. Various unpleasant phrases are used to describe the experience called hell. The water seen by Lehi in his dream was, Nephi tells us, "filthiness" and was a "representation of that awfull hell, which the angel said unto me was prepared for the wicked" (1 Ne. 15:27, 29). Nephi referred to the river of water as an "awful gulf, which separated the wicked from the tree of life, and also from the saints of God" (1 Ne. 15:28). King Benjamin, speaking the words that the angel had spoken to him, called hell "a state of misery and endless torment" (Mosiah 3:25). It is a "place of filthiness" (1 Ne. 15:34), a drink from the "dregs of a bitter cup" (Alma 40:26), an "endless night of darkness" (Alma 41:7), a time of "weeping, and wailing, and gnashing of teeth" (Alma 40:13). The terms *fire* and *brimstone* are used, but always symbolically; for example, the anguish of hell is "*like* an unquenchable fire" (Mosiah 2:38, emphasis added) or "*as* a lake of fire and brimstone" (Mosiah 3:27, emphasis added).

We learn that there will be no change in one's personality as one passes into the spirit world, "for that same spirit which doth possess your bodies at the time that ye go out of this life, that same spirit will have power to possess your body in that eternal world" (Alma 34:34). While the statement that "they who are filthy shall be filthy still" (2 Ne. 9:16; Morm. 9:14) refers to the post-resurrection life, undoubtedly the same principle will apply to the wicked in the spirit world.

We also learn that the torment of the damned is described as mental and emotional suffering. (Note, however, that some of the passages that follow are not always explicitly clear as to whether the context is the spirit world or the final judgment; no doubt the same kind of spiritual anguish characterizes "hell" in either circumstance.) King Benjamin's last discourse mentions the individual who "cometh out in open rebellion against God . . . and becometh an enemy to all righteousness." If the person does not repent, he warns, and "remaineth and dieth an enemy to God, the demands of divine justice do awaken his immortal soul to a lively sense of his own guilt, which doth cause him to shrink from the presence of the Lord, and doth fill his breast with guilt, and pain, and anguish, which is like an unquenchable fire, whose flame ascendeth up forever and ever." (Mosiah 2:37–38.) Later in the same sermon, Benjamin, delivering the words of the angel, tells us that the wicked will be "consigned to an awful view of their own guilt and abominations, which doth cause them to shrink from the presence of the Lord into a state of misery and endless torment, from whence they can no more return; therefore they have drunk damnation to their own souls" (Mosiah 3:25). Moroni spoke in similar language. To "those who do not believe in Christ," the judgment of God will fill them with a "consciousness of guilt." He continued: "When ye shall be brought to see your nakedness before God, and also the glory of God, and the holiness of Jesus Christ, it will kindle a flame of unquenchable fire upon you." (See Morm. 9:1–5.)

Some have experienced this tormented mental state in mortality, which in turn brought them to repentance. One such case was that of the lawyer Zeezrom. Fearing that Alma and Amulek were dead because of his iniquity, he experienced "great tribulations of his mind" and "began to be scorched with a burning heat" (Alma 15:3). Similarly, when the sinful Alma was visited by an angel he lapsed into a paralytic state for three days. Of his mental condition during this time, he states, "I did remember all my sins and iniquities, for which I was tormented with the pains of hell." He was "racked, even with the pains of a damned soul." (Alma 36:13, 16.)

Why this suffering? Is the purpose only punitive, or is it reformatory and healing? In the cases of Zeezrom and Alma, their painful recognition of sins was beneficial because it led to repentance. Could this be the purpose of suffering in the world of spirits? Given the teachings of traditional Christianity, this would be a most revolutionary concept of "hell." Instead of being a place of God's eternal punishment, it becomes a part of his redemptive work, a place where sinners sense deeply the consequences of their sins, turn from their evil ways, and receive some degree of glory as a result. This is, in fact, the Latter-day Saint teaching; and though the Book of Mormon may not fully explain these ideas, the essence of the concept is there. Elder Joseph Fielding Smith, who later became the tenth President of the Church, clarified these ideas in the following statement: "The wicked of the earth who do not repent in this life and who do not receive the gospel, shall be assigned to the telestial kingdom. . . . All of these, however, will be called upon to repent. They will have to suffer the torments of the damned until they do, and through that suffering they will be brought to repentance and to acknowledge Jesus Christ as their Redeemer and the Son of God."[1]

As to the duration of hell's torments, we can say that they come to an end when a sinner repents and turns to Christ (exceptions to this will be discussed below). When Alma threw himself on the mercy of Christ he could remember his sins no more (see Alma

36:19). He told his son Helaman that "there could be nothing so ex-quisite and so bitter as were my pains," and "on the other hand, there can be nothing so exquisite and sweet as was my joy" (Alma 36:21). On another occasion Alma spoke of his father and others who es-caped from King Noah and who when converted were "loosed from the bands of death, yea, and also the chains of hell" (Alma 5:10). We say this despite the fact that most Book of Mormon prophets seem to speak of hell as a permanent condition (see, for example, 2 Ne. 9:16; 28:24; Mosiah 2:38; 3:25; Alma 41:7). This issue was clarified in 1830 when the Lord revealed to the Church that scriptural phrases such as "eternal punishment" and "endless punishment" had reference to God's punishment, not unending suffering (see D&C 19:6–12).

The Second Death

The hell spoken of above is temporary and reformatory, but there may be some who still refuse to change and repent, or maybe cannot repent. This needs some explanation. Lehi eloquently spoke of mankind being "free to choose liberty and eternal life, through the great Mediator of all men, or to choose captivity and death, according to the captivity and power of the devil; for he seeketh that all men might be miserable like unto himself" (2 Ne. 2:27). Is that power of choice still present in the spirit world? It would appear from Book of Mormon teachings that a person (in the spirit world or in mortality) gradually loses free agency as the devil gains power in that person's life. Nephi informed us that the devil leads people "carefully down to hell" until he "grasps them with his awful chains, from whence there is no deliverance" (2 Ne. 28:21–22). Those who procrastinate their repentance until death, according to Amulek, will become sealed to the devil. "The Spirit of the Lord hath withdrawn from you, and hath no place in you, and the devil hath all power over you; and this is the final state of the wicked." (Alma 34:35.) These and other passages seem to teach that there is a point in evil living when an individual is so controlled by the devil that his ability to change direction is lost. Frightening thought! For these, hell is possibly a permanent condi-tion. Samuel the Lamanite speaks of a "second death": "But behold, the resurrection of Christ redeemeth mankind, yea, even all mankind, and bringeth them back into the presence of the Lord. . . . But whosoever repenteth not is hewn down and cast into the fire; and there cometh upon them again a spiritual death, yea, a second death, for they are cut off again as to things pertaining to righ-teousness." (Hel. 14:17–18; see also Alma 40:26.) These souls are apparently those designated as "sons of perdition," and are cut off from the influence of God to suffer a fate not fully revealed but unmistakably terrible (see D&C 76:31–38, 45–48).

The Resurrection of the Dead

The spirit world is an interim period "between death and the resurrection" (Alma 40:11). But "death and hell must deliver up their dead, . . . and the bodies and the spirits of men will be restored one to the other; and it is by the power of the resurrection of the Holy One of Israel" (2 Ne. 9:12). The prophet Abinadi taught, "If Christ had not risen from the dead, or have broken the bands of death . . . , there could have been no resurrection" (Mosiah 16:7; see also Mosiah 15:20; Alma 21:9). This glorious truth was known from the beginning of Nephite history. Lehi, the first among Nephite prophets, said that Christ "layeth down his life according to the flesh, and taketh it again by the power of the Spirit, that he may bring to pass the resurrection of the dead, being the first that should rise" (2 Ne. 2:8). Lehi's son Jacob saw clearly what our fate would be without the Atonement (and the attendant blessing of the resurrection): "The first judgment which came upon man [physical and spiritual death] must needs have remained to an endless duration. And if so, this flesh must have laid down to rot and to crumble to its mother earth, to rise no more." (2 Ne. 9:7.) If the resurrection was not a reality, our spirits would eventually become subject to the devil, "to be shut out from the presence of our God, and to remain with the father of lies, in misery, like unto himself" (2 Ne. 9:9). The resurrection, brought about by Christ's atonement, alone saves mankind from a horrible fate! That is why Jacob exults in his praise to God—"O how great the goodness of our God, who prepareth a way for our escape from the grasp of this awful monster; yea, that monster; yea, that monster, death and hell" (2 Ne. 9:10).

The Universality and Perfection of the Resurrection

Amulek explained that the resurrection will "come to all, both old and young, both bond and free, both male and female, both the wicked and the righteous; and even there shall not so much as a hair of their heads be lost; but every thing shall be restored to its perfect frame, as it is now" (Alma 11:44; see also vss. 41–43). The resurrected body will come forth in a perfected condition. All mortal deformities, infirmities, and maladies will be done away. The younger Alma declared: "The soul shall be restored to the body, and the body to the soul; yea, and every limb and joint shall be restored to its body; yea, even a hair of the head shall not be lost; but all things shall be restored to their proper and perfect frame" (Alma 40:23; see also Alma 41:2). The body is raised from mortality to immortality, from "corruption to incorruption" (Alma 41:4). Death will be no more, said Amulek; body and spirit are united, "never to be divided; thus the whole becoming spiritual and immortal, that they can no more see corruption" (Alma 11:45).

God's law of restoration, according to Alma, will bring to pass not only the resurrection of a perfect body but also an appropriate repayment of goodness or badness, happiness or misery. "Do not suppose," Alma counseled his son Corianton, "because it has been spoken concerning restoration, that ye shall be restored from sin to happiness. Behold, I say unto you, wickedness never was happiness." (Alma 41:10.) And further:

> It is requisite with the justice of God that men should be judged according to their works; and if their works were good in this life, and the desires of their hearts were good, that they should also, at the last day, be restored unto that which is good.
>
> And if their works are evil they shall be restored unto them for evil. Therefore, all things shall be restored to their proper order, every thing to its natural frame—mortality raised to immortality, corruption to incorruption—raised to endless happiness to inherit the kingdom of God, or to endless misery to inherit the kingdom of the devil, the one on one hand, the other on the other—
>
> The one raised to happiness according to his desires of happiness, or good according to his desires of good; and the other to evil according to his desires of evil. (Alma 41:3–5.)

The First and Second Resurrections

The Nephites believed in essentially two resurrections—one to salvation and one to damnation. The prophet Abinadi stated that all will stand before the judgment bar of God "to be judged of him according to their works whether they be good or whether they be evil—if they be good, to the resurrection of endless life and happiness; and if they be evil, to the resurrection of endless damnation, being delivered up to the devil, who hath subjected them, which is damnation" (Mosiah 16:10–11; see also 3 Ne. 26:3–5).

These two resurrections would not occur at the same time. Christ, of course, was the first who broke the bands of death (see Alma 40:2); after him there soon followed the resurrection of "many saints" who came from their graves and appeared to many (Hel. 14:25; 3 Ne. 23:9–10; compare Matt. 27:52–53). Samuel the Lamanite had predicted this miraculous happening, and the Nephites, who had neglected to include this prophecy in their records, were commanded by Christ to add the prophecy to their history (see 3 Ne. 23:9–14).

Those included in the first resurrection, according to Abinadi, will be (1) "the prophets, and all those that have believed in their words, or all those that have kept the commandments of God"; (2) those "that have died before Christ came, in their ignorance, not having salvation declared unto them"; and (3) "little children" (Mosiah 15:22, 24–25). It might also be mentioned that the Nephites also believed that the righteous who lived before Christ will be resurrected before the righteous who live after. Abinadi made some remarks on the subject (see Mosiah 15:21), as did Alma. The latter prophet explained that the first resurrection "meaneth the reuniting of the soul with the body, of those from the days of Adam down to the resurrection of Christ," and that "their resurrection cometh to pass before the resurrection of those who die after the resurrection of Christ" (Alma 40:18–19). He confessed his uncertainty as to the time the wicked would be resurrected (see Alma 40:19).

Those who would have "no part in the first resurrection," concluded Abinadi, were those "that rebel against him and die in their sins . . . , that have wilfully rebelled against God, that have known the commandments of God, and would not keep them" (Mosiah 15:26). These will come forth in the second resurrection, or the resurrection of the unjust.

The Final Judgment

The Lord uttered this warning in a modern revelation: "I revoke not the judgments which I shall pass, but woes shall go forth, weeping, wailing and gnashing of teeth, yea, to those who are found on my left hand" (D&C 19:5). God will bring us to judgment; we are accountable to him for our actions.

Judgment is a common theme of Book of Mormon prophets. Jacob felt impelled to awaken his people to the "awful reality of these things" (2 Ne. 9:47), and thus he gave them powerful admonitions such as this: "Prepare your souls for that glorious day when justice shall be administered unto the righteous, even the day of judgment, that ye may not shrink with awful fear; that ye may not remember your awful guilt in perfectness, and be constrained to exclaim: Holy, holy are thy judgments, O Lord God Almighty—but I know my guilt; I transgressed thy law, and my transgressions are mine; and the devil hath obtained me, that I am a prey to his awful misery" (2 Ne. 9:36).

Alma challenged Church members in Zarahemla with these piercing questions: "Can ye imagine yourselves brought before the tribunal of God with your souls filled with guilt and remorse, having a remembrance of all your guilt. . . ? I say unto you, can ye look up to God at that day with a pure heart and clean hands? . . . And now I ask of you, my brethren, how will any of you feel, if ye shall stand before the bar of God, having your garments stained with blood and all manner of filthiness? Behold, what will these things testify against you?" (Alma 5:18, 19, 22.)

Is it not significant that the prophets Jacob, Nephi, Enos, and Moroni all concluded their writings with warnings of the Judgment? And Mormon, the principal writer of the Book of Mormon, declared it to be a major motive for his writing: "Therefore I write unto you all. And for this cause I write unto you, that ye may know that ye must all stand before the judgment-seat of Christ, yea, every soul who belongs to the whole human family." (Morm. 3:20.) After including the allegory of Zenos in his record, Jacob speaks of the importance of not rejecting the God of heaven, then testifies of the coming judgment:

> Behold, will ye reject these words? Will ye reject the words of the prophets; and will ye reject all the words which have been spoken concerning Christ. . . ?
>
> Know ye not that if ye will do these things, that the power of the redemption and the resurrection, which is in Christ, will bring you to stand with shame and awful guilt before the bar of God?
>
> And . . . ye must go away into that lake of fire and brimstone.
> . . .
> O be wise; what can I say more?
>
> Finally, I bid you farewell, until I shall meet you before the pleasing bar of God, which bar striketh the wicked with awful dread and fear. Amen. (Jacob 6:8–10, 12–13.)

Moroni's final words strike a similar chord: "And now I bid unto all, farewell. I soon go to rest in the paradise of God, until my spirit and body shall again reunite, and I am brought forth triumphant through the air, to meet you before the pleasing bar of the great Jehovah, the Eternal Judge of both quick and dead. Amen." (Moro. 10:34.)

Notice that both these prophets referred to the "pleasing bar" of God. Enos was one who anticipated the time of his accounting with pleasure: "And I rejoice in the day when my mortal shall put on immortality, and shall stand before him [the Redeemer]; then shall I see his face with pleasure, and he will say unto me: Come unto me, ye blessed, there is a place prepared for you in the mansions of my Father. Amen." (Enos 1:27.) On the other hand, as Jacob pointed out in the passage quoted above, the judgment bar "striketh the wicked with awful dread and fear" (Jacob 6:13). We are told that the mental state of the wicked in the spirit world will be an "awful, fearful looking for the fiery indignation of the wrath of God upon them" (Alma 40:14).

How We Will Be Judged

Above all, the scriptures assure us that the Judgment will be fair. There will be no judicial appeals, because, in Alma's words, "when all men shall stand to be judged of him, then shall they confess that he is God; then shall they confess, who live without God in the world, that the judgment of an everlasting punishment is just upon them" (Mosiah 27:31). Abinadi taught that eventually "every nation, kindred, tongue, and people shall see eye to eye and shall confess before God that his judgments are just" (Mosiah 16:1).

Perhaps the greatest sermon on God's justice was delivered by the younger Alma to his son Corianton. Corianton had committed serious transgressions, was worried about his future, and thought it unjust that God would punish the sinner. Alma's great sermon is discussed in the chapter on the Atonement (chapter 12). Let it suffice here to mention Alma's explanation that rewards or punishments will be commensurate with what we have given others, a concept he calls "restoration." "The meaning of the word restoration is to bring back again evil for evil, or carnal for carnal, or devilish for devilish— good for that which is good; righteous for that which is righteous. . . . For that which ye do send out shall return unto you again, and be restored." (Alma 41:13, 15; see also Hel. 14:31.) God, Alma concludes, is bound to be just, or he would "cease to be God" (Alma 42:25). God's mercy cannot "rob justice" (Alma 42:25). In the last days the devil will encourage people to sin by exaggerating God's mercy and leniency, virtually denying divine punishment (see 2 Ne. 28:7–8, 22). While the devil and his spokesmen would minimize the seriousness of sin, the prophets warn us that God "cannot look upon sin with the least degree of allowance" (Alma 45:16), and that "no unclean thing can inherit the kingdom of heaven" (Alma 11:37).

Next, we are certain that the Judgment will be comprehensive. All our thoughts and actions, thoroughly recorded in earthly and heavenly records, will be available at Judgment Day, as will the scriptural records, by which we will also be judged—"for out of the books which shall be written I will judge the world," says the Lord (2 Ne. 29:11; see also 3 Ne. 27:23–26). The wicked Zeezrom learned something about the exactness of the Judgment as he listened to Alma and Amulek. If we harden our hearts against the word of God, said Alma, "then will our state be awful, for then we shall be condemned. For our words will condemn us, yea, all our works will condemn us; we shall not be found spotless; and our thoughts will also condemn us; and in this awful state we shall not dare to look up to our God." (Alma 12:13–14.) Even the "desires of [our] hearts" (Alma 41:3) will be considered. If one "has desired to do evil all the day long," taught Alma, "even so shall he have his reward of evil when the night cometh" (Alma 41:5; see also 42:28).

The Judgment will take account of how faithfully we have fulfilled our responsibilities in the kingdom of God. One reason King Benjamin went to such lengths to deliver a final discourse to his subjects was to make certain that he had done all within his power to discharge his duty to God. "I at this time have caused that ye should assemble yourselves together," he explained, "that I might be found blameless, and that your blood should not come upon me, when I shall stand to be judged of God of the things whereof he hath commanded me concerning you" (Mosiah 2:27). Jacob and Mormon made similar statements about the necessity of giving one's best to free oneself of guilt (see Jacob 1:19 and Moro. 9:6).

I remember once feeling very uneasy while listening to Elder Bruce R. McConkie speak of the strictness and thoroughness of the Judgment. Just when my uneasiness was about to become despair, he ended with these encouraging remarks:

> You could take the expressions that I've made and say they're a little severe, or they're harsh or difficult, and hence, it's hard to gain eternal salvation. . . .
>
> We don't need to get a complex or get a feeling that you have to be perfect to be saved. You don't. . . . What you have to do is stay in the mainstream of the Church and live as upright and de-

cent people live in the Church—keeping the commandments, paying your tithing, serving in the organizations of the Church, loving the Lord, staying on the straight and narrow path. If you're on that path when death comes—because this is the time and the day appointed, this the probationary estate—you'll never fall off from it, and, for all practical purposes, your calling and election is made sure.[2]

As we come to the end of our study of the Book of Mormon, it must be mentioned that another aspect of the Judgment is our accountability for living what truth God has revealed to us. Joseph Smith put it simply: "God judges men according to the use they make of the light which He gives them."[3] The prophet Jacob taught the same truth: "Where there is no law given there is no punishment; and where there is no punishment there is no condemnation. . . . The atonement satisfieth the demands of his justice upon all those who have not the law given to them. . . . But wo unto him that has the law given, yea, that has all the commandments of God, like unto us, and that transgresseth them, and that wasteth the days of his probation, for awful is his state!" (2 Ne. 9:25–27.)

This book, *A Testament for Our Times,* is another reminder that God has given to the modern world a magnificent new revelation of his will—the Book of Mormon, Another Testament of Jesus Christ. The great prophet-writers of the Book of Mormon testify that "the nations who shall possess them [the Nephite records] shall be judged of them according to the words which are written" (2 Ne. 25:22). Those who accept the Book of Mormon and "work righteousness" are promised "a crown of eternal life," while those "who harden their hearts in unbelief, and reject it, it shall turn to their own condemnation" (D&C 20:14–15).

In conclusion, I add my own testimony to those of the ancients. Through this study I have come to know more certainly than ever before that the Book of Mormon is divine in its origin and profoundly inspired in its contents. It is my hope that President Ezra Taft Benson's vision of the book's future impact will be a reality:

> I have a vision of homes alerted, of classes alive, and of pulpits aflame with the spirit of Book of Mormon messages.
> I have a vision of home teachers and visiting teachers, ward and branch officers, and stake mission leaders counseling our people out of the most correct of any book on earth—the Book of Mormon.
> I have a vision of artists putting into film, drama, literature,

music, and paintings great themes and great characters from the Book of Mormon.

I have a vision of thousands of missionaries going into the mission field with hundreds of passages memorized from the Book of Mormon so that they might feed the needs of a spiritually famished world.

I have a vision of the whole Church getting nearer to God by abiding by the precepts of the Book of Mormon.

Indeed, I have a vision of flooding the earth with the Book of Mormon.[4]

NOTES

Preface

1. Joseph Smith, *Teachings of the Prophet Joseph Smith,* sel. Joseph Fielding Smith (Salt Lake City: Deseret Book Co., 1976), p. 194.

2. Bruce R. McConkie, *Doctrines of the Restoration: Sermons and Writings of Bruce R. McConkie,* ed. and arr. Mark L. McConkie (Salt Lake City: Bookcraft, 1989), p. 267.

3. Grant Underwood, "Book of Mormon Usage in Early LDS Theology," *Dialogue: A Journal of Mormon Thought* 17 (Autumn 1984): 53.

4. Gordon B. Hinckley, "'An Angel from on High, the Long, Long Silence Broke,'" *Ensign* 9 (November 1979): 8.

5. Joseph Smith, *History of the Church* 1:252–53.

6. This argument is convincingly presented in the article "How Long Did It Take to Translate the Book of Mormon?" in *Reexploring the Book of Mormon: The F.A.R.M.S. Updates,* ed. John W. Welch (Salt Lake City: Deseret Book Co., and Foundation for Ancient Research and Mormon Studies, 1992), pp. 1–8.

Chapter 1. The Mission of the Book of Mormon to a World in Religious Decline

1. Ezra Taft Benson, "Flooding the Earth with the Book of Mormon," *Ensign* 18 (November 1988): 6.

2. Ezra Taft Benson, "Jesus Christ—Gifts and Expectations," *Ensign* 18 (December 1988): 4.

3. See Benson, "Flooding the Earth," p. 5.

4. There are four major writers of the Book of Mormon as we have it: (1) Nephi, who wrote 1 and 2 Nephi; (2) Jacob, who wrote the book of Jacob; (3) Mormon, who wrote the Words of Mormon and abridged

the record from Mosiah through Mormon, chapter 7; and (4) Moroni, who wrote Mormon, chapters 8 and 9, abridged the Jaredite record entitled the book of Ether, and then finished with the book of Moroni. Of course, these four occasionally quoted others, sometimes at great length (e.g., Nephi quotes Lehi, Isaiah, and Jacob; Moroni quotes Mormon; etc.). The other Book of Mormon writers who penned the books of Enos, Jarom, and Omni wrote only a small portion of the record compared to the four major writers mentioned above.

5. Harvey Cox, *The Secular City* (New York: Macmillan Co., 1965), pp. 2, 3.

6. Robin Keeley, *The Quiet Revolution* (Grand Rapids, Mich.: Eerdmans, 1985), p. 26.

7. W. T. Stace, *Religion and the Modern Mind* (New York: J. B. Lippincott Co., 1952), p. 91.

8. Stace, *Religion and the Modern Mind,* p. 90.

9. Allan Bloom, *The Closing of the American Mind* (New York: Simon and Schuster, 1987), pp. 25–26.

10. Rudolf Bultmann, *Jesus and the Word,* trans. Louise Pettibone Smith and Erminie Huntress Lantero (New York: Charles Scribner's Sons, 1958), p. 8.

11. Jeffery L. Sheler, "What Did Jesus Really Say?" *U.S. News & World Report,* 1 July 1991, p. 57.

12. See Sheler, "What Did Jesus Really Say?" pp. 57–58.

13. See William Hordern, *A Layman's Guide to Protestant Theology,* rev. ed. (New York: Macmillan Co., 1968), pp. 44–46.

14. See Hordern, *A Layman's Guide,* p. 74.

15. William R. Hutchison, "Protestant Modernism," in *Eerdmans' Handbook to Christianity in America* (Grand Rapids, Mich.: Eerdmans, 1983), pp. 383–84.

16. Ezra Taft Benson, "The Book of Mormon—Keystone of Our Religion," *Ensign* 16 (November 1986): 7.

17. Ezra Taft Benson, "The Book of Mormon Is the Word of God," *Ensign* 18 (January 1988): 3–5.

Chapter 2. The Book of Mormon and the Restoration of the Gospel

1. Rollo May, *Man's Search for Himself* (New York: W. W. Norton and Co., 1953), p. vii.

2. Viktor E. Frankl, *Man's Search for Meaning* (Boston: Beacon Press, 1962), p. 99.

3. Harold Kushner, *When All You've Ever Wanted Isn't Enough* (New York: Simon and Schuster, 1986), pp. 18–19.

4. Bruce R. McConkie, *Mormon Doctrine*, 2d ed. (Salt Lake City: Bookcraft, 1966), p. 576.

5. *Lectures on Faith* 1:10.

Chapter 3. Counsel for a Time of War and Political Turmoil

1. The description of the objectives and methods of secret combinations that follows in the text is based on material presented in Hugh Nibley, *Since Cumorah*, vol. 7 of *The Collected Works of Hugh Nibley* (Salt Lake City: Deseret Book Co., and Foundation for Ancient Research and Mormon Studies, 1988), pp. 370–71.

2. See Nibley, *Since Cumorah*, pp. 371–72.

Chapter 4. Guidance for a Day of Demonic Power

1. A survey among Catholics, for example, showed that "while 70 percent of Roman Catholics believe in life after death, only a third believe in hell." "For many," says the Reverend James Breig, "hell is sort of a whimsical place, more of a joke than an eschatological reality. It is a fictional domain, created from one part Dante and one part Milton with a dash of religious art thrown in." ("Pastor Says Hell Losing Its Oomph," *Deseret News*, 19 October 1977.) In an article entitled "Hell Hath Little Fury These Days," Alan Bernstein, a professor of medieval history at the University of Arizona, says, "Hell today is enveloped in silence." Donald Bloesch, a United Church of Christ minister, says, "The doctrine of hell has passed out of conversation and preaching, even in conservative evangelical churches." (Derk Kinnane Roelofsma, "Hell Hath Little Fury These Days," *Insight*, 29 December 1986–5 January 1987, p. 48.)

2. See Stephen E. Robinson's helpful article on this topic: "Early Christianity and 1 Nephi 13–14," in *The Book of Mormon: First Nephi, The Doctrinal Foundation*, ed. Monte S. Nyman and Charles D. Tate, Jr. (Provo, Utah: Religious Studies Center, Brigham Young University, 1988), pp. 177–91.

3. Joseph Smith, *Teachings of the Prophet Joseph Smith*, sel. Joseph Fielding Smith (Salt Lake City: Deseret Book Co., 1976), p. 181.

4. See D&C 50, 129; and *History of the Church* 4:571–81.

Chapter 5. The God of Nations

1. Joe David Brown, *Can Christianity Survive?* (New York: Time-Life Books, 1968), p. 17.

2. Brown, *Can Christianity Survive?* p. 26.

3. See "The Father and the Son: A Doctrinal Exposition by the First Presidency and the Twelve," 30 June 1916, cited in James E. Talmage, *The Articles of Faith* (Salt Lake City: Deseret Book Co., 1975), pp. 466–73.

4. See B. H. Roberts, "Relation of Inspiration and Revelation to Church Government," *Improvement Era* 8 (March 1905): 360–64; John Taylor, in *Journal of Discourses* 25:263–64; George Q. Cannon, *Gospel Truth,* comp. Jerreld L. Newquist, 2 vols. in 1 (Salt Lake City: Deseret Book Co., 1987), pp. 242–43; and First Presidency statement, 15 February 1978, reproduced in Spencer J. Palmer, *The Expanding Church* (Salt Lake City: Deseret Book Co., 1978), p. v.

5. For an extended analysis of Zenos's allegory, see Joseph Fielding McConkie, Robert L. Millet, and Brent L. Top (volume 4), *Doctrinal Commentary on the Book of Mormon,* 4 vols. (Salt Lake City: Bookcraft, 1987–92), 2:46–78. See also Wilford M. Hess, "Botanical Comparisons in the Allegory of the Olive Tree," in *The Book of Mormon: Jacob Through Words of Mormon, To Learn with Joy,* ed. Monte S. Nyman and Charles D. Tate, Jr. (Provo, Utah: Religious Studies Center, Brigham Young University, 1990), pp. 87–102.

Chapter 6. Jesus Christ, the Heart of the Book of Mormon

1. Richard N. Ostling, "Who Was Jesus?" *Time,* 15 August 1988, p. 37.

2. Ostling, "Who Was Jesus?" pp. 37–38.

3. Information cited in Robert J. Matthews, "What the Book of Mormon Tells Us About Jesus Christ," in *The Book of Mormon: The Keystone Scripture,* ed. Paul R. Cheesman (Provo, Utah: Religious Studies Center, Brigham Young University, 1988), p. 33.

4. Susan Easton Black, *Finding Christ Through the Book of Mormon* (Salt Lake City: Deseret Book Co., 1987), p. 16.

5. Black, *Finding Christ,* p. 5.

6. There is disagreement over the exact time of Jesus' coming to America. Was it "soon after [his] ascension" in Jerusalem—that is, a matter of a few days or weeks? (See 3 Ne. 10:18; 11:1–2.) Or was it "in the ending of the thirty and fourth year"? (3 Ne. 10:18.) The first option is preferred in Joseph Fielding Smith, *Answers to Gospel Ques-*

tions, comp. and ed. Joseph Fielding Smith, Jr., 5 vols. (Salt Lake City: Deseret Book Co., 1957–66), 4:25–29.

7. Extended analysis of the Sermon at the Temple is also thought unnecessary here because the intent of this volume is to investigate those teachings that are peculiar to the Book of Mormon. For this same reason, this work does not contain a thorough consideration of the Isaiah passages found in the Book of Mormon (this, plus the fact that there are already several scholarly works on the Book of Mormon that address this topic).

8. See *The Interpreter's Bible,* ed. George Arthur Buttrick (New York: Abingdon Press, 1951), 7:295.

9. See John W. Welch, "Ten Testimonies of Jesus Christ from the Book of Mormon," in *Doctrines of the Book of Mormon: The 1991 Sperry Symposium,* ed. Bruce A. Van Orden and Brent L. Top (Salt Lake City: Deseret Book Co., 1992), pp. 223–25.

Chapter 7. How God Works Through Angels, Prophets, and the Priesthood

1. From "The Westminster Confession of Faith (1646)," chapter 1, article 6, cited in *Creeds of the Churches: A Reader in Christian Doctrine from the Bible to the Present,* ed. John H. Leith (Garden City, N.Y.: Anchor Books, 1963), p. 195.

2. James Cardinal Gibbons, *The Faith of Our Fathers* (New York: P. J. Kennedy & Sons, 1917), pp. 99, 101.

3. This categorization of the different types of angels comes from Monte S. Nyman, "'Confirmed to Others by the Ministering of Angels,'" in *Book of Mormon, CES Symposium Book* (August 1986), pp. 104–5.

4. Joseph Smith, *Teachings of the Prophet Joseph Smith,* sel. Joseph Fielding Smith (Salt Lake City: Deseret Book Co., 1976), p. 170.

5. See Joseph Fielding Smith, *Doctrines of Salvation,* comp. Bruce R. McConkie, 3 vols. (Salt Lake City: Bookcraft, 1954–56), 3:87, and Joseph Fielding Smith, *Answers to Gospel Questions,* comp. and ed. Joseph Fielding Smith, Jr., 5 vols. (Salt Lake City: Deseret Book Co., 1957–66), 1:123–26.

Chapter 9. The House of Israel: Tragedy and Destiny

1. These words do not appear in our biblical Isaiah (comp. Isa. 49:1 and 1 Ne. 21:1).

2. A widely accepted theory of Book of Mormon geography

places the Nephites and Lamanites in a limited area in Central America. If this is accurate, it is likely that the majority of descendants of Lehi would still live in the area. (See John L. Sorenson, *An Ancient American Setting for the Book of Mormon* [Salt Lake City: Deseret Book Co., and Foundation for Ancient Research and Mormon Studies, 1985], pp. 1–48.)

    3. See Bruce R. McConkie, *The Millennial Messiah* (Salt Lake City: Deseret Book Co., 1982), pp. 241–42, 248.

    4. See McConkie, *Millennial Messiah*, p. 320.

Chapter 10. The Gentiles in the Promised Land

    1. Historically the most common use of the term *Gentile* has been to designate anyone who is not an Israelite. When used prophetically in the Book of Mormon, the term is usually meant to designate the modern Christian nations occupying Europe, the United States, and Canada. (See 1 Ne. 13:12–19; Bruce R. McConkie, *Mormon Doctrine*, 2d ed. [Salt Lake City: Bookcraft, 1966], pp. 310–11; Monte S. Nyman, *An Ensign to All People* [Salt Lake City: Deseret Book Co., 1987], p. 49–50.)

Chapter 11. The Fortunate Fall

    1. Bruce R. McConkie, *Mormon Doctrine*, 2d ed. (Salt Lake City: Bookcraft, 1966), p. 491.

    2. McConkie, *Mormon Doctrine*, pp. 756–57.

    3. Erastus Snow, in *Journal of Discourses* 26:217.

    4. See David O. McKay, in Conference Report, October 1967, p. 8.

    5. M. Scott Peck, *The Road Less Traveled* (New York: Simon and Schuster, 1978), pp. 16–17.

Chapter 12. The Atonement: The Savior's Crowning Work

    1. Bruce R. McConkie, *Mormon Doctrine*, 2d ed. (Salt Lake City: Bookcraft, 1966), p. 60.

Chapter 13. The Concept of Conversion in the Book of Mormon

    1. The four phases of the conversion experience were suggested

to me in a significant study by James Harris entitled *Patterns of Conversion in the Book of Mormon* (Provo, Utah: Brigham Young University Press, 1968).

2. Bruce R. McConkie, "What Does It Mean to Be Born Again?" *New Era* 1 (August 1971): 36.

Chapter 14. The First Principles: God's Way of Conversion

1. *Lectures on Faith* 1:10.

2. See James E. Talmage, *The Articles of Faith* (Salt Lake City: Deseret Book Co., 1975), pp. 96–97.

3. B. H. Roberts, *The Gospel and Man's Relationship to Deity* (Salt Lake City: Deseret Book Co., 1965), p. 170.

Chapter 15. The Virtuous Christian

1. "TV Disturbing the National Psyche," *Salt Lake Tribune*, 25 February 1992, pp. A1–A2.

2. David Whitman, "The War over 'Family Values,'" *U.S. News & World Report*, 8 June 1992, p. 36.

3. Nicols Fox, "What Are Our Real Values?" *Newsweek*, 13 February 1989, p. 8.

4. Ezra Taft Benson, "Beware of Pride," *Ensign* 19 (May 1989): 4.

5. Benson, "Beware of Pride," p. 6.

6. Bruce R. McConkie, *Mormon Doctrine*, 2d ed. (Salt Lake City: Bookcraft, 1966), p. 370.

Chapter 16. The Spiritual Christian

1. On one occasion the Nephite Twelve prayed to Jesus Christ rather than to the Father (see 3 Ne. 19:18, 24–25, 30), but Jesus offered this explanation regarding this apparent exception to standard practice: "They pray unto me because I am with them" (3 Ne. 19:22).

Chapter 17. The Serving Christian

1. M. Scott Peck, *The Road Less Traveled* (New York: Simon and Schuster, 1978), p. 83.

2. Brigham Young, in *Journal of Discourses* 2:299.

3. E. Douglas Clark and Robert S. Clark, *Fathers and Sons in the Book of Mormon* (Salt Lake City: Deseret Book Co., 1991), p. 287.

4. See Clark and Clark, *Fathers and Sons*, p. xiii.

5. *History of the Church* 4:227.

Chapter 18. On Resurrection, Judgment, and the Life to Come

1. Joseph Fielding Smith, *Doctrines of Salvation*, comp. Bruce R. McConkie, 3 vols. (Salt Lake City: Bookcraft, 1954–56), 2:183–84. There is another category of the damned, namely the "sons of perdition." These commit the "unpardonable sin," which is to turn against God after receiving by revelation a sure knowledge of the truth of the gospel. (See Joseph Smith, *Teachings of the Prophet Joseph Smith*, sel. Joseph Fielding Smith [Salt Lake City: Deseret Book Co., 1976], p. 358.) No one knows the severity of their fate save those "who are ordained unto this condemnation" (D&C 76:48).

2. Bruce R. McConkie, "The Probationary Test of Mortality," address delivered at the Salt Lake Institute of Religion, 10 January 1982, pp. 12–13.

3. Joseph Smith, *Teachings of the Prophet Joseph Smith*, p. 303.

4. Ezra Taft Benson, "Flooding the Earth with the Book of Mormon," *Ensign* 18 (November 1988): 6.

INDEX

ABOUT THE AUTHOR

C. Kent Dunford is an instructor at the institute of religion adjacent to the University of Utah. He has also served as an institute director in Boston, Massachusetts, and Boulder, Colorado. He received a bachelor's degree from Brigham Young University and a master's degree from the University of Colorado. He received a doctorate in history of religions from Brigham Young University and has studied religion at Harvard Divinity School and Weston School of Theology in Boston.

The author has been a curriculum writer for the Sunday School and has written several articles that have appeared in Church publications. He has served as a full-time missionary, Gospel Doctrine teacher, counselor in a bishopric, high councilor, bishop, and counselor in a stake presidency. He and his wife, Carolyn Barlow Dunford, are the parents of six children.